Making the Case

Essential Tools for Essay Writing

Making the Case

Essential Tools for Essay Writing

Tom Tyner

Breadan Publishing

Making the Case: Essential Tools for Essay Writing
First Edition
Tom Tyner

Publisher, English	Pat Nishimura
Editor, Writer	Susan Wiesick
Marketing	Lori Jones

Copyright 2011 by Breadan Publishing Co.

Address for Domestic and International Orders
Breadan Publishing, 4706 N. Quail Lake Dr., Clovis, CA 93619
Website: www.breadanpublishing.com
Telephone: 559-291-2152
Fax: 559-291-1978

Printed in the United States of America
Breadan Publishing
ISBN: 978-0-615-43863-4

Contents

Unit 3 | Logical Evidence

Unit 4 | Comparative Evidence

Unit 7 | Synthesis

The textbook *Making the Case: Essential Tools for Essay Writing* was created on the assumption that it is of great benefit to college students, and all adults for that matter, to be able to write effective issue-oriented essays. The main intent of this text is to help provide students with the tools to accomplish that goal.

Essay writing requires a number of skills that can be applied to both educational and "real world" experiences: the ability to think and reason clearly, to research, analyze, and evaluate information, to support your beliefs convincingly, to organize your thoughts logically, to distinguish facts from opinions, and to communicate with others in effective ways. In short, the skills you develop through writing essays can benefit you in most endeavors that require some serious thinking.

The need for textbooks such as *Making the Case* is born out in much of the writing available to the public today: a myriad of online articles, newspaper editorials, magazine and periodical essays, and letters to the editor. There are plenty of writers who will offer an opinion on any issue of the day, which is not a bad thing. The problem is that much of the writing falls apart under careful scrutiny: opinions disguised as facts, unsubstantiated claims, logical fallacies, appeals to emotion at the expense of logic, demagoguery in place of reasoned argument.

As with any kind of learned skill, there are things that writers need to know and practice to become effective essayists, and the better writers operating in the world of opinion have developed those skills. The intent of this text is to provide you with the basics for writing the kind of effective, compelling essays that make the greatest impact on readers.

Making the Case

As you write essays, this text requires one thing of you that should be required of all writers: to make your case. You believe that women in the military should not be battlefield participants? Convince us. You believe that political term limits hurt the legislative process in your state? Prove it. You believe that students who "cram" for exams actually do better than those who study systematically over time? Show us the evidence. The text presupposes two things about the people who read your essays: first, that they may take some convincing to agree with your opinion on an issue, and second, that as discerning readers, they will find merit in a well-reasoned, strongly supported viewpoint.

But how does a writer best make his case, you may ask. It is the job of this text to answer that question in detail and give you many opportunities to apply what you learn.

Types of Evidence

Writers make their case in a variety of ways, all with the intent of convincing readers to support, accept, or seriously consider their viewpoint. One of the most common and effective ways to support your opinion on a topic is to provide *evidence*: information that helps to confirm that your opinion is valid, reasonable, or true. The text devotes a unit each to six of the most frequently used and effective types of evidence:

Empirical: evidence that is based on personal experience and observation
Factual: evidence that is *verifiable*, that can be proven to be true
Logical: evidence that is based on reason and common sense
Comparative: evidence that provides comparisons to make a point
Causal: evidence that validates the cause of an occurrence or problem
Moral: evidence that is based on standards of right and wrong

In each unit, your writing emphasis focuses on incorporating the type of evidence presented in that unit to help make your case. As you move through the text, you supplement this evidence with other types of evidence presented in previous units. By the end, you have an arsenal of evidence to choose from for any essay writing you may do.

Other Writing Considerations

While providing effective evidence is an important aspect of essay writing, there are other writing considerations which the text covers in some detail:

Thesis: Your thesis expresses your viewpoint on the topic and gives you something concrete to support in the essay.

Opposing Viewpoints: Writers often acknowledge and respond to opposing viewpoints to their thesis to show their understanding of the topic and disarm readers who may hold those viewpoints.

Audience: You will write essays for specific audiences of your choice: readers that you feel may benefit from reading your essay or whose viewpoint you would like to influence.

Purpose: Your purpose in writing - the reason you are writing on a particular topic for a specific audience - will help to shape your essay in ways that will accomplish that purpose.

Research: For many potential writing topics, a writer's interest is often greater than her knowledge. For a number of your essays, you will investigate your topic to learn more about the subject and find the best possible evidence to support your thesis.

Writing Process

Making the Case is a process-oriented text that takes into account what we have learned about how writers move from contemplating a particular writing topic to completing the final essay. In each unit, the writing process is repeated in the following manner:

Prewriting: During each "Prewriting" section, you are given a number of suggestions and activities in preparation for writing your first draft.

Drafting: In each "Drafting" section, you write the first draft of your essay taking into consideration the drafting suggestions presented in the text.

Revision: During each "Revision" section, you are presented a number of suggestions for revising your draft, such as improving sentence wording, organization, or thesis support, and you make the revisions that you feel will improve the essay.

Editing: In the "Editing" section, you do activities to help eliminate some of the more common errors that writers make, and you proofread your final draft for errors and make any necessary corrections.

Readings

Throughout the text you will find sample essays reflecting each unit's writing emphasis to read, evaluate, and get ideas from. In the "Readings" section of each unit are professionally written essays to read, discuss, and analyze. At the end of each unit in the "Writing about Writing" section, you are given the opportunity to write a critique of an essay by subjecting it to the same critical evaluation that you give your own essays. The text recognizes the interconnectedness between writing and reading and provides you with amply opportunities for doing both.

Readings

Unit One
Empirical Evidence

I n the world of print, writers regularly express their opinions on a variety of issues and problems: global warming, health care reform, soaring college costs, outsourcing of American jobs, deteriorating urban centers, the national debt, surviving the recession. We read such opinion pieces in magazine and journal articles, newspaper editorials and letters to the editor, essay collections, and online articles.

On any issue, the perspectives of writers vary widely. For example, depending on the writer's viewpoint, governmental involvement in health care is an essential part of reform, an insidious step towards socialism, the only chance for millions of uninsured Americans, or a costly experiment that will raise everyone's taxes. Given the complexity of the issue and range of opinions, what is a reader to believe?

Opinions are not hard to come by, judged by the wealth of information available on all sides of practically any issue. Any writer can say that a government-sponsored health care program would be a costly disaster or the salvation for millions of uninsured children. Any writer can say that the war in Iraq will ultimately help spread democracy throughout the Middle East or create a fundamentalist Islamic government hostile towards the U.S. Therefore, readers should have one requirement for any writer with an opinion: *make your case.*

A writer's opinion, or *viewpoint*, can best be evaluated by the evidence he provides to support it. Without such evidence, an opinion is of little value. For example, a writer claims that illegal aliens in the U.S. are a boon to the American economy rather than a drain on it. This may be true, or it may be false. That a writer claims something certainly doesn't make it true. However, if the writer provides credible evidence that the money that illegal aliens put into the economy far outweighs what they cost the country in health and educational services, many readers may believe his claim.

As writers, it is our job to convince readers that our opinions have value. An important part of that job is to provide evidence that what we write about a particular issue is true or valid. A major emphasis of the text is on what discerning readers expect of writers: to prove their claims. To that end, each unit focuses on a different type of evidence - *empirical, factual, logical, comparative, causal, and moral* - that writers use to support their viewpoints. You will learn to incorporate these different types of evidence in your writing to help validate your opinions, substantiate your claims, and make an impact on readers.

Of course, there are other considerations besides providing evidence for writing effective essays, including audience awareness, effective organization, acknowledging differing opinions, providing explanatory information, writing clearly and vividly, having a definite purpose, crafting strong openings and conclusions, and revising for improvement. All of these topics will be covered throughout the text.

We are all both writers and readers, and the two are inextricably connected. Learning to read critically and carefully no doubt makes us better writers, and writing effectively makes us more discerning readers. As writers, we learn to hold our writing to a similar standard by which we judge other writing, and as readers, we judge the writing of others in comparison to our own. The readings at the end of each unit are intended to sharpen your critical reading skills, which will in turn enhance your own writing, and provide you with essays to evaluate and write about.

A great deal of what we know, understand, and believe derives from *empirical* evidence: what we have personally experienced and observed. Writers draw heavily upon their experiences and observations to write about the reality that they have known. Of course, life experiences differ greatly among individuals, creating a multitude of perspectives from which writers approach their work.

For one person, for example, her job may be a valued part of her life where she finds challenges, fulfillment, and friendship. For another, his job may be merely a means to an end, a joyless task necessary to pay the bills. Their perspectives on work, based on experience, would differ greatly. Or two people raised in very different households - one loving, protective, and stable, the other cold, indifferent, and threatening - may hold very different opinions on what family means to them.

Since personal experience and observation are both subjective and limited to an individual's unique situation, how can they be used by writers to support opinions that go beyond that experience? For example, a person may hold the opinion, based on her experience, that grade school is a wretched place, full of fear, failure, and ridicule. Based on that experience, can she generalize that going to school is a negative experience for children? Probably not. However, this does not discredit her own experience or its poignancy. And therein lies the writer's challenge in using experience-based support. To what extent does that experience embody a greater reality, if at all?

Using Experience and Observation

Experience and observation can help any writer make her case if she is aware of both their potential and limitations. The following suggestions will help bring your experiences to bear on your writing most effectively.

1. **Keep in mind the uniqueness of your personal experiences and observations**. For example, a successful businessman who didn't go to college and who knows of other successful people with similar backgrounds may conclude that you don't need a college education to be successful. This certainly may be the case for some, but is it true for most people? In using such personal experience and observations to make a point, keep in mind that what holds true for some may not hold true for others. A reasonable conclusion that the businessman might draw is, "There are some people who can be very successful in business without going to college."

2. **The greater degree to which an individual experience reflects the experience of others, the more convincingly it can be used to make a point.** When readers identify with the experience or observation of the writer, they are most inclined to agree with him. For example, based on her experience and observations, a writer might conclude that there is a strong correlation between how successful a person is at a job and how much she enjoys doing it. She knows that she has had success at jobs that she liked doing. Most readers might agree with her conclusion based on their own job experience.

3. **Often the greater the frequency of the experience or observation, the more valid it is for making a point.** For example, a person who has owned six American-made cars and had mechanical trouble with all of them can make a better case for the poor quality of American vehicles than a person whose transmission went out on one Chevrolet. In addition, observing a particular politician evade taking a position on controversial issues at numerous press conferences would strengthen the conclusion that she dodges critical issues more than if she had sidestepped a question on abortion at one press conference.

4. **Personal experience and observation can be used to provide support for a factual assertion.** The police chief in a particular city, for example, may claim that based on the number of teen arrests and complaint calls, the juvenile crime rate in a particularly crime-ridden part of town had declined significantly since the city opened two teen activity centers. By way of personal observation, a writer living in the area might confirm this assertion by noting that fewer teens have been hanging out in the streets, that the teen centers are always full of people, and that gun shots are heard less frequently at night. Used in this way, a personal observation by someone from the area may convince some residents of the reduced crime rate who may be skeptical of any claim that the police chief makes.

5. **Personal experience and observation can put a human face on an issue.** It is with clear intent that presidential candidates provide the experiences of average Americans to highlight particular issues in their campaigns: Joe Atkinson, who lost his health insurance when he changed jobs and had to postpone a serious operation, or Mildred Ortiz, who was denied health care coverage due to a pre-existing health condition. Putting a human face on an issue can create interest,

stir the emotions, and help readers relate personally in a way that presenting hard facts may not.

Activity 1.1

From the topics below with which you have some experience, select three topics and draw a conclusion on each topic based on your experience and observation. Provide your empirically based reasons for arriving at this conclusion. Then consider how you might "test" each conclusion to determine its broader validity.

EXAMPLE

Issue: The relative difficulty of college compared to high school

Personal experience/observation: I have been through high school and am in my second year of college.

Conclusion: College is more difficult than high school

Reasons:
1. My grade point average is a full point below my high school average.
2. I have to read significantly more for my classes than I did in high school.
3. The course work is more challenging and complex.
4. I have to spend more time studying.
5. Many of my friends' experiences have been similar to mine.

Test conclusion: Ask a number of other students about their comparative experience.

Topics:
1. What it is like to work and go to college at the same time?
2. The challenge of paying for one's college education
3. Being raised in a one-parent household
4. The pressure on young people to be sexually active
5. Should the drinking age be lowered to eighteen?
6. Should marijuana be legalized for recreational use?
7. Is religion an important part of students' lives?
8. Are police prejudice against minorities?

Activity 1.2

For one of the topics that you selected from Activity 1.1, take your analysis a step further to probe the topic more deeply by answering the following questions:

1. What are the possible consequences, outcomes, or effects of your conclusion?
2. Based on your conclusion, what, if anything, needs to be done: what action or steps might be taken?

EXAMPLE

Topic: The relative difficulty of college compared to high school

Conclusion: College is more difficult than high school.

1. Consequence: In college, students have to study harder and longer, they feel more pressure and stress than in high school, they take their college work more seriously than in high school, and they sometimes lose confidence in their abilities.
2. Action: Students need to be made more aware of the changes that college brings, be prepared to study harder, and expect that their grades might drop off a little.

Writing an Experienced-Based Essay

In this first unit, you write a paper based primarily on empirical evidence: what you have discovered through personal experience and observation. Later you are introduced to other types of evidence that writers use to support their viewpoints, and in the end you will be able to draw from a variety of evidentiary sources to write most effectively and convincingly.

The "Writing" section of each unit is divided into four parts: *prewriting, drafting, revising,* and *editing.* In each "prewriting" section you prepare to write your paper; in each "drafting" section you write the first draft of your paper; in each 'revising" section you make changes in the draft that you feel will improve the paper; and in each "editing" section you proofread your paper for errors and make corrections. This basic *process* approach to writing is one that is used in some manner by most writers, one that you have probably used yourself. Each section also provides some suggestions and guidelines you may find useful for writing the particular type of essay that is the focus for that unit.

Writers do a variety of things in the "prewriting" phase to prepare to write a paper. They decide what they want to write about and perhaps what they want to say. They may also decide on a particular reason for writing about a subject (*purpose*) and whom they would like to read their writing (*audience*). They may also get some ideas on paper that they want to include in their paper. They may think about the structure of their upcoming paper (*organization*) and how they'd like to develop it.

Some writers like to plan out a paper in some detail before writing while others prefer launching into their writing with little more than a general idea of where they want to go. The variety of approaches that writers take during the prewriting phase reflects the individuality of the writing experience and the different ways in which writers' minds work. Writers ultimately rely upon what seems to be the most productive and natural way to proceed, something that each writer usually discovers for herself.

Topic Selection

Where do writers find topics to write about? We have all sat hunched over a paper waiting for a brainstorm. Sometimes it comes and other times it doesn't. However, there are different questions that writers can ask themselves to help come up with something that they may want to write about. Here are a few:

1. **What am I interested in?** Without doubt, writing is most pleasurable when we write about something that interests us. Whether our interest lies in politics, sports, computers technology, fitness, music, or helping others, there are always topics to write about that fall within those interests.

2. **What do I know?** Writers often write on topics that they have some knowledge of or experience with. For example, novelists often fill their books with the types of people they grew up with and places they have lived. Essayists often focus their writing on topics that lie within their area of expertise: science, sociology, psychology, art, or political science.

3. **What do I want to know?** Writing is often a source of discovery, and for most of us, our interests in the world exceed our knowledge. Writers learn by writing and by doing the investigation necessary to write knowledgeably on a topic. Is global warming a man-made condition or a natural phenomenon? Is a person heterosexual or homosexual due to

biological wiring or learned behavior?   We may think we know the answers to these questions, but in order to be most certain, or to convince others of the validity of our position, we may need to learn a great deal more about the topic.

4. **What topics are *substantive* enough to write about?** All writers make the subjective decision as to whether a particular subject is significant enough to merit readers' attention. For example, the censoring by the school administration of an article in the student newspaper critical of the college's treatment of part-time instructors may be a litmus-test issue regarding the freedom of a college's student press. On the other hand, the decision of the administrative advisor to change the weight of the paper on which the newspaper is written from twenty to ten weight to save money may be considered insignificant to most readers. In considering possible topics, ask yourself questions like, "What impact or effect does the topic have on readers? Would the topic be of interest to readers? Is the topic serious or substantive enough to engage readers' interest?"

5. **What needs to be said?** Sometimes there is a situation occurring, a condition existing, or something being proposed that needs to be addressed. You think, someone really needs to say something on this issue, and that someone may be you. When we ask ourselves questions like, "When is the city ever going to get a stop light installed at that dangerous intersection?" or "Why isn't the college doing anything about that sexist sociology instructor?" or "How can the college possibly consider raising tuition?" or "How can drug dealers in the neighborhood operate in the open?", the answer may lie in part in someone writing about the situation.

Activity 1.3

Select a possible writing topic for your empirically based paper keeping in mind the points just presented, along with the following criteria:

1. Select a topic from any area provided it is substantive enough to provide some interest for readers: school-related issues, work-related issues, family/relationship issues, health/fitness/nutrition issues, political issues, computer or online-related issues, gender issues, financial issues, child welfare issues, and so on.

2. Select a topic for which you can rely on empirical evidence

- your personal experiences and observations - to develop your paper. In other words, select a topic that you are knowledgeable about through your own personal involvement or observation.

3. Select a topic that you can write about within the length parameters set by your instructor. For example, a general topic such as "Student Safety on College Campuses" may be too extensive for the assignment but a more specific topic such as "Nighttime Safety Problems at Fremont College" may work well.

Sample student topic: The college's new five-week class drop date

Focusing Your Paper: Thesis

Now that you have selected a writing topic, your next step is to decide what you want to say about the topic. In other words, based on your personal experience and observations, what conclusion can you draw about your topic? What viewpoint does your experience and observation support?

Your viewpoint provides the focus for your paper: the main point or *thesis* that you are supporting primarily with empirical evidence. This focus helps you develop your paper and helps readers follow and understand what you want to say. Your *thesis* basically says, "This is what I believe," and your paper explains to readers *why* you believe as you do.

For example, a student writing on the topic "Injuries Caused by Weightlifting" had serious shoulder and knee problems due to heavy weightlifting. As much as he enjoyed the challenge of bench pressing or squatting as much weight as possible, he would inevitably end up injuring or reinjuring a shoulder or knee until he had to give up the heavy lifting. His doctor also told him that due to the injuries, he could suffer from arthritic joints in the future.

He had also observed that many of his fellow weightlifters had similar problems over the years, so he reached the conclusion that heavy weightlifting over time inevitably results in serious injuries, his thesis for the essay. He recommended to readers that although heavy lifting was a great temptation, particularly for men, they should resist the temptation and lift lighter weights with more repetitions for the best and healthiest results.

Activity 1.4

Based on your experience and observations regarding your topic, decide on a viewpoint that your experience supports and that can form the *thesis* for your essay. Your thesis will provide the writing focus for your upcoming paper: the main idea that you are presenting and developing for readers.

In addition, generate some reasons for reaching this conclusion based on your experience: *why* you believe as you do.

EXAMPLE

Topic: The college's new five-week class drop date

Thesis: The college's new five-week drop date is detrimental to students.

Reasons for thesis based on experience and observation:

1. Students don't have enough time to decide whether a class is for them.
2. Not enough happens in the first five weeks to give students an indication of how they might perform in the class.
3. Students make hasty decisions about dropping or remaining in the class that they may later regret.
4. The new drop date was not created with the students' best interests in mind.

Testing Your Thesis

Your thesis for the upcoming paper is based on what you believe about the topic as a result of your personal experience and observations. Such empirical evidence is *subjective* in nature, based on your personal interpretation and perspective. It may lead to a valid conclusion that most readers would accept or believe, or it may lead to a conclusion that is contrary to the experience of readers or to factual findings on the topic.

For example, based on her experience and observations, a writer concluded that the state's tax on small businesses is driving owners out of business and forcing others to relocate out of state. She cites her parents' family-run business as an example, which is barely making a profit, which she blames primarily on the business tax. She also references other businesses in town that have closed over the past few years as a result of what she considers the exorbitant state tax.

The broader reality, however, may not support her conclusion. First, the size of the business tax in her state is about average compared to other states. Second, the loss of businesses in her city is a common occurrence in the business world, and she neglects to say that, as most frequently occurs, other businesses have taken their places. Finally, state economic records show that the number of small businesses (defined as those with ten employees or fewer) in the state has actually increased in the past two years, raising doubts of her claim that businesses are leaving the state.

By testing her conclusion - comparing the size of business taxes in other states, investigating whether the number of small businesses in the state is dwindling, understanding the typical business cycle of loss and replacement - the writer may have arrived at a different, more valid thesis. That her experience-based conclusion does not prove to be valid in a broader sense, however, does not invalidate the subjective experience of the individual. It does mean, however, that in some cases, the subjective experience can not be generalized to provide an accurate broader picture.

Activity 1.5

Test your conclusion in ways that you feel will either help to confirm or bring into question its validity. If your findings don't concur with your thesis, you may want to reanalyze your interpretation of your experience or consider a different topic from which your empirical evidence may produce a more valid conclusion. If your findings support your thesis, you may have additional evidence to help make your case.

EXAMPLE

Topic: The college's new five-week class drop date

Thesis: The college's new drop date is detrimental to students.

To test the thesis:
1. Do a survey of students regarding the effects of the five-week drop date.
2. Talk to instructors about their opinions regarding the new policy.
3. Find out from the admission's office whether the number of drops have in fact increased.

Addressing Different Viewpoints

As writers, we need to be aware of the different perspectives that readers may bring to their reading. There is more than one way to look at most issues, and writers who address differing viewpoints often do the best job of connecting with their readers. This does not mean that a writer abandons her position on a particular issue because her readers may believe differently. It may mean, however, that she shows an awareness of other perspectives in her writing and an understanding of why readers may hold different beliefs.

To acknowledge and respond most effectively to different perspectives in your writing, consider the following suggestions.

1. **Before writing, consider viewpoints on the topic of your essay that differ from your thesis.** For example, on the issue of a new college policy that requires security officers to carry guns, a writer may be opposed to the policy for a number of reasons. However, she also knows that there are other students who support the new policy or see no harm in it. To reach these readers, she may need to acknowledge their viewpoints and address their concerns.

2. **To respond best to readers' opposing viewpoints, try to determine and understand *where* those viewpoints come from**. Do they come from the readers' life experiences? their religious conviction? their self-interest? their misunderstanding of the issue? For example, if students from a particular college reside in a conservative part of a state, those who are opposed to same-sex marriage may be influenced by the conservative values of parents, friends, or local clergy. Understanding that influence may help a writer who supports same-sex marriage address their concerns most effectively.

3. **Consider the strongest arguments that readers with differing viewpoints may hold and how you might respond.** It may be impossible to address all arguments that support a particular perspective, so focus on the most critical arguments. For example, the strongest arguments for an armed college security force may center on student safety and the recent violent crimes that occurred on campus. Addressing those arguments effectively may be the most important thing that the writer does to further her purpose.

4. **A writer is not required to give opposing perspectives equal time with his own viewpoint**. A writer presenting and supporting a thesis is not writing an objective pro-and-con paper. He is making a case in support of his viewpoint. While opposing arguments are often addressed, they are secondary in importance to the writer's support for his thesis. Writers address differing perspectives in an essay to further their writing purpose, not to cast doubt on their viewpoint.

Activity 1.6

For any two of the following topics and theses, think of an *opposing viewpoint* and two or three arguments that would support that viewpoint. Then decide how you might respond to those arguments in a way that would get readers to question them.

EXAMPLE

Topic: Legalization of marijuana

Thesis: Marijuana should be legalized for recreational use.

Opposing viewpoint: Marijuana should *not* be legalized for recreational use.

Opposing Argument 1: Marijuana usage leads to harder drugs.
Response: There is no research or studies that support that contention, but there are studies that show otherwise.
(Provide evidence of studies that refute argument.)

Opposing Argument 2: Legalizing marijuana would lead to much greater usage.
Response: That has not been the case in other countries that legalized marijuana.
(Provide studies from other countries where marijuana use has been decriminalized.)

1. **Topic:** Serving beer on campus at a four-year college
   Thesis: Providing a beer license to an on-campus restaurant is a bad idea.
2. **Topic:** Condom machines in college rest rooms
   Thesis: The college should put condom machines in men's and women's restrooms on campus.
3. **Topic:** Student parking fee
   Thesis: Students should not be required to pay an annual fee to park on campus.
4. **Topic:** Sex education in elementary school (grades 4-6)
   Thesis: Sex education should be introduced in all elementary schools.

Activity 1.7

Consider an opposing viewpoint to your thesis, the arguments that support it, and how you might respond to them in your essay.

EXAMPLE

Topic: The college's new five-week class drop date

Thesis: The college's new drop date is detrimental to students.

Opposing viewpoint: The new drop date is a good idea.

Opposing Argument 1: Students shouldn't be allowed to stay in a class nearly half the semester and then drop with impunity.
Response: Why not? Who does it hurt to allow students more time to make an educational decision? It may be tough on a student to spend eight weeks in a class and get no credit, but that should be her decision.

Opposing Argument 2: Instructors need to "firm up" their class enrollment earlier and not waste time on students who won't be around in the end.
Response: Are school policies made for the benefit of the instructors or the students? If a policy hurts students but makes life a little easier for instructors, the school has its priorities backwards.

Audience and Purpose

Issue-oriented writing is most frequently a communication between a writer and readers. Those readers form the writer's *audience*, the person or persons who will read the writer's essay, letter, article, editorial, or story.

In addition, writers usually have a *purpose* for writing to a particular audience: to inform, persuade, convince, enlighten, entertain, amuse, or move to action. For example, letters to the editor during the weeks preceding an election often encourage readers to vote for a particular candidate or ballot measure. The writers' *audience* is the newspaper's subscribers who read the "letters to the editor" section. The writers' *purpose* is to convince and encourage those readers to vote a particular way in the upcoming election. A writer's *audience* and *purpose*, then, help determine *what* a writer says about a particular issue and *how* he says it to accomplish his purpose.

Audience Considerations

To consider the most appropriate reading *audience* for a particular piece of writing, consider the following questions:

1. Who might be most interested in reading about this particular topic?
2. Who may be most affected by this particular topic: college students? women? a particular ethnic group? voting age residents? The general population?
3. Whom do you want to "reach" with this particular essay? What people do you want to have a particular impact or effect on?
4. What do you need to keep in mind about your audience regarding this particular essay: their degree of interest in it? their opinions on the issue? their knowledge of the issue? the degree to which they are affected by the issue? the types of emotional response this issue may elicit? the degree to which their age, gender, ethnicity, or education level might influence their viewpoint?

Purpose Considerations

To determine your *purpose* for writing to a particular audience, consider the following questions.

1. What do you want to accomplish in writing to this particular audience? Do you mainly want to inform them so they will be more knowledgeable on the issue? Do you want them to believe as you do on the issue, or at the least, consider your viewpoint seriously? Do you want to alert them to the importance of the issue and its affect on them? Do you want to encourage them to take some action?
2. How might you best accomplish your writing purpose? Given the particular reading audience that you want to reach, what can you write to have the greatest impact on those readers?
3. To best accomplish your purpose, what *tone* should your writing take? Your writing tone is the attitude you convey to readers and the mood you create with your writing. Your tone may be courteous and respectful, angry and challenging, light and playful, serious and concerned, kind and solicitous, or ominous and threatening, or it may change during the course of your writing according to your audience and purpose.

For example, if a writer writes an essay for high school students on the value of sexual abstinence, she may lose her audience if she writes in a condescending or judgmental tone. On the other hand, if the writer's tone shows her understanding and respect for her readers and their situation, her audience may be more receptive to her message.

Activity 1.8

For your upcoming paper, determine the best reading audience for your essay and your purpose in writing to them.

EXAMPLE

   Topic: The college's new five-week class drop date

   Audience: The college's board of trustees who approved the new policy

   Purpose: To get the board to reconsider their policy change in light of the problems

When writers write the first draft of a paper, they are seldom composing a final product. As writers, we are usually thinking our way through the paper, not knowing exactly how one sentence will follow from the previous or how we may word it. In addition, new ideas may come to us as we write - new experiences to include, a new point in support of our thesis, a new thought on best accomplishing our purpose - that we work into the paper. With so much going on, it is not surprising that the first draft of a paper is not a perfectly worded, perfectly organized essay. Instead, it is a work in progress which will improve as we review, evaluate and revise it. This is how the writing process works for most writers, including the most gifted, for a simple reason: it usually produces the best results.

In writing the first draft of your current paper, then, there is no pressure to write the "perfect" essay. The first draft is not the best place for fine tuning your sentence wording or your organization, which will come later. With the first draft, you deal with the broader concerns of presenting and supporting your thesis, including providing the empirical evidence on which your thesis is based. The following suggestions may help you work through this first draft.

Organization

Most essays include a beginning, middle, and ending. What writers do within these sections can vary greatly, but they provide a customary framework for writer and readers to follow. In writing your upcoming draft, keep in mind these general functions of the beginning, middle, and ending of an essay.

Beginning

In the beginning of an essay, writers generally do the following:

1. **Introduce their topic in a way that creates interest for readers**. You can engage your readers' interest in different ways: a brief anecdote, an interesting and important fact, a compelling incident, a relevant scenario.
2. **Present their thesis in a sentence called the *thesis statement*.** By presenting your thesis in the beginning of the essay, readers have a clear idea of your intent and will read the essay with that intent in mind.
3. **Indicate the seriousness or importance of the topic in some manner.** Readers may be compelled to read beyond the opening with keen interest if they are made aware of the importance of the topic and how it may affect them.

The beginning part of an essay is usually brief, no more than a paragraph or two, with the thesis statement often coming towards the end. The following paragraphs of the essay on a college's new five-week class drop policy provide examples of three different opening options that the writer considered. The *thesis statement* in each is underlined.

Opening Option #1:

After having an eight-week class drop date for several years, the college decided to switch to a five-week drop date two years ago. Students made little fuss over the change, and it largely went unnoticed. However, as students began receiving "F" grades in classes that they dropped after the five-week period, they started waking up. Since then, students have become more and more frustrated with the early drop date and its consequences, none of which are good. <u>After a one-year trial, it is clear that the new five-week drop date is not working well, and the policy needs revisiting.</u>

Opening Option #2:

Allison Wong had a decision to make. It was the fifth week of her physiology class, the last week to drop the class without penalty. She knew that it would be a difficult class for her, one of the most challenging for nursing majors, and one she needed a good grade in. However, the first major test wasn't for another week, so she had no indicator of how she might do in the class. She was flying blind, but the five-week drop date was still looming.

Allison's dilemma is shared by thousands of students due to the college's new five-week class drop date policy. Students are often making critical decisions on whether to drop or remain in a particular class before they are ready. <u>The new five-week drop date often forces students into a premature decision with negative consequences, and it needs to be changed.</u>

Opening Option #3:

Jonathan Connors has a timing dilemma. With his newly acquired bachelor's degree in psychology, he has been offered a full-time job in a clinical research lab, which starts in a week. However, Jonathan has also applied for admission to a graduate program, but he won't know whether he was accepted for at least two weeks. In other words, he must decide whether to take the job before he knows his graduate school status. A full-time job right out of college is extremely inviting, but getting into grad school would ultimately provide greater opportunities. If he only knew whether he was going to be accepted.

Each semester our college students basically face the same dilemma:

having to make a decision on whether to drop a class before they have enough information to make an informed decision. They may make the right decision or they may not; it's a roll of the dice. The new five-week class drop date has made dropping a class a game of chance, which is not the way to make important educational decisions. <u>The new drop date is creating serious problems for students, and it needs to be changed.</u>

Middle

The middle of an essay, several paragraphs in length, often contains the following:

1. **The reasons in support of the writer's thesis.** The middle paragraphs answer the question: Why does the writer believe as she does about the topic? Typically, the reasons are presented in separate paragraphs and in an order that seems the most effective: most important to least important, least important to most important, or similar or related reasons presented together.

2. **The empirical evidence upon which each reason is based.** Each reason is "backed up" by the personal experience and observations on which the reason is based.

3. **Information to help readers understand the topic better.** Any background history, explanations, or definitions that will help familiarize readers with the topic are usually presented at the beginning of the middle paragraphs. For example, for an essay on global warming, a writer may first want to explain exactly what it means.

4. **Responses to differing viewpoints.** Opposing viewpoints which readers may hold are addressed in a manner that may get readers to reconsider their beliefs. Writers often respond to opposing arguments near the end of the middle paragraphs.

Read the middle paragraphs of the essay on pages 20-22 to see how the writer organized and presented her material, paragraphed her ideas, used her empirical evidence to substantiate each reason, provided some background information at the beginning, and addressed opposing viewpoints towards the end.

Ending

Now that the topic and thesis have been introduced in the beginning and developed and supported in the middle paragraphs, what is there left to do? Endings of essays vary a great deal depending on the topic, what has come before in the essay, and the writer's purpose. An essay's ending can, among other things, do the following:

1. Reinforce the thesis in some manner.
2. Summarize the main points of support.
3. Present a final compelling point to support the thesis.
4. State, clarify or emphasize the writer's purpose.
5. Speculate on the future regarding the issue.
6. Leave the reader with a question or final thought to ponder.

Whatever the ending includes, it should leave readers with a sense of completion, follow logically from what has come before it, go beyond what was presented in the beginning and middle, and emphasize the readers' purpose.

Read the ending two paragraphs of the essay on pages 20-22 to see what the writer included, how it related to her thesis, how it furthered her purpose, and the impact it may have had on its intended readers.

Activity 1.9

Write the first draft of your essay following the organizational suggestions presented and keeping in mind your reading audience and purpose. Use your best empirical evidence - personal examples and observations - to substantiate the reasons in support of your thesis. Keep in mind that this is a first draft, not the time to worry about fine-tuning your sentences or making an occasional error, concerns you will address later.

Sample First Draft (reading audience: board of trustees)

The College's Five-Week Drop Deadline

For many years the college had an eight-week class drop policy, during which time students would not be penalized for dropping a course by receiving a failing grade. Two years ago, however, the college adopted a new five-week policy, compelling students to make a decision earlier on whether to drop or remain in a class.

On first glance, the change seemed innocuous enough, merely moving the drop date up a few weeks. However, the first year, the change caught many unsuspecting students off guard, who received an "F" grade for dropping a class after the five-week deadline.

The second year, as students became more fully aware of the new policy, the number of failing grades from late drops diminished, but other problems associated with the earlier drop date became apparent. The new drop-date policy simply isn't working well for many students, and it needs to be reconsidered.

It is unclear exactly who first came up with the idea to change the drop date, but a few vocal instructors who let their thoughts be known to students apparently got the ear of the administration. These instructors simply didn't like the idea of students having eight weeks to drop their classes, and they didn't want to waste their time and effort on students who might be dropping. Some of them even admitted that they liked to get their class sizes down as soon as possible, which an earlier drop date would accomplish. In other words, the new drop date was initially promulgated by instructors whose main motivation was to make life easier on themselves. Whether it was good for students was not an important point of discussion.

Dropping a class is a serious decision for most students. First, we do not like to drop classes because we have already paid for them and of course don't get reimbursed for dropping. Second, we reduce our unit load, which means having to increase the load in future semesters to stay on track for graduation, or take longer to get our credits and graduate. Certainly there are some students who sign up for additional classes with the intent of dropping those classes that prove the most difficult, but who has the money or time to play such games?

Most students drop a class for a clear-cut reason: the likelihood of receiving a poor grade, a heavier class load than they can handle, or a circumstance beyond their control that requires their dropping (e.g. change in work schedule, loss of a babysitter, health problems). The few times I have personally dropped a class, I was simply in over my head for the semester, and not dropping the class would not only have led to a poor grade in that class but poorer grades in other classes as well. With the emphasis that graduate schools place on grade point average for admittance, many students can't afford a bad grade, so they feel they have no choice but to drop a class.

Which brings us to the new drop policy. At eight weeks, students had a good handle on whether they were going to fare well in a class. There were grades on tests and assigned papers to measure their performance, and eight weeks to estimate their progress. They were also nearly half way through the class, meaning fewer weeks ahead where some unforseen circumstance could derail their attending. In short, they were in a position to make an informed decision on whether to drop, and if they remained in the class, they deserved whatever grade they earned.

At five weeks, however, the situation is quite different. For all intents and purposes, the semester has just begun and students seldom have a good grasp on how the class is going to go. They may have not had a major test nor an assigned paper to measure their performance. I have had classes where instructors record no grades for the first part of the semester, letting students get a good feel for the class before they are tested. In other classes, there may be only two or three major tests for the semester, none of which fall within the first five weeks. Not enough has gone on during the first five weeks of the semester in many classes for students to make a wise decision on whether to drop. They are doing little more than flipping a coin.

In addition, the earlier the drop date, the more time left for the unforseen circumstances to crop up such as the new work schedule or the sick child that needs her mother at home. Many times I have seen students quit showing up for classes that they were doing well in, only to discover that they had to drop the class due to an outside circumstance. The old eight-week drop policy narrowed that negative window of opportunity, and the new five-week drop date widens it, so students who are caught between the new five-week drop and the old eight-week drop now receive a failing grade that they wouldn't previously have received.

Although I don't have conclusive evidence, I also suspect that the five-week drop date results in a greater number of drops rather than fewer, due to the number of students in my classes that I have seen drop after five weeks. With a five-week drop date looming shortly ahead, it is easy to panic and think, "I only have three days left to decide whether to drop and I have no performance indicators to make a decision on. I'd better drop and not take a chance." I know that I have felt that way more than once, and I still regret dropping one class after five weeks because now I think I would have done fine in it; at the time, however, I really had no idea. After eight weeks, I would have had a good idea.

For those who see dropping classes as game playing by students who simply drop when the going gets tough, I can understand how a shorter drop period might make sense. "Let them either drop early or stay in the course and get what they earn, for better or worse," the thinking might go. However, to the vast majority of students, dropping classes is not a game and neither is it a way to avoid challenging classes. It is done after serious deliberation and almost a half semester of performance in the class. It means losing money for a class not completed and falling behind in credits, which may also affect a student's financial aid status. Dropping a class is serious business for students, and it is a difficult decision that they need to have good input on. In eight weeks, they can get that input. In five weeks, they can't. If the pressure to maintain a high GPA weren't so great, students may be more inclined to muddle through a course. However, graduate schools have created that pressure as well as the resultant pressure on students to drop classes they are struggling in. That is not the students' fault.

The current five-week drop deadline is not working well, and it needs to be changed. Eight weeks worked much better, and I believe that statistics will prove that it resulted in fewer drops than the five-week deadline. Students don't drop a class on a whim, they only drop when they feel it is absolutely necessary. As students who pay dearly for their education, they deserve the right to make that choice at a point in the course when they can make an informed decision. Five weeks simply doesn't give them enough time. A student's educational decision should not be made with the roll of a dice.

Revision

All writers share the task of revising their drafts to make improvements and get them into more "publishable" form, ready to turn over
to readers. Writers often wait until they have completed a draft before
beginning to revise so that they can view the writing as a whole to see
how well all parts fit together: beginning to middle to end, paragraph
to paragraph, and sentence to sentence.

   While writers revise specific aspects of a draft based on its particular strengths and weaknesses, they generally consider revisions
to accomplish the following: strengthen the beginning and ending
sections; improve the wording and syntax of individual sentences;
improve the organization of the essay as a whole; improve the paragraphing of the essay; add new material or delete irrelevant material
to improve the content; and make any other changes that would help
accomplish their purpose.

Revision Guidelines

As you read and revise your draft, consider the following suggestions.

1. **Strengthening the beginning or ending.** The beginning
    and ending of any essay are critical components, the first and
    last things that readers read. To evaluate the beginning, ask
    yourself, Have I clearly introduced my topic? Have I engaged
    my readers' interest in some way? Have I presented my thesis
    clearly so that readers will understand the main point that I am
    going to develop in the essay?

    To evaluate your ending ask yourself, Will my ending have
    an impact on readers? Is there something in it for them to con-
    sider that I haven't presented in the beginning or middle para-
    graphs? Does it flow logically and smoothly from the middle
    paragraphs? Does it help to accomplish my writing purpose?

2. **Improving wording and syntax.** For most writers, a significant
    part of revising a draft involves improving the wording and
    syntax of individual sentences. When you first put an idea on
    paper, the wording is seldom perfect and the sentence may not
    flow smoothly.

    To improve your sentences, consider the following:

    a. **Look for sentences that appear overly wordy and
    lengthy.** Problems that lead to wordiness include need-
    lessly repeating words or phrases or using more words than
    necessary to make your point.

b. **Look for sentences that sound awkward and don't flow smoothly.** To improve such sentences, you may need to move words or phrases around, delete or replace certain words, or restart the sentence in a different way.

c. **Look for sentences where one or more of the words don't look or sound quite right**. All writers struggle to find just the right word to make a point, and that word doesn't always come to mind initially.

d. **Look for sentences whose meaning may not be clear to readers**. Sometimes a writer has in mind what she wants to say, but when first put on paper, the idea doesn't quite make sense or is too vague for readers to understand.

e. **Look for sentences that appear stilted and unnatural**. Some writers mistakenly believe that readers are impressed with pretentious verbage rather than meaningful content. Don't write, "The verisimilitude of the loquacious seller of previously owned automobiles was unimpeachable" when you can write "The talkative used-car salesman was good to his word."

3. **Improving organization.** An essay should be organized so that its content is most accessible to readers and makes the greatest impact. To evaluate the effectiveness of the draft's organization, consider the following:

a. **As you read your draft, make sure that readers have a clear sense of its overall organization: its beginning, its middle, and its ending**. Does each section follow naturally and smoothly from the previous section? Do readers know when they have moved from beginning to middle to ending?

b. **Evaluate the order in which you have presented your supporting points in the middle paragraphs.** Would a particular point be more effective if placed in a different location? Do the strongest, most important points stand out?

c. **Evaluate the order of the sentences in each individual paragraph.** Are the sentences organized in the most logical, sequential order? Are there any sentences that appear out of place in a particular paragraph and would fit better in a different location?

d. **Read the entire draft a final time to make sure that each paragraph follows logically and seamlessly from the previous paragraph**. A writer's goal is to create a unified paper whose content is presented in the best possible order for readers to follow. That goal is accomplished paragraph by paragraph, sentence by sentence.

4. **Improving paragraphing.** The purpose of paragraphing is to help readers follow a writer's thoughts most clearly. This is accomplished by putting related thoughts together in the same paragraph and by changing paragraphs when moving to something new: a different idea, a new reason of support, a different piece of empirical evidence. To revise your paragraphing most effectively, consider the following suggestions.

a. **In general, most paragraphs develop one main idea or thought, and all of the sentences within the paragraph are related to that idea.** As you check the paragraphing of your draft, see whether each paragraph develops a particular point on your topic and whether all of the sentences tie together logically.

b. **Paragraphs frequently begin with a topic sentence that introduces the main idea to be developed in the paragraph**. For example, reread paragraphs two-seven in the sample draft on pages 20-22, all of which begin with topic sentences which introduce the idea that is developed in the paragraph. As you revise your paragraphing, see whether you are using topic sentences to introduce the main point or thought of a paragraph.

c. **Writers usually change paragraphs as they move to something new within their writing: a new section (beginning to middle to end), a new reason in support of their thesis, a new explanation, example, or step in a process**. As you read your draft, see whether each paragraph change indicates the beginning of something new in your paper.

d. **An overly long paragraph can be a problem for readers**. They can get bogged down in the paragraph and lose sight of its main focus or get lost in the details. Usually it is not difficult to spot an overly long paragraph or find a natural break within the paragraph where it can be divided into two more readable paragraphs.

e. **Strings of two or more short paragraphs - two or three sentences each - often indicate a problem.** One of two things is probably occurring: the writer is separating related material that could fit in a single paragraph, or he is not providing much development for his ideas. If the material within two or three short paragraphs is clearly related, they can be combined into a single paragraph. If the main idea in a paragraph is not sufficiently developed, more support needs to be provided.

5. **Adding and Deleting Material.** As writers reread their drafts,

they often think of things that they want to add that are relevant to their topic. On the other hand, they can also get off topic in their first draft, something which is more noticeable on rereading. To add relevant material or delete irrelevant or unnecessary material during the revision process, consider these suggestions:

a. **As you read your draft, keep your mind open to new possibilities**. Read your draft at least one time with the thought in mind, "What might I add to make the draft more interesting, more complete, or more convincing, or to better accomplish my purpose?

b. **As you read your draft, think of specific ways that you might add material**. Is there something you might add to the beginning to create more interest or show the importance of your topic? Is there anything you might add in the beginning of the middle paragraphs to help readers understand the topic more clearly? Is there one more reason you can add in support of your thesis?

c. **Read your draft one time looking exclusively for sentences or paragraphs that don't relate directly to your topic**. To determine the relevance of a sentence or paragraph ask yourself, "How does this sentence or paragraph relate to my topic, support my thesis, or further my purpose?

If you decide that a particular sentence or paragraph does not relate clearly or directly to your topic, you have two choices: one, delete the sentence or paragraph from the draft, or two, revise the sentence or paragraph so that it *does* relate clearly.

d. **Evaluate the empirical evidence you provide: the experiences and observations that support your reasons for believing as you do.** Is your empirical evidence compelling in making your case? Are there other experiences or observations you might add to strengthen it further?

6. **Responding to opposing viewpoints.** Acknowledging and responding to opposing viewpoints is an important part of essay writing. Check your essay to make sure you have addressed one or two major opposing arguments in a way that will influence readers who hold differing viewpoints to reconsider them.

7. **Accomplishing your purpose.** A final criterion for evaluating your draft is, "How well have I accomplished my purpose?" To evaluate your draft, consider the following suggestions:

a. **Read your draft with your purpose in mind**. Read each paragraph to see whether it furthers your writing purpose in some way, and make revisions that will strengthen your purpose.

b. **Read your ending carefully - the final place in your paper to make your purpose clear to readers.** What might you do to make it even clearer or more convincing?

c. **Read your paper to evaluate its tone: the attitude you present and mood you create with your writing.** Consider the appropriateness of your tone for your topic and audience, and make any changes in tone that will aid your purpose.

d. **Read your draft as if you were one of your reading audience.** Read it as if you needed to be convinced of the validity of your thesis. Question anything that an objective or skeptical reader might question, and make any changes in your draft that would resolve these questions.

Revision Activities

The following activities involve various aspects of the revision process: improving sentence wording and syntax, organization, and paragraphing. Your instructor may have you do some or all of these activities before revising your draft.

Activity 1.10 Sentence Revision

Revise the following sentences from the first draft on page 20-22 to eliminate wordiness, improve word choice, smooth out awkward sentences, and clarify vaguely worded sentences. You may add or replace words, delete words or phrases, move them around, or completely reword a sentence.

EXAMPLE

First draft sentence:
Although I don't have the evidence, I also suspect that the five-week drop date results in a greater number of drops rather than fewer.

Revised:
Although lacking evidence, I suspect that the five-week drop date results in a greater number of drops.

1. Dropping a class is serious business with some negative consequences for the student, and that is why most students take it so seriously and only drop a class out

of what they feel is absolute necessity.

2. However, colleges have created the pressure that students must maintain high grade point averages as well as the resultant pressure on students to drop classes they are struggling mightily in.

3. In addition, the earlier the drop date, the more time left during the remainder of the semester for the unforseen circumstances to crop up such as new working hours or the sick child that needs her mother at home.

4. The second year, as students became more fully aware of the new policy, the number of failing grades from late drops diminished, but other problems associated with the earlier drop date became apparent.

5. The few times I have personally dropped a class, I was simply in over my head for the semester, and not dropping the class would not only have led to a poor grade in that class but poorer grades in other classes as well.

6. For all intents and purposes, after five weeks, the semester has just begun, and students seldom have a good grasp on how a class is going to go.

7. With a five-week drop date looming shortly ahead, it is easy to panic and think, "I only have three days left to decide whether to drop, and I have no performance indicators to make a decision on, so I'd better drop and not take a chance."

8. In short, the students were in a position to make a decent decision on whether to drop the class, and if they remained in the class, they certainly deserved whatever grade they earned, for better or worse.

Activity 1.11 Organization

Reorganize the following first draft by moving some paragraphs to more effective locations in the draft and some sentences to more effective locations within their current paragraph or a different paragraph.

To Rent or Not to Rent

In America, it seems that everyone wants to experience the American Dream of home ownership. Owning our own home has been something that each generation of my family has aspired to: my grandparents, parents, and now myself. I would certainly like to own my own home someday, and I don't know anyone who doesn't.

However, home ownership in many parts of the country has become difficult if not impossible for most people who did not previously own homes and build equity. Where I grew up in the Bay Area of California, modest homes sell for over $500,000, and in San Francisco, you can't buy anything for under $800,000. The possibility of my never being able to afford a home where I want to live is very real. Perhaps the future American Dream needs to be revised, where renting rather than buying a home is an acceptable choice rather than a sign of failure.

When my parents bought their first home nearly thirty years ago, it cost them around $80,000, and they paid $8,000 down. Their monthly mortgage payments were $600, which represented less than 20% of their monthly income. If I were to buy the same house today, it would cost close to $600,000, and I would have to come up with a minimum of $60,000 just for the down payment. Then my monthly mortgage payments would be over $4,000, which if I had a job that paid an excellent salary of $100,000, would still represent well over 50% of my monthly income.

First, I don't know how I could ever save $60,000 to buy a house, and by the time I had saved that much, the cost of houses may have doubled. Second, even if I could somehow save the $60,000, I'd still be strapped to a huge monthly mortgage for the next thirty years. It would probably take both myself and my wife's salary, assuming I was married, to pay such a monthly mortgage, and if one of us were laid off a job, which is not unusual in today's economy, we could be looking at foreclosure.

I know of couples who have gone into foreclosure on their home or who slave away to make monthly house payments with little or no discretionary cash left for enjoying life or starting a savings. They have bought into the American Dream of owning their own home, but for many, it is turning into a nightmare.

My dad was making about $50,000 a year when he bought an $80,000 house. Today, that $50,000 job would be worth perhaps $125,000, but the price of the same house would be close to $600,000. In other words, the value of the house has increased over 700% during the same time that income increased a little over 100%. It is not surprising that with today's home prices, people's incomes are virtually devoured by mortgage payments.

How did home prices get so out of whack with people's income? The answer is quite simple: salary increases over the past twenty years have not come close to keeping pace with rising housing costs fueled by speculators, greedy builders selling houses for the highest possible price, and American home buyers doing anything possible to buy a house, including mortgaging their future.

First, renting a home or apartment means no down payment. The $60,000 for a down payment that I may never have is no longer an issue. Once I graduate and get a job, I will be able to get into a decent home with no money down. I won't own the home, but how much different is that from living in a house that I am "buying" but that the bank owns for most of my life?

Second, it is usually cheaper to rent a home on a monthly basis than to buy it since as a renter, you are not responsible for property taxes or home insurance. By renting a somewhat older home, you are probably making payments for the owner of the home who bought it at a lesser price than it would be worth today, making your payments less than if you bought the same house. When you add the positives of having no down payment and the lower monthly cost, renting a home indefinitely sounds like an attractive option.

Of course, people will tell you what you are missing out on by not buying a home. First, you don't get the tax break for deductible loan interest payments that buyers get, but what you save by not making a $60,000 down payment and having lower monthly payments more than exceeds the tax break for many years. Second, you are not building up equity in your house like the buyer is. However, the reality is that most people never see that equity money since they either don't move or they invest the money in their next house, and it is not the buyers but their offspring who usually reap the equity benefits. In addition, if you invest the money you save monthly by renting compared to buying a house, you may end up with more money than the buyers' equity value in their house.

As we know, the overheated housing market has finally cooled some, but in many parts of the country, the gap between income and house prices remains far too great for millions of people to buy a house. It is time to start looking at renting as a viable lifetime choice, one which doesn't carry the stigma of destroying the American Dream. Let's take a closer look at that option.

Another argument for buying a home is that one day you will have it paid off while the renter keeps on paying for a lifetime. This is true, and if a first-time buyer can survive a thirty-year mortgage without foreclosure and with the sacrifices his family has made, he certainly deserves some years without payments. In addition, while your rent can go up over the years, the house payments remain the same for buyers if they are on fixed-rate loans. However, since the home buyer is probably paying considerably more than the renter to begin with, the cost of rent may never exceed what the buyer pays.

Of course, the arguments for or against renting or buying a home are academic for those who can't afford a home. They are stuck with renting for better or worse, but as we've seen, renting is not such a bad option. The people that are making the tough decision are those like myself who come from generations of home buyers and who have bought into the belief that home ownership means success. That is why people drive four or five hours round trip to work in the city and live far away where housing is cheaper. That is why young mothers work a lifetime to help make the mortgage payments, their children raised in day care facilities eight to ten hours a day. That is why couples can't afford to take a vacation, save money, or have that second or third child. "With the house," I have heard people say, "we just can't afford a lot of things."

The question comes down to what a person is willing to sacrifice to own a home today. Obviously, the answer for many people is, an awful lot. I will be in that same position at some point, and I have grown comfortable enough with renting during college that it is an option I will consider for my future. I believe that renting a home long-term may someday be comparable with the popularity of leasing automobiles. Unless the housing market is absolutely turned on its head, which is unlikely to happen, there may be little choice for most of us.

Activity 1.12

Paragraph the following first draft of an essay by marking off the beginning of each paragraph. Change paragraphs as the writer ends one thought and moves to another.

The Cruel World of Little Girls

I picked up my niece from her second grade class the other day and rather than her usual cheerful self, she seemed a bit distracted. I asked her what was wrong and she said, "Nothing," but her silence and serious face indicated otherwise. I knew something was bothering her and that she'd tell me in her own good time. Driving her to her home, I asked again, "What's wrong, honey?" and she said, "I had a little problem at school." She went on to tell me that one of her friends, Jo Ann, told her that if she played with another one of her friends, Miriam, that she wouldn't be her friend anymore. She had told her this at lunch and it had bothered her the rest of the day, so much that she had trouble concentrating on her math problems. This was not the first troubling incident that she had experienced with one girl in class or another, and while it may appear rather inconsequential and just part of the "girls will be girls" world, it is no trifling matter to my niece or other girls her age. Little girls can be cruel, and it is a problem that affects their daily lives. Some girls seem to be very possessive at an early age. My niece Breanna's friend Jo Ann seems like a nice little girl, but she wants Breanna all to herself. She gets very jealous when Breanna plays with other girls, like her friend Miriam, and threatens her with reprisals. Jo Ann, however, plays with other girls whenever she wants, and doesn't follow the code of loyalty she tries to exact upon Breanna. Jo Ann and Miriam, according to Breanna, are arch enemies, with Breanna caught in the middle of the tug-of-war. "Why don't you just try to get them together and you can all play together?" I asked her naively. "That's impossible," she said. "They absolutely hate each other." Do seven or eight year old girls really know how to hate? I'm not sure, but they do throw the word around a lot as well as a lot of other words meant to demean or humiliate their target: "I hate you!" "Your hair is so ugly!" "Why are you wearing that awful color?" "I'll never play with you again!" You're not invited to my birthday party!" "You smell bad!" Whatever words they can use to get a rise out of another girl, or to deflate her, they throw out. As we all know, words can really hurt, and second grade girls have already learned that and can use them like poison-tipped arrows. When I try and assure Breanna that so-and-so didn't really mean what she said and she should ignore it, she'll say, "Oh no. She meant it." Breanna is fortunate that she is a nice and popular girl who likes just about everybody and doesn't care for disputes. She is more often the observer of the cruel behavior than the recipient. The larger targets are girls like Kendall, who is loud and somewhat hyperactive, dresses differently, and doesn't fit the second-grade norm. Ostracism isn't too strong a word for how Kendall is treated by her classmates: not invited to birthday parties, not asked to play with other girls at recess or sit with them at lunch, not getting many cards at the class Valentine's Day party. When she isn't being ostracized, she is being teased about her hair, her clothes, the way she talks, even about her parents, who appear older than the parents of the other girls. Breanna says matter-of-factly, "No one likes Kendall," my niece being one of the few people who try to be nice to her. When I read about a thirteen or fourteen-year-old girl committing suicide, I am no longer completely shocked. She might have been a Kendall when she was eight years old, and things didn't get better. I love my niece very much, and I feel for her when she comes home upset over the way she or other girls have been treated by their classmates. She usually mentions the same girls who cause most of the problems, but no one seems immune to being hurt or slighted on occasion. Most of the problems occur at recess or lunch, and I don't know how aware the teacher is to what goes on outside the classroom. I do know that the problems have gone on all year, and that seems wrong. Schools need to do all they can to create a safe, non-threatening environment in which all students can learn and be happy. I don't see that happening in my niece's school. It is obvious through my niece's experiences that the often cruel ways that junior high and high school girls treat one another, as depicted in movies and written about in books, begin at a much earlier age. Is there anything that teachers or parents can do about it? I think there is, and the first thing is to acknowledge that the behavior of some young girls towards their classmates is unacceptable. Children need to be taught that it is absolutely wrong to pick on anyone because they are different, to be tolerant of the individual differences that make us all unique, and that being mean to your classmates is inappropriate and unacceptable. They need to understand that snubbing and shutting out others is wrong and that being kind and including others is right. They must also learn that any kind of threatening language is wrong and won't be tolerated: threatening not to be someone's friend if they play with others; threatening never to talk to someone again; threatening to do something to someone if they act a certain way; or saying mean things about someone to their face or behind their back. Finally, teachers need to find ways that young girls can tell them when such behavior is occurring without feeling they are "tattling" and being subjected to retaliation by the accused. Some teachers apparently don't really want to know what's going on, and Breanna told me that her teacher has said, "You girls just work it out together," like it is their problem and not hers. If girls could just "work it out together," these problems wouldn't be occurring, so that is no answer. The world of little girls is not always as bright and fun-filled as it may appear, and the slights, taunts, and threats are real and deeply felt. The casual cruelty among little girls must be stopped. If not, it just gets worse as they get older.

Activity 1.13

Revise your draft keeping in mind the "Revision Guidelines" presented.

Once your essay has been revised to the point that you are satisfied, you are ready to do the final "polishing" before sharing it with readers. Basically, you are eliminating any grammatical, punctuation, or spelling errors and perhaps making a final wording change or two.

Sometimes writers are so ready to let a paper go after revising it that they have little patience with the editing process. Certainly, proofreading a paper for errors isn't the most exciting part of writing. The reality, however, is that even the most accomplished writers make mistakes, and that is why publishing companies have the drafts of all their writers proofread for errors.

While spelling and grammar check programs on word processors certainly help the editing process, they do not necessarily catch all of the mistakes that writers make. And unless a writer knows *why* he made a particular error, he will more than likely continue making it in the future. Writers need to do their own careful proofreading for errors in combination with using spelling and grammar checks.

As a college writer, you no doubt know the "rules" that govern grammar usage, spelling, and punctuation and apply them without thinking, so the majority of your errors probably come from inadvertent slips. Therefore, the "editing" sections will not belabor these rules but devote themselves to specific grammatical or syntactical situations where writers are most prone to make errors.

Editing Checklist

When you're proofreading your paper for errors, the following checklist will help ensure that you don't overlook any aspect of grammar usage, punctuation, or spelling.

1. **Spelling.** Use the spell check on your word processor and also proofread your paper for spelling errors. Most spell checks do not flush out words that are spelled correctly but used incorrectly (e.g. *There* motives aren't as altruistic as one might imagine.), so pay particular attention to *homophones*, words that sound the same but are spelled differently, and similar sounding words.

2. **Punctuation**. Check to make sure you use the following correctly:
    End marks (periods, question marks, exclamation marks) are used to designate the end of each sentence. As you read your sentences, look for any *run-on sentences, comma splices,*

or sentence fragments, and punctuate them correctly to eliminate the problems.

Commas are used to separate words or phrases in a series; after introductory dependent clauses and prepositional, participial, and ~~gerund phrases~~; ~~after~~ [*before*] conjunctions in a compound sentence; after *interrupters* such as "by the way," "incidentally," or "of course" at the beginning or within a sentence; before and after appositives or unrestricted relative clauses; before ending participial phrases; or at a place in a sentence where a pause is necessary for the sentence to be read and understood correctly. [*wrong* ✱ α]

Semi-colons are used to connect two closely related sentences or to separate phrases within a lengthy series that also contain commas within the phrases (See the sentence above beginning with "*Commas.*").

Colons are used to set off a summary, series, or example following a main clause.

Dashes are used to set off a summary, series, or example *within* a sentence: The most difficult part of helping a child with school work - letting her learn from her own mistakes - is also one of the most important.

Apostrophes are used to identify possessive words and contractions.

Quotation marks are used to set off direct quotations.

3. **Grammar.** Check to make sure that your verbs agree with their subjects, pronouns agree with their antecedents, the correct pronoun subject and object forms are used, the correct comparative and superlative adjective forms are used, the correct adverb forms are used, and the correct irregular past tense verb forms are used. (See the upcoming section on subject-verb agreement.)

Subject-Verb Agreement

While subject-verb agreement is not a frequent problem for most college writers, errors can occur in complicated sentences where the subject is separated from the verb and the incorrect verb form doesn't necessarily "sound" wrong to the writer.

For example, in the following sentence, the subject-verb agreement problem doesn't necessarily jump out at a reader:

> An extensive report by the National Dropout Prevention Center, "Dropout Risk Factors and Exemplary Programs," highlight the type of programs across the country that have proven effective in reducing the high school dropout rate.

However, a careful proofreading of the sentence identifies the verb error: the verb "highlight" does not agree with the singular subject "report." Here is the corrected sentence with the subject and verb in italics:

> An extensive report by the National Dropout Prevention Center, "Dropout Risk Factors and Exemplary Programs," highlights the type of programs across the country that have proven effective in reducing the high school dropout rate.

For such a sentence, many writers would have to proofread it carefully and rely on their knowledge of the rules rather than their "eye" or "ear" to detect the error.

In proofreading a draft for subject-verb agreement problems, consider the following suggestions.

1. Look for longer, more complicated sentences written in the present tense.
2. Look for sentences where the subject(s) and verb(s) are separated by other words.
3. Look for a word or words between the subject and verb that are *opposite* in number to the subject (e.g. plural instead of singular or singular instead of plural) and that might influence you to use the incorrect verb form.
4. In complicated sentences, identify the subject(s) and make sure that the verb(s) agrees with it.

Activity 1.14

Proofread the following sentences for subject-verb agreement problems and correct any verb that doesn't agree with its subject.

EXAMPLE

Demographics across most colleges in the country shows an increasing percentage of women and a decreasing percentage of men attending college.

Corrected:

Demographics across most colleges in the country *show* an increasing percentage of women attending college and a decreasing percentage of men.

1. The fee increase apparently was done behind doors with considerable input from the athletic department, and the exclusion of student input and the lack of transparency over why the increase was enacted makes the process appear somewhat shady.
2. Dropping out of school comes from a culmination of negative experiences that often goes back to elementary school.
3. You have learned how to establish a purpose for your writing and craft your essay in ways that best accomplishes that purpose.
4. However, the longstanding success of government-sponsored health care programs such as Medicare, Medicaid, SCHIP, and FEHB (Federal Employees' Health Benefits) fly in the face of such criticism.
5. Noted archaeologist Marcus Freeman believes that the greatest archaeological discoveries of the earliest forms of man lies ahead of us.
6. When using sources for a writer's information, evidence from acknowledged experts in a field or from highly regarded journals or periodicals often carry the greatest weight.
7. There appears to have been no similar efforts to provide medical services to children of uninsured workers.
8. Public opinion is changing, however, as more research on the subject and studies on the effects of weightlifting on seniors has been publicized.
9. Acknowledging sources in your writing - letting readers know where you found particular pieces of information - have a definite purpose.
10. The reason for the fee increase was never made public

although anyone following the alleged travails of the athletic department know that reason.

11. A survey of Wolfe State's part-time instructors, as well as similar surveys at other colleges, reveal widespread dissatisfaction with colleges' hiring practices.

12. Longitudinal studies by the state's Department of Pre-school Education clearly shows that children who do well in elementary school continue to do well in middle school and high school.

13. Figurative analogies, which use words metaphorically rather than literally, often appeal to the creative fancy of readers and remains in their minds.

14. Downloading a CD illegally from the Internet or stealing it from a record store result in the same thing: depriving the recording artists and the recording companies of the revenue from their creations.

15. A wealth of potential writing topics are no farther away than the morning paper or the latest Internet news flashes.

Activity 1.15

Proofread your revised draft for errors and make any necessary corrections.

Readings

Birth Order: Fun to Debate, but How Important?
By Perri Klass, M.D.

The older girl was smart, neat and perfectly behaved in school; in her spare time, she won dance trophies. At every checkup, her mother would tell me what a good girl she was.

She is the oldest, her mother would say, so she gets lots of attention, and she works very hard. When her younger sister turned out to be an equally good student, the proud mother explained that naturally she wanted to be just like her older sister. Then a long-looked-for baby boy was born. When he was a toddler, I began to worry that his speech seemed a little slow in coming. His mother was perfectly calm about it. He is the only boy, she said, so he gets lots of attention, and he doesn't have to work very hard. Everyone takes it personally when it comes to birth order. After all, everyone is an oldest or a middle or a youngest or an only child, and even as adults we revert almost inevitably to a joke or resentment or rivalry that we've never quite outgrown. Children and parents alike are profoundly affected by the constellations of siblings; it is said that no two children grow up in the same family, because each sibling's experience is so different. But that doesn't mean the effects of birth order are as clear or straightforward as we sometimes make them sound. Indeed, birth order can be used to explain every trait and its precise opposite. I'm competitive, driven — typical oldest child! My brother, two years younger, is even more competitive, more driven — typical second child, always trying to catch up! I surveyed some experienced pediatricians about when parents are likely to bring up birth order. Many cited the issue of speech, especially when a second child doesn't talk as well or as early as the first. And parents are likely to talk about mistakes they think they made the first time around. This time, we're going to solve the sleep thing good and early. This time, we're going to get it right with potty training. This time, we're going to sign the child up for soccer. "Too many parents are haunted by experiences both good and bad that they identify with their birth order," said Dr. Peter A. Gorski, a professor of pediatrics, public health and psychiatry at the University of South Florida. And that might lead them to classify their own children according to birth order, he went on, which in turn can lead to a sense of identification or even rejection and to "self-fulfilling prophecies."

Frank J. Sulloway, a visiting scholar at the University of California, Berkeley, and the author of "Born to Rebel: Birth Order, Family Dynamics and Creative Lives" (Pantheon, 1996), points out that second-born children tend to be exposed to less language than eldest children. "The best environment to grow up in is basically two parents who are chattering away at you with fancy words," Dr. Sulloway said. He cited a huge and well-publicized Norwegian study published in 2007, which found that eldest siblings' I.Q.'s averaged about three points higher than their younger brothers'.(The study made use of Norwegian military records, so all the subjects were male.)

Those differences in verbal stimulation, like the differences in I.Q., are "relatively modest," Dr. Sulloway continued, and unlikely to result in clinical speech delays. But in a child who is already vulnerable, a child who may be temperamentally less likely to evoke adults' attention, or a child growing up in a less stimulating home - well, then, being the second child might be the added risk that makes the difference, he said. Birth order doesn't cause anything," Dr. Sulloway said. "It's simply a proxy for the actual mechanisms that go on in family dynamics that shape character and personality." We can all cite examples and counterexamples, from our own families, our friends, history and literature. There are plenty of families where the younger child is brighter or more academic, and plenty of literary and historical examples (Jane and Elizabeth Bennet, Meg and Jo March, Dmitri and Ivan Karamazov — and you can think about those authors and their older siblings as well, and draw any comparisons you like). And then there are plenty of examples of brilliant eldest siblings, but given my own eldest status, I will refrain from citing any. (I told you this always gets personal.) I.Q., though it does grab headlines, may shape family life less than personality and temperament. "It's a part of a bigger picture that really involves family dynamics," Dr. Sulloway said. "Child and family dynamics is like a chessboard; birth order is like a knight." Then there are all the other influences, from family size to socioeconomic status. "Typically firstborns tend to boss their younger siblings around, but what if you're a very shy person?" Dr. Sulloway said. "Napoleon was a second-born and his older brother was a very shy guy, and he usurped the older-sibling niche because his older sibling didn't occupy that niche. "And why didn't he occupy that niche? Temperament."

Now, of course birth order played into my patients' patterns, but so did gender and birth spacing and, above all, temperament. That little boy was more even-tempered, more placid than either of his sisters, easily soothed, and I think he would have shown that temperament no matter what.

But temperament also helped define his relationship to the four larger people in his immediate circle. "I wouldn't discount the impact of birth order," Dr. Gorski told me. "It sets up the structure of one's place in relation to others from the beginning, as we learn how to react to people of different ages and different relationships."

Pediatricians are always being warned not to let a speech delay slip past because of parents' beliefs that boys talk later or that youngest children talk later. I did eventually insist on a hearing test and speech therapy for this little boy. As it turned out, his hearing was fine, and his sisters drilled him over and over with "use your words" exercises until his speech improved. That is one of the advantages of having hardworking older sisters.

DISCUSSION

1. What is the thesis of the essay: the main point the author is making on the effects of birth order?
2. What empirical evidence does Klass provide in the essay, and to what purpose does he use it? How does it help him make the case for his thesis?
3. Discuss the essay statement, "...it is said that no two children grow up in the same family, because each sibling's experience is so different." How true is this statement based on your own experience and observation, and what impact, if any, might it have on children?
4. Discuss the meaning of the statement, "Child and family dynamics is like a chessboard; birth order is like a knight." How does the statement relate to the essay's thesis?
5. How well do you think the essay made the case for its thesis? What impact, if any, did the essay have on you?
6. Based on your own experience and observations, what role, if any, do you think that birth order has in determining the intelligence or personality of a child, or in the way that he or she is treated by parents or siblings?

A T-Shirt Campaign To Bring Students Out of the Closet
by Greg Bloom

In 1999, my freshman year at Duke, the Princeton Review's college guide ranked my university No. 1 in the nation under the category, "Alternative Lifestyles Not An Alternative." This embarrassing citation of homophobia at Duke became a factoid that popped up in conversation throughout my time there. There was no better shorthand way to complain, "Our school is *so lame.*"

But aside from typical fratty juvenilia, you'd probably never see an open display of intolerance at Duke. On the other hand, you were equally unlikely to see an openly gay couple together on campus. In fact, I could count the number of "out" people I knew on two hands. That was Duke's sexual orientation "problem"--it wasn't so much that "alternative lifestyles" were actively discouraged, but rather that they were not really acknowledged in the first place. They were invisible.

Before I graduated, however, that changed unexpectedly and significantly. In the final few weeks of 2003, a distinctive T-shirt appeared on campus, hardly more conspicuous than your standard ironic hipster garb, except for its wholly un-ironic slogan: Gay? Fine by Me. That tee-shirt eventually made its way across campuses throughout the country, opening a dialogue among students on homosexuality and creating a more accepting college environment for gays.

The shirts had been designed, ordered and distributed by Lucas Schaefer, a junior at the time, and Leila Nesson Wolfrum, a graduate student, along with a group of their friends. "A lot of people we know support equal rights and oppose homophobia, but weren't vocal about it because there was the perception that everyone else was homophobic," explained Nesson Wolfrum, who is straight. The group deliberated carefully about the most effective way to shatter that perception, and crafted a plan that was both simple and, in its way, greatly ambitious. Schaefer, who is gay, added: "Ultimately, we wanted to create a community where people felt more comfortable coming out of the closet."

I ordered my T-shirt in the first batch. The first thing I noticed while wearing it was that this was actually a great way to meet women. But within a few days, the shirts were everywhere, and I noticed something else: With this personal statement painted on my chest, I shared a bond with every other person who was making the same statement. In those spring days, with prospective freshmen walking everywhere around campus, the Duke community was colorfully, proudly accepting of diverse sexual orientations.

This year, the *Advocate*, a national gay and lesbian news magazine, ranked Duke among the top 20 LGBT-friendly schools in the country. And since 2003, the Fine By Me project has taken on a life of its own. Word of mouth spread through friends, gay-straight alliances, and other support groups, and orders for more T-shirts came in from colleges across the country. For almost two years after that initial program, Nesson Wolfrum herself coordinated the distribution of over 14,000 "gay? fine by me" shirts. And that was before the 2004 election, when things got really serious.

"That was the 'moral values' moment," Nesson Wolfrum recalled, in reference to the widespread interpretation that homophobic "moral values" was a major factor that November. "Pundits and various anti-gay groups made it seem as if the vast majority of Americans were unsupportive of gay rights," Schaefer remembered. "That's just not true in my experience. Of course, I know that there is a great body of people out there who vehemently oppose me having the same rights as they do. But my hunch--and this is backed up by what we've learned through doing the T-Shirt Project in communities across the country--is that most Americans aren't homophobic, they're just shy about advertising their acceptance. They think that most other people condemn gays, and so they're afraid to stand up and say that they don't."

In 2005, Schaefer and Nesson Wolfrum relaunched Gay? Fine By Me, and incorporated it as a nonprofit organization. Today, Fine By Me campaigns have run in over 200 communities. Last month alone, at least 50 college campuses were treated to the coordinated display of 12,000 students, faculty, and staff who are openly tolerant of a diverse spectrum of sexual orientation.

Schaefer regularly travels to new campuses to give presentations about what the program is all about. From there, the effect is viral--the T-shirts have a way of moving themselves around--and every week a new group or two decides to launch their own campaign. "Our basic philosophy is that you know your community better than we do," says Schaefer of his organization's relationship with the groups that run Fine By Me campaigns. "Our experience is that this program can work in any community, and we'll tell you what worked for us and what worked for other groups, but how you want to implement it is pretty much up to you."

The resulting campaigns have been remarkably diverse. For instance, at Boston College, over 1,000 shirts were worn to a march in demand of a change to the administration's non-discrimination policy to include sexual orientation (the administration is currently "re-evaluating" the policy).

At the conservative Christian Messiah College in Pennsylvania, 25 student activists wore the shirt to an impromptu picnic. Marten Beels, the initial organizer of Messiah's Gay? Fine By Me campaign, had already attended one religious school--the traditionally-Mennonite Goshen College--before transferring to Messiah. "In Goshen, it wasn't totally open...but there was an active conversation with many people involved," Beels explained. "I was used to that comfortable atmosphere....But at Messiah, it felt like a big void, a prohibitive and even threatening void." Beels knew he wanted to do something for some time before he learned of Gay? Fine By Me.

Reaction to the campaign was, predictably, mixed, but in response, the Messiah faculty convened a panel discussion entitled "How to Have Civil Discourse." The program continues at Messiah this year, although it has now changed: Shirts read "homophobia is a social disease"--less succinct, but subtly poised to be more palatable on Messiah's campus." In Christian circles, we often say you have to separate the sin from the sinner. Accept homosexuals as people, but not homosexuals. So a statement that homophobia is a social disease, that's more toward common ground," Marten said.

One of the most remarkable Gay? Fine By Me campaigns occurred at Notre Dame, a school that had also, in 2003, ranked first on the Princeton Review's "Alternative Lifestyles not an Alternative" list. That year, Notre Dame's gay-straight alliance was once again denied recognition as a student group--first by the student government, and then by the board of trustees. Recognition would have provided not just access to money for programming, but even the basic permission to advertise meetings and events. In response to the administration's refusal, the students ordered 3,000 bright orange shirts.

Joe Dickmann, who was at the time a board member of the unrecognized LGBT support group OutreachND, wrote over email about their campaign: "University administration...gave us no support and repeatedly tried to sabotage our efforts, [so] we ran on volunteer labor, credit card debt, favors, donations, and an outpouring of support that inspires me to this day. Our fliers got torn down, so we worked through email and word of mouth, ultimately delivering 2,300 T-shirts by year's end. We drove our big gay truck through every loophole we could find."

Ultimately, it will take more than a few boxes of T-shirts to change the policies of a school with strong formal ties to the Catholic church, but as a first step toward dialogue, the campaign was widely held as an overwhelming success. "The board of trustees could try to assert what the school was about, but the students themselves still had more control over who was an accepted member of the school's community," Nesson Wolfrum said. "They couldn't change the rules, but they could completely overwhelm as a visible presence."

The Gay? Fine By Me project does have its critics. Some argue that it sets the bar too low by calling only for individual tolerance, instead of complete societal acceptance. Joy Pugh, program coordinator of the LGBT Resource Center at the University of Virginia, acknowledged this limitation, but said that within these limits, the project is uniquely valuable.

"A lot of...LGBT work can gloss over the importance of allies, and this is the perfect program for allies," she said. "This is a big step, to get someone to put it on their body. It gives people a different experience than just talking about these issues in a safe space--there is a personal risk in taking a stand on an issue in a public environment where people might feel differently, and in doing that, their consciousness is raised about how LGBT people have to move around in the world between places that are 'safe' or otherwise. Several of our heterosexual partici-pants told me that they found the experience empowering, in a way."

Many schools have made "Fine By Me" into an annual campaign, and though the novelty might wear off, there are always fresh students who are interested in participating. Gay? Fine By Me is also consider-ing other settings and messages that might be effective, including, "gay marriage? fine by me" campaigns, and more subtle steps like "fine by me" pins for hospital nursing staff and social workers.

Of course, Pugh adds, "I would not want to see us doing this pro-gram 10 years in a row, because it would mean that we haven't been moving forward."

Schaefer is quick to acknowledge that "this is a first step, not a final step.... The purpose is not to create a country in which everyone has a Fine By Me shirt. It's to create a country where you don't need the shirts in the first place."

DISCUSSION

1. What is the thesis of the essay: the main point the author is making regarding the "Gay? Fine by Me" tee-shirt campaign?
2. What empirical evidence does Bloom use to support his thesis and develop the essay, and how effectively is it used?
3. How and to what extent is Bloom's empirical evidence cor-roborated by the experiences presented at other college cam-puses where the "gay? fine by me" campaign was launched?
4. What critical reaction to the campaign was presented in the essay, and how was it addressed?
5. What limitations did the Gay? Fine by Me campaign admit-tedly have according to both supporters and detractors, and in what way is it considered a "means" rather than an "end?"
6. Based on your empirical experience and observations, what is the attitude towards gays on your college campus, and how would a "Gay? Fine by Me" tee-shirt campaign be taken?

The Case Against Quick-Fix Marriage
By Anna Monardo

Apparently stupidity is the new intelligence. That was my first thought after reading Lori Gottlieb's much-discussed article "Marry Him!" in a current issue of *The Atlantic*. And I'm not referring to Gottlieb's stupidity - which is just immaturity - but rather that of the magazine editors who published the piece. Gottlieb's premise: All women want to marry and have a family; therefore, women under 35 should seriously consider "settling" and marrying "Mr. Good Enough," the man who is not a soul mate but who in time may end up being an adequate partner in the business of parenting. Okay, whatever. What's dicey here is that Gottlieb supports her marry-quick-now scare with a recurrent riff on her loneliness as a single mother by choice. The hard data providing backbone to her argument: episodes of *Sex in the City* and *Friends*. And The Atlantic editors went along with it.

Gottlieb admits that her plan was "that I would continue to search for true connection" after the birth of her child. I'm a single mother by choice and what I'm wondering is this: When did dating, rather than parenting, become the logical aftermath of childbirth? In her discussion of her post-birth struggle to meet men, date men, find a man to marry who will help raise her child and take out the garbage, Gottlieb did mention her concern for her child's well-being - but not until the last few paragraphs. Way too late. The news is this: For a single mother by choice, the search for the man of your dreams ends the minute the child enters your life. From that point on, if you're looking, you're looking for a father for your child, and for that role, settling" is simply not an option. Talk about slim pickin's.

Yes, it is absolutely true that when women - and men - are pre-middle-age, their pool of potential mates is larger and less, shall we say, compromised by the natural consequences of aging: weight gain, hair loss, infertility, libido dip, illness and death, to say nothing of the bitterness and financial assaults caused by divorce. So it's just common sense to urge young women - and men - to give themselves a chance by urging them to give the undazzling a break. But why call it settling when what you're advocating is simple human decency: Give someone your attention for a minute or two longer and with a bit more concentration than is required to fill out an on-line dating questionnaire or to sit through a 60-minute tele-drama? Hubris and vanity often make it difficult for young women - and men - to offer that kind of attention. Our quick-fix culture, and the decades-long adolescence Americans enjoy, suggests that finding true love is as easy as hitting the refresh button on your laptop. Gottlieb is correct in her suggestion that love may lurk where you haven't yet bothered to look, or where you haven't looked long enough. But all for the purpose of getting that pesky marriage task off your list?

Gottlieb anticipates that readers of her article will think she's been "co-opted by the cult of the feminist backlash," which is an unavoidable conclusion since her battle cry is directed only at women and since it presents marriage as a cure-all solution and single parenting as a problem rather than a choice. Her argument is an insult not only to single women - and men - but also to married people. The goodenough marriage, from what I've observed, is not something that is settled for but rather something that is achieved over time and with a certain amount of effort, something like what's required for raising a child. Why does the media - particularly forums that are reputedly dedicated to the thoughtful exchange of ideas - continue to showcase banter about how women can, and should, manipulate themselves into marriage?

As for Gottlieb's discussion of single mothering, I don't understand why *The Atlantic* didn't push for a substantial examination of the trend of single-parenthood-by-choice, which is not only a social phenomenon but also a hard-earned opportunity. Many of us who have opted for this chance are awash in gratitude daily that we can, without social stigma and ostracism, enjoy a way of life that was never available to past generations, when, let us never forget!, woman - and men, too - were often prisoners of wildly compromised marriages because otherwise they would not have been able to have or raise children. An intelligent article could have considered the benefits as well as the pitfalls of single parenting and perhaps would have explored ways in which single parents - indeed all parents - can be more adequately supported by employers, federal and state government policies, neighborhood organizations and their own extended families. The last thing those of us who head single families need is for our home lives to be trivialized by tantrums like "Marry Him!"

So, yes, on first glance Gottlieb's rant is all backlash. On second glance, though, I recognized her vision of settling. I know it very well. It is that mirage that taunts every exhausted parent of a young child - the idea that out there somewhere is comfort, support, deus ex machina, an uninterrupted night of sleep, a weekend of nothing but movies and museums. She mentions in passing that her days right now are about potty-training and day care, and I want to tell her what people told me a few years back when my own son was that age (but I was too tired to really hear it): It gets easier as they get older. Lori, you need a nice glass of wine, you need a night out with friends, you need maybe a good cry, but what you don't need - what no one needs - is a quick-fix marriage because there is no such thing. And I'm not saying that single mothers don't need a social life, a romantic life, a sex life; oh my, we do! But looking across the candlelight at a date, we can't start thinking husband until we're also able to see him very clearly as father.

Ultimately I feel empathy for Ms. Gottlieb, both as a woman for whom romantic love has been elusive and as a single mother. I adopted my son when he was four months old and I was 44. I'd spent my twenties to mid-thirties dating in New York City. In my late thirties I had a brief and chaotic marriage. I'm grateful I had that marriage and equally

grateful I'm not in it now. I'm even grateful I didn't manage to have
children then, even though I wished for them mightily throughout the
course of the marriage, which was my first and my husband's third.
Fun, intellectually stimulating, sexy, marked by times of true kindness and intimacy, that married life was completely settle-able. Sure,
there were unpredictable emotional episodes. My husband's previous
wives could have predicted them, and some of the chaos was of my
unique brand. Since marriage had brought me to a small town in the
Midwest, I sometimes affectionately thought of my husband as my own
personal New York City -- sparkling and invigorating, unpredictable
and chaotic, but nothing that a woman who'd managed 17 years of
urban life couldn't deal with.

Reader, I divorced him. Why? Because I wanted a child.

Though I could more or less manage the chaos, any child born of
that marriage would have had to learn how to cope, too, and at what
price? Those personality-distorting accommodations that children
make in order to navigate the storms of their parents' troubled marriage? Accommodations that have repercussions into their adulthood
and on into the next generation? Bequeath that to my child? Never.
Talk about settling. One sadder-but-wiser mother trumps a we're-not-
sure-why-we're-together *folie a deux* any day.

Is single-parenting lonely and difficult? Yes. Are there moments of
despair? Absolutely. Do I wish I'd "settled" and married when I was
young? Absolutely not. God knows, I was as confused as any 30-some-
thing who ever sat on a barstool on Third Avenue, but I trusted my
gut and I still do. If there was a reason not to marry the men I was
with when I was young, well, then there was a reason not to marry.
When you're a single parent there definitely are those times Gottlieb
chronicles, when you look around and see families that are "whole"
or at least look that way from the outside, and you long for what you
imagine is going on over there at that other picnic blanket. Most painful are the moments when you realize that your child is noticing those
families, too, and perhaps wishing that his or her home life included a
fuller cast of characters. There are lonely nights of the soul in every life,
in every family. But that's when, as a parent, you just have to settle in,
show your kid that you believe what you believed the day you chose to
become a single parent: Our family is a fine family just the way we are.

Looking in the recent media, I found a bit of news that seems more
cogent and relevant than *The Atlantic*'s hysteria headlines. It was hidden in the Style section of Sunday's *New York Times*. Yes, back there
near the marriage announcements, which I read weekly, looking in
particular for those weddings between people who are middle-age
or older. I may be without illusions but I am not without hope that

perhaps someday I'll meet a man who is not only the love of my life but also, and more importantly, an excellent father for my son; what I found last Sunday was an unexpected bit of comfort. Daniel Jones, editor of the "Modern Love" column, wrote that while "trying to make sense of the preceding Year in Love" he came across data that shows that earthly happiness hits twice in a person's life: in youth and in old age. Between those two high points is the "trough" of middle age, when most of the heavy lifting gets done - child rearing, career building, relationship negotiating, mortgage paying - a time of struggle no matter what a person's circumstances are.

By mid-life, choices have been made, which is to say that options have been eliminated, which is to say that there is loss. Loss causes pain. When we choose to marry or not to marry, choose to have a child or not, choose to live here rather than there, we are makir.g life-altering decisions not only about what we want but also about what we believe we can manage to live without. Maturity means you are able to live not only with your choices but also with your losses. Every child deserves a parent who can sit still - let's call it settle down - and take in that bit of news.

DISCUSSION

1. What is the thesis of the essay?
2. What empirical evidence does the author provide to support her thesis, and how convincingly does she use it?
3. What major fault does the author find in the article that she is evaluating? Do you agree with her?
4. Discuss the statement that made an impact on the author: "... earthly happiness hits twice in a person's life: in youth and in old age. Between those two high points is the "trough" of middle age, when most of the heavy lifting gets done - child rearing, career building, relationship negotiating, mortgage paying - a time of struggle no matter what a person's circumstances are." Do you agree with the statement, and why?
5. According to the author, what should the priorities of a single mother be? Do you agree with her?

Writers often analyze and evaluate the writing of others, as in the previous essay "The Case Against Quick-Fix Marriages," to provide readers with an assessment of a particular essay, article, editorial, or book. The writers' purposes are varied: to review a writing and recommend to others whether it is worth reading; to analyze a writing and evaluate the validity and significance of its message; to support and champion the ideas of a particular writing; to disagree with and refute the arguments of a particular writing; or to analyze and evaluate the quality of a particular writing: the strength of support for its thesis, its organization and coherence, and its overall impact.

Book reviewers for a periodical such as *The New Yorker*, for example, critique novels and short stories for its readers. Newspaper editorialists often analyze and comment on non-fiction books involving politics, the environment, or other issues of national concern. Writers of letters to the editor of newspapers often respond favorably or unfavorably to letters from other writers. Writers of letters to periodicals often comment on the contents of a particular article from a previous issue. A particular letter to the editor, newspaper editorial, periodical article, or book often illicits a strong reaction from readers, moving them to write a response.

During the essay-reading section of each unit, you will have the opportunity to write a *critique* of a particular essay of your choice, analyzing and evaluating the merits of the essay. Through analyzing and evaluating your own essays, you are also developing the tools to critique the essays of others. Subjecting them to the same scrutiny that you do your own essays, you look for elements such as a clear thesis, strong supportive evidence, organizational coherence, good writing, compelling openings and conclusions, a definite purpose, and a strong overall impact.

Critical Reading

Writing an effective critique begins with a close and careful reading of the essay itself. When we read critically, we attempt to understand the essay in the deepest sense, analyze and evaluate the parts that comprise the whole, scrutinize the arguments in support of the thesis and the evidence to support each argument, determine whether the conclusions drawn follow logically from what has been presented, and consider the value and importance of the essay. In short, we dissect and reconstruct the writing in a manner that leaves us with a thorough understanding and a clear opinion of the essay.

To read an essay critically in preparation for writing a critique, consider the following suggestions:

1. **Read the essay more than once to gain the best understanding.** The second reading of an essay often results in a much greater understanding than the first, and sometimes a third or fourth reading can be useful.

2. **As you read, determine the topic of the essay and the writer's perspective on it - the essay's thesis.** A clear understanding of the topic and the writer's perspective allows you to evaluate how well the writer presents the topic and supports his thesis.

3. **Evaluate the reasons (arguments) the writer uses to support his thesis and the evidence he provides to validate the reasons.** Are the supportive reasons clear and sensible? Does the evidence convincingly validate each reason?

4. **Evaluate other forms of support for the thesis that the essay may include.** Do any examples provided help you understand the essay's ideas more clearly? Does the essay present and address any opposing points of view effectively? Do any comparisons in the essay help make the writer's case?

5. **Does the essay have a strong conclusion that follows logically from what has been presented?** Is the writer's purpose clear? Is the thesis reinforced in some manner?

6. **Evaluate the quality of writing of the essay.** Are the sentences clearly, smoothly worded? Does the writing enhance the overall quality of the essay and make it easy to follow the writer's thoughts?

7. **What if anything may be left out that weakens the essay?** Are there crucial opposing arguments that the essay doesn't address? Are there issues regarding the topic on which the essay is silent? Is there not enough explication of the topic for readers to understand it clearly?

8. **What are the greatest strengths of the essay?** The writer's command of the topic? The wealth of supportive evidence? The clear and compelling examples? The interesting and provocative conclusion?

9. **Do you agree with the writer's perspective?** If so, how does the essay help you reach that conclusion? If not, how does the essay fail in convincing you?

10. **What is the overall impact of the essay?** Is the topic important enough to take seriously? Did you find the topic and the essay interesting? Did the essay make an impres-

sion on you that may be lasting? Did it change your way of thinking about the topic or present some ideas you hadn't considered? How might you think or act differently as a result of having read it?

Activity 1.16

Read, analyze, and evaluate the following essay by applying the critical reading suggestions presented.

Trying Juveniles as Adult Offenders
by Terence Gorsky

Should children and adolescents be sentenced as adults when they commit serious crimes such as murder? It is my position that they should not. Here's why. According to Amnesty International, a human rights watch dog organization, the United States is the only Western democracy that sends youthful offenders to adult court and sentences them to adult prisons. According to Amnesty International the imprisonment of youthful offenders in adult prisons violates United States international treaty obligations prohibiting cruel and inhumane treatment of children and adolescents.

Is this an unwarranted or extreme position to take? I don't believe that it is. Most youthful offenders will be physically and/or sexually assaulted within seventy-two hours of admission to adult correctional facilities. Such abuse will continue to occur on a regular basis for the duration of their incarceration. The effects of this abuse are horrific and include suicides, suicide attempts, severe personality damage, and the development of severe and permanent psychiatric symptoms. These effects make youthful offenders sentenced as adults more dangerous, not less. Our willingness to do this to our children sends a strong message that the level of moral development of elected officials, judges, prosecutors and the general public is rapidly and dangerously declining. We need to ask ourselves an important question: Are we the kind of people who are capable of inflicting cruel and inhumane punishment upon our children and adolescents?

As a nation, we answered that question decades ago with an emphatic no. At that time we recognized that most kids deserve a second chance and can turn their lives around with proper no-nonsense treatment in rehabilitation-oriented juvenile correction centers. We backed up our answer by developing a Juvenile Justice System that protects kids from cruel and inhumane punishment while providing rehabilitation, and teaching the skills necessary to become a productive member of society.

We did all this because it's the right thing to do. We did it because to do less would have been beneath us as one of the most moral nations in the civilized world.

We built our Juvenile Justice System around three critical principles:

1. It is wrong to hold children and adolescents who have not reached legal age to adult standards. They are developmentally immature and often unclear about the nature of right and wrong and without proper adult supervision can have problems with judgment and impulse control causing them to act out impulsively without forethought.

2. With appropriate treatment most children who commit crimes, even the most violent crimes, can be rehabilitated and become responsible adults.

3. A moral society feels obligated to give kids a second chance whenever possible by having a Juvenile Justice System designed to help kids change rather than punish them for past offenses.

Our Juvenile Justice System is based upon the recognition that moral societies value their children and seek to help rather than hurt, treat rather than punish, and rehabilitate rather than destroy. However, not all youthful offenders can be rehabilitated. Some pose a real and present danger and need to be segregated from society. The period of confinement, however, should be designed to give youthful offenders a chance to learn, grow, and change. If long-term protective segregation is required, it should be done in adolescent correctional facilities which protect the children from harm.

It is important to remember that *punishment does not work*. The threat of punishment is an ineffective deterrent to crime, especially for children and adolescents. Punishment is a failed strategy for changing behavior, teaching new skills, or developing new and more positive attitudes and beliefs. The only justification for inflicting harsh punishment is to deliver vengeance in accord with the old testament standard of an eye-for-an-eye.

Loved ones of victims may feel justified in crying out for vengeance. The result is tragic. Vengeance does not relieve the grief and loss. It also instills a sense of inner conflict and guilt. On a deep level most human beings intuitively know that vengeance breeds more vengeance and violence breeds more violence. When people mature to higher levels of moral development, they recognize the obligation to break the cycle of vengeance and retribution.

Tiffany Eunick, age 6, was the victim of violence perpetrated by an unsupervised twelve year old, Lionel Tate. Lionel thought he was playing when he emulated the moves and tactics of the professional wrestlers who were his heroes and role models. He watched professional wrestling week after week. He witnessed hundreds if not thousands of savagely brutal acts perpetrated by professionally wrestlers assuming the personas of theatrical psychopaths. He watched as they savagely body slammed, knee-dropped, and kicked each other.

In his immaturity, he couldn't see that it was all a show. He had inadequate adult supervision. There was no one to point out the dangerousness and immorality of the violent displays he was witnessing. There was no adult present to impress upon his immature mind the danger of using such savage tactics on others.

Lionel, an immature 12 year old, assumed he could do to other kids what these heroic wrestlers did to each other. He assumed the outcome would be the same – no one would really get hurt. Thinking he was playing, Lionel body-slammed, head kicked, and knee dropped Tiffany. It was over quickly. Lionel was shocked and traumatized to see that he killed Tiffany.

Is Lionel a hopeless psychopath who should be locked away for the rest of his life? He doesn't appear to be. Will throwing away Lionel's life bring back Tiffany or sooth the grief of her parents and friends? Probably not. Will Lionel be helped to become a better person as a result of his life-long imprisonment? Definitely not. There is a strong possibility he will attempt suicide to try and escape the torturous consequences of his imprisonment.

So why are we as a nation allowing this to happen? Part of the reason is because our adolescent treatment professionals, the experts trained and educated to know better, are standing silently on the sidelines. The clinical professionals who are obligated to advocate for our youth and to protect our Juvenile Justice System from destruction have failed to act decisively and effectively. As a result the safety of all children is progressively going at risk.

How many children need to be tried, convicted, and imprisoned in adult facilities before it becomes wrong? How many children must be destroyed by a criminal justice system going out of control before we do something?

Writing a Critique

After you have done a critical reading of an essay and formed an opinion, you are ready to write your critique. A critique generally follows a format similar to the following:

Opening

Introduce the author, the essay, and the topic that it discusses without going into detail. Next, present the perspective the essay presents on the topic - the essay's thesis or main focus. Finally, present your viewpoint on the essay - the thesis for your essay.

Middle

Provide a synopsis - a brief summary - of the essay, including the main points in support of the writer's thesis, critical evidence she includes, any opposing arguments that the essay addresses, and pertinent examples or comparisons provided. Next, analyze and evaluate the essay based on the quality and amount of support for the thesis, the impressiveness of the evidence, the response to opposing arguments, and the thoroughness with which the topic is treated, including what may have been left out. The analysis and evaluation often follow the supportive arguments point by point rather than coming at the end of the middle section. (See upcoming critique of the Gorski essay.)

Ending

Based on the analysis and evaluation in the middle section, draw conclusions on the overall impact of the essay and its success in achieving its presumed purpose, all in keeping with the thesis of your critique.

SAMPLE CRITIQUE

Sentencing Children as Adults
by Terence Gorsky

In Terence Gorsky's essay "Sentencing Children as Adults," he makes the case that children should not be tried as adults for committing violent crimes and that America needs to changes its laws regarding youthful offenders. While I agree with the position that the essay takes, I question whether it would convince readers who strongly believe otherwise.

First, the essay contends that America is the only Western democracy that tries juveniles as adults according to Amnesty International. This is certainly a damning comparison, indicating that as a country, we treat juvenile offenders more harshly and less compassionately than similar countries.

Next, the essay claims that juveniles who enter the adult prison system suffer cruel and inhumane treatment, subjected to physical and sexual abuse for the duration of their imprisonment. As a result, they often become suicidal or suffer severe psychiatric damage, and ultimately leave prison more dangerous than they came in. While all of this may be true, the essay provides no evidence to that effect, relying on readers to believe the claims without proof. Many readers may remain skeptical.

The essay makes the argument that imprisoning kids as if they were adults is morally wrong, that children are still developing mentally, that they don't know right from wrong in the same sense as adults, and that as children, they deserve a second chance in any country that cares about its children. That is why we created America's Juvenile Justice System, where children have a chance at rehabilitation rather than being thrown away in adult prisons. It does seem morally wrong to give up on children before they realize the full import of their actions and basically throw their lives away, and the moral argument against adult incarceration is the essay's strongest.

The essay makes a final argument that punishment does not work and that punishing children as adults has absolutely no deterrent effect on other children who may commit violent crimes. That may certainly be the case, but readers are left to rely solely on the say-so of the author since no evidence is provided.

Gorsky addresses two arguments that proponents of the current system would make. First, there are some violent children who are beyond rehabilitation and need to be removed from society. The essay concurs, but says they should be placed in an adolescent rather than adult facility where they can be protected from harm, a sensible response. Second, there are those who believe that the loved ones of victims who have met horrendous fates have the right to expect justice that is commensurate with that fate. This type of vengeance, Gorski says, does no one any good and does nothing to relieve the loss and grief. I question whether advocates of the status quo would agree with him, given the sense of retribution in a country that supports the death penalty and fears the ever-rising occurrence of violent crime.

The essay concludes with the example of a twelve-year old boy who killed a six-year old girl by pummeling and body slamming her like the professional wrestlers he watched on television. He was acting just like his television heroes and had no inkling of the effect of his actions on the young girl. He was tried and sentenced as an adult for the crime, a prime example of a child who did not fathom the consequences of his action and who should never have been tried as an adult. While it is difficult not to agree with the injustice in this case, skeptics would argue that it isn't representative of many of the violent crimes perpetrated by juveniles who shoot, stab, smother, and sexually abuse their victims.

There is little that I disagree with in the Gorsky essay, but in my case the essay is preaching to the choir. However, in a country where violent juveniles have been treated as adults for years, where the death penalty is favored by the majority, where juveniles are committing violent, often horrific crimes at ever-younger ages, and where no politician wants to be seen as soft on crime, any essay aimed at swaying public opinion must be very convincing.

Unfortunately, Gorsky doesn't provide the necessary evidence to convince skeptics that adult punishment isn't a crime deterrent for juveniles, that youthful offenders treated as adults become more dangerous, or that juveniles placed in adult facilities are subjected to interminable physical and sexual abuse. If there is evidence that all of this is true, it needs to be provided in detail. While the moral argument that we need to help our children rather than throw them away is impassioned, I'm afraid that given the current environment, it is overwhelmed by those whose compassion runs much higher for the victims than for the perpetrators.

Activity 1.17

Write a critique on an essay from the text or another essay approved by your instructor.

Unit Two
Factual Evidence

——————————————

Perhaps the strongest evidence that writers use to make their case to readers is *factual*: evidence that is difficult to dispute based on its *verifiable* nature. Although not all readers may be swayed by the power of facts, such evidence is the most frequently used by writers to convince readers that what they are writing is true or valid.

Of course, something is not a fact just because a writer presents it as such. For example, someone may write, "The polar ice cap is melting at a rate of 5% per year." In actuality, this may or may not be the case, and discerning readers would want the writer to provide some evidence before accepting it, such as who conducted the study and how it was done. Beyond that, assuming the information were factual, readers would probably want to know the significance of the information. Is a 5% melt rate cause for alarm?

At other times, a writer may present an *opinion* - a particular belief on a topic - as if it were a fact. For example, someone may write, "Zoo animals would be much better off in their natural environment." This is the writer's opinion, and there may or may not be a factual foundation to support it. If the writer could provide factual evidence that animals live longer in their natural habitat, live healthier lives, and are more physically and mentally active, then many readers may agree with the writer's opinion.

How do writers use factual evidence most effectively in their writing, and how are fact and opinions integrated most successfully in an essay? In addition, what facts can stand alone without need of verification and what facts need substantiating before many readers will accept them? In this unit, answers to these questions will help prepare you to write your next essay, which emphasizes the use of factual evidence in making your case.

Facts and Opinions

In general, a *fact* is something that can be proven or verified as true or existing. It is a fact, for example, that ice will melt at above-freezing temperatures, something that we have all observed many times. An *opinion*, on the other hand, is a belief or viewpoint held by someone which may or may not be based on fact. It is the opinion of some writers, for example, that America's war on Iraq was a mistake. It is the opinion of others that the war was justified. Which viewpoint readers embrace may depend on the factual evidence that writers on each side can produce to support their opinion.

Writers use both facts and opinions in their writing to make their case to readers. A writer's thesis for a particular essay - her viewpoint on the subject - is often an opinion that she supports with factual evidence.

For example, a writer may believe that the strong emphasis on testing in the elementary grades does more harm than good to young students, her thesis for an essay on grade-school testing. To support her thesis and convince readers of its validity, she may rely primarily on facts. She may find that test scores show that students are not reading or computing significantly better than they did prior to the emphasis on testing. She may also be able to prove that teachers today are devoting significantly less classroom time to music and art as a result of the testing emphasis. If such facts do exist, they could lend credibility to the writer's opinion.

Writers need to be aware of how they are integrating facts and opinions within an essay so as not to confuse the two. If a writer is presenting opinions as if they were facts and providing no factual support for them, many readers may ignore them. If a writer is presenting facts without showing clearly how they relate to or support his opinions, readers may not see the connection. The following sections will help you distinguish between fact and opinion in your writing and use them most effectively.

Using Facts

Facts provide perhaps the strongest support for a writer's position on an issue. If a writer can prove that what she is writing is true, she has provided compelling evidence for readers.

The following information will help you use factual evidence most effectively in your writing.

1. **A fact is something that is true or that exists**. A fact can be

proven or verified in a manner that is credible to most people. For example, many people did not want to believe in the monstrous atrocity of the Jewish holocaust perpetrated by the Nazis in World War II. However, as pictorial evidence appeared of thousands upon thousands of skeletons buried together, people began believing the unthinkable: that the horrific tragedy did in fact occur.

2. **An *accepted fact* is one that most people would agree upon *without further verification*.** For example, most people know that the earth and other planets in our solar system revolve around the sun, that boys in general are more physically aggressive than girls, and that the cycle of poverty among our country's poorer citizens tends to perpetuate itself from one generation to the next. When you present a generally accepted fact in your writing, you usually don't have to verify it with some type of evidence. It can stand by itself and be accepted by most readers.

3. **An *alleged fact* is one that many people may either not be aware of or necessarily agree is factual.** When a writer presents *alleged facts*, she needs to verify or prove their existence is a manner that is convincing to readers.

    For example, it is an accepted fact that rivers flow into the oceans rather than away from them. However, at certain times with certain bodies of water, rivers at the mouth of an ocean can *reverse* their course and flow backwards *away* from the ocean. Since this is such an unusual phenomenon, a writer presenting this information would probably need to provide factual evidence to convince readers.

    First, he could present a scientific explanation for it, namely that when the water in an ocean bay or harbor rises with the tide to a level higher than the incoming river, it forces the river to reverse its flow. Second, he can reveal specific bays or harbors in the world where the phenomenon exists. Third, he can use the "testimony" of expert oceanographers to confirm the fact based on their research and observation.

    Whenever you present a fact that is not common knowledge or that some readers may question, you need to prove its existence. This may be accomplished by providing research, studies, statistics, or expert testimony that help verify the fact.

4. **All factual evidence is not equal in weight and influence.** To provide the most convincing evidence, consider the following suggestions:

    a. **When finding sources for your information, evidence**

from acknowledged experts in a field or from highly regarded journals or periodicals often carries the greatest weight. For example, a writer's reference to a study in *Scientific Journal Quarterly* on the positive effects of riding horses for autistic children may be more credible than a story in *People* magazine on the same subject.

b. **In general, the greater the size of a research or study sample, the more influential it is.** For example, a two-year study of hair growth on one thousand subjects testing a new hair regeneration product would carry greater weight than a two-month study on ten subjects.

c. **Evidence that readers can clearly understand and relate to often has the greatest impact.** For example, in providing evidence to support the alleged fact that Americans suffered as a result of the skyrocketing gasoline prices in the summer of 2008, what evidence would seem most compelling to readers: that truck drivers had to cut their intra-state driving by 30%, or that 40% fewer Americans took vacations compared to typical summers? Most readers would probably relate to the vacation statistic since it may well have included them.

Activity 2.1

Decide which of the following statements are *accepted facts* or *alleged facts*. For each alleged fact, decide what kinds of factual evidence might be used to verify it.

EXAMPLE

The moon casts no light of its own, and the moonlight on a lake is actually created by sunlight. (accepted fact)

On average, children who attend pre-school do better in kindergarten than children who do not. (alleged fact)

Possible evidence: Compare kindergarten-level skill development in reading and math for students who did and did not attend pre-school; secure testimony from kindergarten teachers regarding comparative social development and adjustment of students who did and did not attend pre-school; compare percentage of students held back in kindergarten who attended and didn't attend pre-school.

1.   Nationwide, rap music is waning in popularity.

2. Adults who were physically abused as children are more likely to abuse their own children.

3. America's history has shown a long migration from the country to the city, and farmers, who once constituted a large majority of the country's workers, are now a small minority.

4. Sexually transmitted diseases (STDs) are reaching epidemic proportions among teenagers.

5. Steroid use among baseball players was responsible for the tremendous home-run records established in the 90's.

6. Although women still tend to live longer than men, the age difference between when men and women die has shrunk significantly in the past twenty years.

7. College tuition is more expensive for today's students than it was for their parents' generation.

8. Throughout history, new immigrants to America have added to its population growth.

9. During the economic recession of 2008 and 2009, the movie industry was one of the few that thrived as Americans continued going to theaters in large numbers.

10. In the last ten years, more pre-teen boys have committed violent crimes than in any ten-year period in history.

Activity 2.2

Read the following short essay and determine where the writer needs to provide some evidence to prove or verify an alleged fact. What type of evidence might she use in each case? The writer's *thesis statement* - her viewpoint on the topic - is underlined.

The Benefits of Weight Lifting for Older People

At fitness centers throughout the country, you see men and women in their seventies and eighties working out. That they are turning out in greater numbers and coming back month after month indicates that they are benefitting from their workouts. It is becoming apparent that if done properly, lifting weights can be a healthy activity for older people.

Of course, the value of aerobic exercise for older people - brisk outdoor walking or walking on a treadmill - has been long accepted. However, until recently, weight lifting has not been a highly recommended activity for seniors. That is changing, though, as more research on the subject and studies on the effects of weightlifting on seniors have been publicized.

First, weight lifting increases muscle strength for people at any age. For seniors, stronger arm and leg muscles enhance their ability to be more active - gardening, working, playing -, which leads to a more productive, enjoyable life. The longer that seniors can remain active the better, and stronger muscles through weight lifting can help them remain active.

Second, in strengthening the leg muscles, seniors can maintain their walking strength and stability. Serious falls among seniors are often caused by weakened leg muscles that the body teeters on, so strengthening the leg muscles through weightlifting helps seniors walk on sturdier legs, which helps to prevent those dreadful falls.

Third, when a senior does fall or has some other sort of accident, the more brittle bones of the elderly break more easily, often with debilitating or life-threatening results. However, when the muscles around the bones are built up and strengthened, they form a protective cushion around the bones which keeps the bones from cracking or breaking as readily. These muscles are best strengthened by weight-lifting, another great benefit for senior lifters.

Finally, weight lifting among seniors has been found to be good for the heart and respiratory system. Although different from aerobic exercise, where the goal is to get the heart rate above normal to strengthen the muscles, weight lifting produces the same heart-strengthening results. All things being equal, seniors who lift weights regularly have more endurance than people who don't. They are able to walk farther, work longer, and exert themselves greater.

If done properly in moderation with lots of stretching and warming up, weight lifting for seniors has a lot of benefits and little downside. It is not surprising that more and more seniors are getting involved in an activity that will improve their health and prolong their lives.

Using Opinions

Writers often have opinions that they share with readers. The degree to which readers are influenced by those opinions often depends on how well the writer *supports* them as well as whether the readers hold similar or differing opinions themselves.

There are times when writers share opinions with like-minded readers in order to move them to action, like getting out the vote for a particular political candidate or to oppose a particular ballot measure. Frequently, however, writers share opinions with readers who hold different opinions or who are neutral on the issue. In such cases, the writer's purpose may be to change the readers' minds, one of the more challenging tasks for any writer.

The following information will help you use *opinions* most effectively in your writing.

1. **An *opinion* is a belief or viewpoint held by a writer that may or may not be based on fact.** The degree to which a writer can support an opinion usually determines the readers' response.

2. **Some opinions are based on feeling and have no factual basis**. A writer may believe that the neighborhood in which she lives is becoming more dangerous because of an influx of immigrants into the area. Her belief may be completely unfounded, based on her fear of people who are different from herself. When you consider writing an opinion on a topic to which you are emotionally attached, make sure that opinion can be supported in ways that readers will accept who may not share that attachment.

3. **Some opinions have a factual basis which supports their validity**. For example, a writer may have the opinion that it is worthwhile for students to decide on a college major and career path before they are out of high school. She may be able to provide factual evidence to support her opinion: that students who decide on a college major in high school graduate on average in a shorter time than those who don't, and that students who choose a career path in high school stick to that path more frequently than students who decide later.

4. **As you write, be aware of when you are stating an opinion and what you need to do for readers to accept it.** For example, if a writer presents the opinion that pre-med is the most difficult of college majors, he needs to provide ample support for those English, philosophy, or engineering majors who may not agree.

Activity 2.3

Decide which of the following opinions may have a factual foundation and the type(s) of support a writer might use to convince readers of their validity.

EXAMPLE

The Swine Flu scare in the United States is overblown.

Opinion that may have a factual foundation. For support, determine the actual number of cases of swine flu compared to other serious communicable diseases; compare latest swine flu "scare" with the swine flu scare of 1986; determine the odds that a person would contract swine flu compared to other serious communicable diseases; compare the health and sanitary conditions in countries where swine flu outbreaks occurred with those in the United States.

Women lawyers don't have the mental toughness to litigate successfully against their male counterparts. (Opinion that likely has no factual foundation.)

1.   The four-day forty-hour work week is better for both the employees and the companies for which they work.
2.   Workers who want to change from a five-day to four-day work week are just lazy.
3.   Most companies that have changed to the four-day forty-hour work week have been satisfied with the results.
4.   The longer ten-hour work days in a four-day week can result in more accidents.
5.   With the three-day weekends created by the four-day work week, workers spend more time with their families.
6.   Managers who are against the four-day work week should be fired.
7.   Productivity actually increases when employees go from a five-day to a four-day work week.
8.   Most of the problems that skeptics of the four-day work week envision never materialize once the new work week is implemented.

Activity 2.4

Read the following short essay and identify both factual statements and opinions. Next, determine which opinions may be based on facts, and which facts are "alleged" and need substantiating. For the opinions and the alleged facts, decide on the types of evidence that the writer might use. Also determine which opinion statements seem unsupportable, and whether they should be deleted or revised.

Our Broken Health Care System

America's health care system is not working well. Health insurance premiums are far too expensive. Many Americans who are sick and need health care can't get insurance because of "pre-existing conditions." Millions of others aren't covered by health care at all, including children. We need to change our health care system so that all Americans have affordable health insurance.

Doctors today are not in the profession to help people. They are in it to make as much money as possible, which is why our health insurance premiums are so high. If doctors charged less, medical costs would go down and insurance premiums would drop. In countries where doctors receive a flat salary rather than getting as much money as they can charge, medical costs are lower and the people benefit as a result.

Pharmaceutical companies contribute to the high cost of health care.. They charge ridiculously high prices for prescribed drugs. Americans pay much higher prices for most prescription drugs than residents of other countries. The government is in collusion with the pharmaceuticals by not allowing Americans to buy their prescription drugs from other countries at considerably lower costs. It is no coincidence that the pharmaceutical lobby is one of the biggest in the country and one of the largest political donors.

Medical insurance companies form the third barrier to affordable health care. These companies exist to make a profit, pure and simple. Profits of medical insurance companies have gone up considerably during the time when insurance premiums have skyrocketed out of control. These companies have one goal: maintain the greatest margin between the price of health insurance and the cost of the actual claims. That is why most of these companies won't accept people with "pre-existing health conditions" such as cancer. They are less concerned about the person's health than about having to pay out the claim money for treatment.

Universal health care could help to solve many of the problems of the current health care crisis. First, all Americans would be insured. Second, medical insurance companies would be eliminated, drastically reducing the cost that comes from insurance profits. Third, with a government-managed system, physicians' salaries could be regulated, as could the cost of prescription drugs. Similar universal systems have been very successful in other countries, and there is no reason that universal health care could not work well in America.

Prewriting

For your upcoming writing assignment, you will write an essay with a thesis supported primarily by factual evidence. During the prewriting phase, you may do a number of things to help prepare to write the paper, including selecting a topic, deciding on a probable thesis, considering some alleged facts that may support it, determining the types of factual evidence needed to verify each alleged fact, investigating your topic to find relevant information, and deciding on a purpose for your essay and a reading audience you would like to reach.

Each "Prewriting" section includes an extensive set of prewriting considerations that often help prepare writers for their first draft. The extent to which you incorporate these considerations into your prewriting process depends on how you best prepare to write a paper. You might write out each prewriting task as presented in the text, do the preparation mentally rather than on paper, or pick and choose those tasks that you feel will best prepare you to write. You might also incorporate other elements that have become a regular part of your prewriting process. With your instructor's guidance, use the prewriting suggestions in the text in ways that you find most productive.

Topic Selection

To select a topic for your upcoming essay, consider these suggestions.

1. Select a topic from any field of interest: political issues, college issues, social issues, health-related issues, educational issues, gender issues, children's issues, legal or ethical issues, criminal issues, media-related issues, family-related issues, financial issues, technological issues, local, state, national, or international issues, and so on.
2. Select an issue that people have differing opinions on.
3. Select an issue that you are interested in, that you know something about, and that is serious or compelling enough to engage readers' interest.
4. Select a topic that you think can be developed through factual evidence, the main source of support for your thesis.

Activity 2.5

Select a topic for your upcoming essay. Take your time and consider different issues of interest to you. You may want to look through newspapers, in periodicals, or on the Internet to find current issues in fields that interest you, or learn more about issues affecting students at the college or residents of the local area.

Sample topic: Increase in the college activity fee

Thesis

The *thesis* for your upcoming paper reveals your opinion or viewpoint on the topic: the position you are taking and supporting in your essay. You may already have a definite opinion on the topic, or you may form an opinion as you learn more about it. You may even change your initial opinion if you find that the factual evidence supports a different conclusion.

For example, let's say that you are writing an essay about the electoral college voting system we use to elect the president every four years. Initially, you may believe that the system should be abolished and that the president should be elected by the popular vote. However, as you learn more about the purpose behind the electoral college and how it helps to provide a voting voice for smaller states, you may reconsider your opinion. Keeping an open mind as you investigate your topic allows you to consider different viewpoints and reach a conclusion based on the best evidence available.

To decide on a thesis for your upcoming paper, consider the following suggestions.

1. Select a thesis that truly reflects your opinion on the topic and that you can support enthusiastically.
2. If you are uncertain about your opinion, learn more about the topic before making a decision, and base your thesis on the conclusion that you draw from your investigation.
3. For your upcoming paper, you need to develop your essay and support your thesis primarily with factual evidence. Therefore, select a thesis for which such factual support is available, something that your topic investigation will help determine.

Activity 2.6

Decide on a tentative thesis statement for your essay, one which expresses your opinion on the topic and that can be supported through factual evidence. You may want to do some investigation of your topic before deciding on a thesis.

Sample topic: Increase in the college activity fee
Thesis statement: Not only should the college activity fee not be increased, it should be reduced.

Providing Support

The development of a thesis-directed essay is quite simple in intent: to explain to readers *why* the writer believes as she does about the topic. The explanation itself may be long and complicated, but the simplicity of intent should not be lost. It provides a litmus-test question for anything that a writer considers including in the essay: will this information help readers understand and accept my opinion on the topic?

For an essay based on factual evidence, most of its development comes in two types of support. The first type is direct support of the thesis: the *reasons* that the writer believes as he does, which are often presented as *alleged facts*. The second type is support of the alleged facts: *factual evidence* that confirms their validity. The two types of support form the core of an essay's middle paragraphs, with each alleged fact often followed by factual evidence supporting it.

For example, let's say a writer's thesis in his essay on ocean pollution is, "Pollution of the oceans is causing irreparable damage to the ecosystem." In the essay, he presents four main reasons for his belief, each an *alleged fact*: 1) The great reefs of the earth's major oceans are being damaged; 2) The marine life that the reefs support is being harmed; 3) Pollution is contaminating the water in many ocean areas and killing marine life; 4) Pollution is drastically affecting the natural order of sea life, causing the extinction of marine and plant species.

Each of these alleged facts strongly supports the essay's thesis, but to convince readers of their validity, the writer needs to provide factual evidence. To that end, he may present studies by marine biologists confirming the destruction of the reefs and its effect on marine life, first-hand accounts of expert divers who have witnessed the destructive effects of contamination on marine and plant life, and statistics revealing significant decreases in the size of various marine and plant species. For each alleged fact, some form of factual evidence is presented to validate it.

To provide the most effective support for your thesis in the upcoming essay, consider the following suggestions.

1. **Generate as many reasons as you can in support of your thesis**. You may not know which reasons are most valid until you investigate your topic. In general, the more verifiable reasons that you can provide to support your thesis, the better you can make your case.

2. **For each reason, consider the types of factual evidence you might provide to confirm its validity, and where you might find such evidence.** For example, in supporting the electoral college as the best way to elect presidents, a writer may point out that in almost every election, the electoral college and the popular vote would have elected the same person. To support

this *alleged fact*, he presents factual evidence showing that in the past twenty elections, only twice did the elected candidate not receive a majority of the popular vote. His source for the information was credible: the historical record of voting results from the Federal Elections Office.

3. **In some cases, you may find no factual evidence to support an alleged fact, or what evidence you find may actually invalidate it.** For example, if the writer had discovered in her investigation that the electoral college and the popular votes were frequently at odds, she couldn't use the alleged fact that the opposite were true. In such a situation, you might rely upon other verifiable reasons to support your thesis, or you might need to reconsider it.

Activity 2.7

For your upcoming paper, generate some reasons in support of your thesis. Then decide on the types of factual evidence you might use to verify each reason and how you might find such evidence.

Topic: Increase in the college's activity fee

Thesis: Not only should the college activity fee not be increased, it should be reduced.

Reasons:
1. The activity fee is already higher than other colleges.
2. The 40% increase will be a burden on many students.
3. The students shouldn't subsidize the athlete program.
4. A reduction, not an increase, in the fee is justified.
5. Students had no say in the fee increase.

Potential factual evidence:
For reason 1: Compare the size of fees at comparable state colleges.
For reason 2: Include all of the college expenses that students already incur.
For reason 3: Show small percentage of students who attend athletic events, and show high percentage of the fee that goes to athletics.
For reason 4: Show that if percentage of the fee that goes to athletics is in proportion to other activities, it could be reduced considerably.
For reason 5: Show that student council wasn't consulted and there was no student referendum on the issue.

Activity 2.8

Based on your topic and the kinds of factual evidence that you might include, do some research on your topic to obtain the best supportive evidence you can find. Depending on your topic, you might be looking through online information, books, periodicals, or newspapers, or talking to school officials or experts on your topic. Make note of any evidence you might use in your essay and the source where you found it.

Differing Perspectives

As presented in Unit One, acknowledging and responding to opposing viewpoints is an important part of writing opinion essays. Writers are often trying to change the viewpoints of their readers, and if they can cast doubt on the underpinning arguments, they may be successful.

It is not realistic to believe that readers will always move off of their position and embrace the writer's. Sometimes writers look for a "middle ground" which can both serve their purpose and bring their readers along. To that end, writers sometime employ the following "strategies."

1. **Considering the perspectives of others may lead to a *qualified* conclusion, one that leaves room for compromise.** For example, a writer opposed to an armed college security force understands how a woman who attends college alone at night would feel safer with armed security officers patrolling campus. This may lead her to *qualifying* her position by conceding that having armed officers patrolling the huge, largely unlit parking lots at night may be the one justified use of armed officers.

    As another example, some anti-abortion advocates qualify their opinion by supporting abortions for rape victims or women with life-threatening pregnancies. Many issues are complicated, and all people may not be affected the same way by them. Therefore, a writer may sometimes qualify his viewpoint to acknowledge this reality.

2. **In responding to differing perspectives, a writer sometimes suggests *alternative measures* in keeping with his thesis.** A writer, for example, opposes the creation of a large downtown lake as part of the city's urban revitalization plan, citing the tremendous expense and questionable drawing power. However, to bring along current supporters of the lake, he suggests that the city look at other watery alternatives such as fountains throughout the mall or a "stream" meandering through the downtown area.

    Another writer who opposes an increase in the local college's tuition acknowledges the school's financial problems and suggests alternative ways to increase income: student enrollment drives, donor drives, budget reductions, larger class sizes. In short, the writers are saying, "We understand the problem, but perhaps there is a different and better way to solve it," one in keeping with their viewpoint.

3.   **Writers often show an understanding of a reader's viewpoint without embracing it.** For example, residents living near a high school opposed the creation of a new event center, citing the noise and traffic in the neighborhood that would be created by large public events. A writer who strongly supported the center wrote that she understood the local neighbors' concerns, and that no residents want more traffic and noise in their neighborhood. She went on to point out, however, that none of the other high school event centers in the city held more than one or two major events a year, so the problem of traffic and noise would be very infrequent, not serious enough to offset the students' need for the center. The writer provided both understanding and reassurance to the neighbors who opposed the center without wavering from her position.

4.   **To gain reader support, a writer sometimes emphasizes how much she and her readers have in common.** If a writer can establish a bond with her readers, they may consider her viewpoint more seriously. For example, the writer who opposed the creation of a downtown lake assured readers that she too supported downtown revitalization, agreed that something new and unique should be tried, and applauded their bold approach to revitalization. The only difference she suggested was an alternative course to the lake, a slightly different means to the same common end. Pointing out what a writer and his readers have in common may help to close the gap between what they differ on.

Activity 2.9

Consider opposing arguments to your thesis that readers might hold and how you might address them most effectively in your essay.

EXAMPLE

   Topic: Increase in the college's activity fee

   Thesis: Not only should the college activity fee not be increased, it should be reduced.

Opposing arguments: Supporters of the fee increase would cite the need for the increase to help the athletic budget, but I will point out that students shouldn't subsidize the athletic program and that there are other, fairer ways to raise money for athletics. Supporters may also feel the increase won't really hurt students, but I will point out that added to all of the other mounting college expenses, it will in fact hurt many students.

Audience and Purpose

Two final considerations for your essay are your reading audience and writing purpose. To decide on your audience and purpose for your upcoming paper, consider these questions:

1. **Whom would I like to read this essay?** Who could benefit from reading it, who could be influenced by it, and who might help to affect a change?
2. **What do I need to keep in mind about my audience?** Their knowledge of the topic? Their viewpoints on the topic? Their ability to affect the topic in some positive way? Their level of interest in the topic? How the topic may affect them?
3. **What would my purpose be in writing to this audience?** To inform or enlighten them? To move them to action? To change their minds? To get them to consider a different perspective?
4. **What writing *tone* should my essay take to help accomplish my purpose?**
5. **Given my reading audience and purpose, how might I best accomplish my purpose with this essay?** Provide the best possible factual evidence? Show how serious the topic is and how it will affect readers? Clear up all of the existing misinformation on the topic? Specify exactly what readers can do to make an impact? All of the above?

Activity 2.10

To consider your reading audience and purpose for your upcoming essay, answer the five previous questions.

EXAMPLE

Topic: increase in college activity fee

1. I would like to reach a broad reading audience including students, instructors, administrators, and college trustees to get as much support as possible.

2. College sports are important to a lot of people in my reading audience, and writing an anti-sports paper will probably just alienate them. These are also educated, basically reasonable people who might listen to a well-supported argument.

3. My ultimate purpose would be to get the fee increase rescinded. I need to convince all readers that the increase is unfair and has a negative impact on students. I need to get students engaged enough to add their voice to my own since that is the only way that the fee increase might be rescinded. I need to get a conversation on the issue going.

4. I don't think an angry tone is best. I think it's best to lay out all the arguments against the fee increase and the evidence supporting those arguments in a calm and reasoned manner. I don't want to rile up the pro-sports element by thinking this is an anti-athletic hit piece, which it isn't.

5. I think the key points to convince readers include the size of the current fee compared to other colleges, the added financial burden on students, and the fact that the large majority of students would not benefit from a fee increase. I also think that it is important to raise the question of whether students should help subsidize the athletic program. I think an emphasis on fairness is important. I also need to pound home the purpose: to get the fee increase rescinded.

Most of the drafting considerations for the first essay that you wrote in Unit I apply to your upcoming draft: having a beginning, middle, and ending to your paper, introducing your topic and thesis in the beginning and developing your topic in the middle, and getting your ideas on paper without concern for perfection.

The new element for your upcoming draft is the inclusion of *factual evidence*, which you may gather from different sources. An important aspect of presenting factual evidence is letting readers know *where* the evidence came from to give credit to your sources and lend credibility to your evidence.

For example, if you wrote that a flying saucer piloted by little green men had landed on a football field in Texas, and noted that your source was the *National Inquirer*, most readers would dismiss the information with a laugh. However, if you wrote that NASA officials had seen strangely hovering objects on a radar screen whose identify they could not confirm, you might take an interest.

Acknowledging Sources

Acknowledging or *citing* sources - letting readers know where you found particular pieces of information - is an important aspect of essay writing. Essayists, editorialists, and article writers who want their ideas to be taken seriously cite the sources for the information that they use to make their case. For example, if an editorialist writes that the earth's oceans are rising as a result of glacial melting caused by global warming, and cites as her source a world-renown oceanographer that has concluded a ten-year study, most readers would tend to take the findings seriously.

There is another important reason for acknowledging sources beyond providing credibility for your evidence. A writer needs to distinguish his own thoughts and ideas from information that he has "borrowed" from other sources, which he does by acknowledging those sources. If a writer mixes his own ideas and his source information without acknowledgment, readers may suspect that he is passing off someone else's ideas as his own, perhaps inadvertently, and is guilty of plagiarism. Clearly acknowledging all sources of borrowed information eliminates that potential problem.

For your essay writing in Units Two - Six, you will acknowledge sources for your information in the body of your essay similarly to how it is done in newspaper, periodical, and online editorials, articles, and essays, and in the readings at the end of each unit. Using this method, you will make clear to readers the source for each piece of evidence you present and distinguish between that source information and your own ideas and responses.

To acknowledge sources effectively in your writing, consider the following suggestions.

1. **Provide the source for any information from your investigation that you include in your essay:**

    According to a study by the State Department of Transportation . . .
    The College Admission's Office reports that . . .
    Noted archaeologist Freeman Johnston has discovered that . . .
    The financial director of the Metropolitan Museum confirmed that . . .
    According to asthma research studies at the UCSF Medical Center . . .

2. **Use the most credible sources available for your evidence since readers will evaluate your sources as well as the evidence.** For example, if you write that the college's student health facility provides outstanding health care, who would be the better source to support that contention: the administrator in charge of the facility or the students who use the facility?

3. **In general, use the most objective sources available and steer away from obviously biased sources.** For example, there is little question that any information on the topic of gun control coming from the National Rifle Association will be in strong opposition, or that "pro choice" organizations will not provide information that does not support their position on abortion.

4. **In general, use sources that readers are most apt to believe**. Experts in their field, studies or research done by universities or established research institutes, polls conducted by credible polling companies, and reputable journals, periodicals, and newspapers are generally the types of sources that carry the most weight with readers.

Activity 2.11

Read the sample first draft on page 80 and note how the writer acknowledges the source for each piece of evidence. You can use this essay as one model for source acknowledgment when writing your own paper.

Drafting Guidelines

When you write the first draft of your essay, keep in mind the following considerations.

1. **In your opening, introduce your topic, engage your readers' interest to motivate them to read further, and present your thesis statement**. Sometimes writers introduce the topic in the opening but withhold their thesis until they have presented their support in the middle paragraphs (See the upcoming sample first draft.). As the evidence grows, there is little question where it is heading, and the intent is to lead readers to the same clear conclusion that the writer reached based on the evidence. Whether you present your thesis in the opening or withhold it until the ending is a decision you make based on your purpose and how you think it can best be accomplished.

2. **In your middle paragraphs, present your reasons - *alleged facts* - in support of your thesis and the *factual evidence* that provides verification for each alleged fact.** When presenting evidence from your sources, *paraphrase* most of the information: *put it into your own words*. Use direct quotes from the source information sparingly for the greatest impact, and when you do, enclose them within quotation marks, along with introducing the source of the quote.

    While providing factual evidence is the focus for this essay, you may also include *empirical evidence* - personal experience and observation - for support if it will help make your case. Use the empirical evidence to *supplement* rather than *supplant* the factual evidence.

3. **Present your supportive reasons in the most effective order for readers.** That order may be from the most to least important reason or vice-versa, grouping related reasons together, or placing the two most compelling reasons at the beginning and end of the middle paragraphs.

4. **Acknowledge sources as you present the factual evidence from your investigation.** Sources can be effectively identified by introductions such as the following: According the County Elections Office clerk, Studies done by the State Department of Education indicate, A survey of ten thousand

asthma sufferers conducted by Duke Medical School reveals that, The chief administrator of the Child Protection Agency confirms.

5. **If readers may not be particularly knowledgeable or well-informed on the issue, provide some explanatory information at the beginning of the middle paragraphs.** Such information may include some background history, a brief overview of the issue, a definition of key terms, or why the issue should be important to readers.

6. **Acknowledge and respond to opposing viewpoints towards the end of the middle paragraphs.** Address only the strongest or most prevalent argument(s), and do so in a way that will help accomplish your purpose.

7. **In your ending, reinforce your thesis in some manner, provide something new for readers to consider, and make your purpose clear.** You might include a summary of your main points, present a final compelling argument, or provide some reasoned speculation on the future of the topic.

8. **Write without great concern for wording or organizational perfection.** The purpose of your first draft is to get your ideas on paper so that you can evaluate both what you have done well and what may need improving.

Activity 1.12

Write the first draft of your essay keeping the drafting guidelines in mind.

Sample first draft

Increasing the Student Activity Fee (audience: students, instructors, school board)

Two months ago, the college increased the student activity fee from $30 to $50 per semester, effective this fall. That represents a sizable 40% fee increase and an additional $40 expense per year for students. While $40 in itself may not sound like a lot of money, when added to all of the other expenses that students incur, it is an additional burden.

Beyond that, many students are questioning the need for such an increase and expressing some concern over how the activity fee money is spent. Why are we seeing such a huge increase in the fee, and is it justified based on the value that students get out of it? The college needs to take a long look at this latest policy change and ask itself if it is truly in the best interests of all students.

Surprisingly, the college's student activity fee was one of the highest among state colleges *before* the fee increase was enacted. Out of ten state colleges, Wellborne State's activity fee was the second highest compared to each college's activity fee as provided by the college's admission's office. In addition, the size of the student population of each school, which is found at each college's online site, has no bearing on the relative amount of the fee. In fact, three out of the four colleges with larger student populations than Wellborne have smaller fees. Since the current fee is among the highest, the 40% increase to $50 would make it by far the highest, a fact that seems difficult to justify.

As most people know, the cost of going to college throughout the state has skyrocketed in the past ten years. The cost of tuition in state colleges, according to a 2008 study by the State Chancellor's Office, has increased by almost 200% in ten years. Over that same period, the cost of living in the state has increased just 25% according to the State's Consumer Price Index (CPI). A student who paid $2000 in annual tuition in 1998 would have to pay over $8000 today. As a result, students are struggling more than ever to pay for college. With the high cost of tuition along with the cost of textbooks, the required health fee, the required parking fee, and required activity fee, now seems like a very bad time to be adding to students' expenses yet another $40.

Where does the money generated by the activity fee go? According to the Dean of Activities' Office, approximately 70% of the fee goes to athletics to help fund the sports' programs. The other 30% is divided among fine arts, the speaker's forum, and social activities. In a recent newspaper article, the college's athletic director said, "Gate receipts from sporting events are down over $2 million from last year, and operating expenses have risen by 5%," so there is little question as to the timing of the fee increase. Students are being required to help replace the athletic department's depleted income.

Wellborne State's mission statement in the student handbook states, "The College is committed to enabling students, including those who have traditionally been excluded from higher education, to realize their educational and personal goals." Perhaps the statement should add, "and to help finance the college's athletic department."

Not only is the practice of students having to help subsidize the school's athletic program highly questionable, what benefit do students get from it? The athletic department ticket office shows that for 2008, 2000 students had tickets to home football games while the other 25,000 tickets were purchased by the public. Of the college's 30,000 students, less than 7% of the students attended football games. The numbers for basketball and baseball are even smaller, according to the ticket office, so the vast majority of students who help support the athletic program derives no benefit from it. In reality, the 70% of the activity fee that goes towards athletics helps keep programs afloat primarily for the benefit of the public.

Who made the decision to increase the activity fee? Certainly not the students, who in a recent poll by the school newspaper opposed the fee increase by a ten-to-one margin among the 3,000 participants. In fact, neither the student body-at-large nor the student council were asked to provide any input on the increase. Nor was the reason for the increase ever made public although anyone following the alleged travails of the athletic department knows the reason. The fee increase apparently was done behind closed doors with considerable input from the athletic department, and the exclusion of student input and the lack of transparency over why the increase was enacted make the process appear somewhat underhanded. The American colonies went to war with their mother country over taxation without representation, so why should students sit by idly when their "taxes" are being raised without any input?

Some people hold those who criticize the fee increase as being anti-athletics, but that is not the case. The athletic program is an important part of the college. However, it should not have to be subsidized by a student population over 90% of whom do not benefit. There should not be a fee increase for students based on decrease in attendance at sporting events. There should not be a fee increase at a time when students are struggling to make ends meet with the high cost of education. There should not be a fee increase when the activity fee at Wellborne is already higher than in all but one other state college. There should not be a fee increase in which students had absolutely not say.

The new fee increase scheduled for the fall needs to be rescinded, and then the entire issue of student subsidization of the athletic department needs to be addressed. When one reads the college's mission statement for students, it becomes obvious how far afield of that statement the increase in the student activity fee has strayed.

After you have completed the first draft of your essay, set it aside for a time before revising it. After distancing yourself from the draft, you will read it more objectively, and elements requiring revision will be more obvious: an awkwardly worded sentence, a sentence that strays from the topic, a paragraph that needs further development, an ending that needs greater punch.

You may be surprised how much professional writers - novelists, essayists, editorialists - revise their work. They may make considerable sentence revisions, move parts of their drafts around, add details, supportive examples, or new points, or completely rewrite the ending. Nothing is sacred in a first draft, and the revision process is often what brings a particular essay or novel to a level of excellence. What readers don't see are all of the revisions the writer made to reach that level.

Revision Guidelines

In deciding what to revise in your current draft, consider the following suggestions.

1. **Read your opening to see whether it clearly introduces the topic, generates interest for readers, and presents the thesis statement.** How might you strengthen your opening, make it more interesting, or sharpen your thesis statement?

2. **Read your middle paragraphs to see whether you have presented each supporting reason (*alleged fact*) in a different paragraph and validated it by providing effective factual evidence.** Have you provided a *source acknowledgment* for each piece of factual evidence in a manner that enhances the credibility of the evidence? Have you presented the source information primarily in your own words (i.e. *paraphrased*) and used quotation marks to enclose any direct quotes? Have you provided any empirical evidence to supplement your factual evidence and provide interest for readers?

    Next, have you presented some explanatory information - background history, definitions, overview - at the beginning of the middle paragraphs to help readers better understand your topic?

    Finally, have you acknowledged and addressed the strongest or most prevalent opposing arguments in a manner that will help accomplish your purpose? Make any revisions in your middle paragraphs that will clarify your supportive reasons, highlight your factual evidence, and strengthen your thesis.

3. **Have you organized the draft effectively?** Are the beginning, middle, and ending sections clearly demarcated? Have you presented the supporting reasons in the best possible order, and does each sentence within a paragraph relate clearly to its topic and follow logically from the previous sentences? Are there any paragraphs or sentences that seem out of order in the draft and that need to be moved? Revise your organization to present your ideas most effectively and make the greatest impact on readers.

4. **Read your draft to see what you might *add* or *delete* to improve it.** As you read, you may think of a new reason supporting your thesis, a personal example to help verify an alleged fact, or a fresh thought to add to your ending. In addition, you may find some sentences or a paragraph that strays from the topic and does nothing to help make your case. Add relevant material to your draft and delete anything that may distract readers from your topic.

5. **Read your ending to see whether it will have the desired impact on readers.** Does it effectively reinforce your thesis, summarize your main supporting points, or present something new and important for readers to consider? Does it make your purpose clear and convincing? Read your conclusion from the perspective that it is the last thing that readers will read. How might you make the strongest final impression?

6. **Read each sentence to see how it might be improved.** Evaluate whether each word in a sentence is critical to its meaning, and delete anything that isn't. Reword awkward or vague sentences, eliminate wordiness, replace questionable word choices with more appropriate ones, and smooth out any rough phrasing.

7. **Reread your draft with your writing purpose in mind.** Is the *tone* of the draft most appropriate for convincing readers? Do the strongest points of your essay stand out clearly? What might you change in any part of the draft to further your purpose and have the greatest effect on readers?

Activity 2.13

Read the sample first draft on page 80 and apply the revision suggestions presented. What revisions might you suggest the writer make to improve the draft and better accomplish her purpose?

Since sentence wording improvement is a major revision concern for most writers, the text provides some sentence revision practice in most units prior to your revising your draft.

Activity 2.14

Revise the following first draft sentences from the sample draft to improve their wording, eliminate unnecessary words, smooth out awkwardly worded sentences, clarify vague sentences, and replace questionable word choices with more appropriate ones. You might divide an overly long, awkward sentence into two more effective sentences. Try out different wording or phrasing options until you are satisfied.

First draft: The huge, massive wave launched itself into the end of the pier out over the water, destroying the railing and gouging out huge sections of wooden two-by-sixes that formed the floor of the pier.

Revised: The massive wave crashed into the end of the pier, destroying the railing and tearing out huge sections of wooden planks.

1. While $40 in itself may not sound like a lot of money, when added to all of the other expenses that students incur, it is an additional burden.
2. Why are we seeing such a huge increase in the fee, and is it justified based on the value that students get out of it?
3. With the high cost of tuition along with the cost of textbooks, the required health fee, the required parking fee, and required activity fee, now seems like a very bad time to be adding to students' expenses yet another $40.
4. With the college's athletic director being quoted in a recent local newspaper article as saying that gate receipts from sporting events were down over $2 million from the previous year and operating expenses had risen by 5% during the same time, there is little question as to why the fee increase was timed as it was.
5. Not only is the practice of students having to help subsidize the school's athletic program highly questionable, what benefit do students get from it?
6. The fee increase apparently was done behind closed doors with considerable input from the athletic department, and the exclusion of student input and the lack of transparency

over the reason for the increase makes the process appear somewhat underhanded.

7.   Some people hold those who criticize the fee increase as being anti-athletics, but that is not the case.

8.   However, the athletic program should not have to be subsidized by a student population over 90% of whom do not attend athletic events at all.

Activity 2.15

Revise the current draft of your essay by applying the six revision suggestions provided and making any changes that would improve the essay.

Once you have revised your paper to your satisfaction, you are ready to proofread it for errors with the goal of producing a cleanly written essay for your reading audience. The following editing checklist is reproduced from the first unit with a new element added from this section so that no aspect of grammar usage, punctuation, or spelling escapes your attention.

Editing Checklist

1. **Spelling.** Use the spell check on your word processor and also proofread your paper for spelling errors. Most spell checks do not flush out words that are spelled correctly but used incorrectly (e.g. *There* motives aren't as altruistic as one might imagine.), so pay particular attention to *homophones*, words that sound the same but are spelled differently, and similar sounding words.

2. **Punctuation**. Check to make sure you use the following correctly:
   End marks (periods, question marks, exclamation marks) are used to designate the end of each sentence. As you read your sentences, look for any *run-on sentences, comma splices, or sentence fragments,* and punctuate them correctly to eliminate the problems.

   Commas are used to separate words or phrases in a series; after introductory dependent clauses and prepositional, participial, and gerund phrases; after conjunctions in a compound sentence; after *interrupters* such as "by the way," "incidentally," or "of course" at the beginning or within a sentences; before and after appositives or unrestricted relative clauses; before ending participial phrases; or at a place in a sentence where a pause is necessary for the sentence to be read and understood correctly.

   Semi-colons are used to connect two closely related sentences or to separate phrases within a lengthy series that also contain commas within the phrases (See the sentence above beginning with "*Commas.*").

   Colons are used to set off a summary, series, or example following a main clause.

Dashes are used to set off a summary, series, or example *within* a sentence: The most difficult part of helping a child with school work - letting her learn from her own mistakes - is also one of the most important.

Apostrophes are used to identify possessive words and contractions.

Quotation marks are used to set off direct quotations.

3.   **Grammar.** Check to make sure that your verbs agree with their subjects, pronouns agree with their antecedents, the correct pronoun subject and object forms are used, the correct comparative and superlative adjective forms are used, the correct adverb forms are used, and the correct irregular past tense verb forms are used.

4.   **Parallelism.** Check to make sure series of words, phrases, or clauses within a sentence are *parallel in construction* (See the upcoming section on "parallelism.")

Parallelism

Within their sentences, writers often include a series of two or more words, phrases, or clauses. The previous sentence, for example, includes the series "words, phrases, or clauses." To produce the clearest, smoothest sentences, writers make each part of a series *parallel* in construction with the other parts, meaning using the same parts of speech and similar word order.

For example, in the following sentence, the phrases in the series are *parallel* in construction.

On our visit to Washington D.C., we enjoyed visiting the National Air/Space Museum, touring the Mt. Vernon estate of George Washington, and taking a cruise on the Potomac.

As you can see, the three phrases in a series - visiting the National Air/Space Museum, touring the Mt. Vernon estate of George Washington, and taking a cruise on the Potomac - are all participial phrases that function as direct objects. The sentence reads smoothly and is easy to follow.

Here is a second version of the same sentence with some parallelism problems.

On our visit to Washington D.C., we enjoyed visiting the National Air/Space Museum, a tour of George Washington's estate at Mt. Vernon, and a Potomac River cruise.

As you can see, the sentence does not read as smoothly as the first version, and the three parts of the series are not parallel. The first part is a participial phrase, the second a noun followed by two prepositional phrases, and the third a noun preceded by two modifiers.

Here are a few more examples of non-parallel sentences followed by revised, parallel versions.

Armand enjoyed science fiction movies, watching romantic comedies, and documentaries of a political nature. (The three parts of the series - science fiction movies, watching romantic comedies, and documentaries of a political nature - are not parallel.)

Revised:
Armand enjoyed science fiction movies, romantic comedies, and political documentaries. (The three parts of the series are parallel, with each containing a noun preceded by modifiers.)

Latrice is compassionate, shows loyalty, is forthright, and with principles. (The four parts of the series aren't parallel and begin with an adjective, a verb, a verb, and a preposition.)

Revised:
Latrice is compassionate, loyal, forthright, and principled. (All parts of the series are adjectives.)

To begin solving the immigration problem, we need to deal in facts rather than opinions, the employment needs of agriculture should be assessed, the children of immigrants must be considered, and maintaining a good relationship with Mexico. (The four parts of the lengthy series aren't parallel and create an awkward sentence.)

Revised:
To begin solving the immigration problem, we need to deal in facts rather than opinions, assess the employment needs of agriculture, consider the children of immigrants, and maintain a good relationship with Mexico. (Each part of the series is parallel, beginning with the "(to) deal," "assess," "consider," and "maintain," each followed by a direct object.)

While a non-parallel sentence is not an "error" in the same way as a grammar or punctuation mistake, it is a syntactical problem that can create awkward, less readable sentences. Therefore, it can be addressed both in the sentence revision and editing processes.

The following suggestions will help you identify and revise any non-parallel sentences in your writing.

1. Look for sentences that contain series of two or more words, phrases, or clauses, which are frequently joined by the conjunction "and" or "or."
2. If a series within a sentence looks or sounds awkward, it may have a parallelism problem. Check each part of the series to see whether it is parallel with the other parts, and if not, how it can be made parallel.
3. Revise the non-parallel sentence to make the series parallel by using the same construction in each part, including parts of speech and word order, and usually, making all parts parallel with the part that is the simplest and clearest.

Activity 2.16

The following paragraph contains some sentences with parallelism problems. Revise those sentences to eliminate the problems and create smoother, more readable sentences.

EXAMPLE

The health care debate contains a mixture of misinformation and inflammatory rhetoric, and to the public's understanding of the issue, it adds little.
Revised:
The health care debate contains a mixture of misinformation and inflammatory rhetoric and adds little to the public's understanding of the issue. (Sentence is parallel with a verb-direct object construction in the two parts of the series.)

Skeptics of global warming have few reasoned arguments against its existence. They may cite historical weather patterns within which the current warmer temperatures fall but as to the scientific data showing that the current warming trend defies all such patterns, they ignore it. They point out accurately that scientists predict an approaching ice age and slowly cooling temperatures, but that such an occurrence is forty or fifty thousand years away, they neglect to mention, and utterly irrelevant to our present situation. As to the accumulation of warming evidence such as melting glaciers, the rise of oceans, air and water temperatures warming, and precipitation conditions that are changing worldwide, skeptics basically lend a deaf ear. Some may even agree that such conditions exist but not to accept man's role in creating global warming. In short, most skeptics remain unconvinced of global warming not because there isn't evidence available but for political or economic reasons, they don't want to be convinced. Fortunately, skeptics are in the minority worldwide, and many nations, including the U.S., are moving forward with an agenda to reduce global warming.

Activity 2.17

Proofread your paper for grammatical, punctuation, spelling, or parallelism problems and make the necessary corrections.

Readings

E-Learning Clicks with Students
by Kim Clark

The timing couldn't be better. Just as millions of working-age Americans are realizing they need extra education and skill-sharpening to thrive in a recession, a flowering of competition promises to dramatically drive down prices and raise the quality of online college courses. Online education is playing a significant role in the college education of millions of students, and its impact will only continue to grow.

Indeed, time-stressed Americans fed up with commuting costs are already choosing online education. More than 4 million enrolled in at least one online course last fall, up from fewer than 2 million in 2003. And some of the biggest online players, such as the for-profit University of Phoenix, say new enrollment has jumped by about 20 percent since the economy began its decline more than a year ago. While online courses have been primarily designed for working adults, younger students in increasing numbers are switching to E-learning. Some, like students at Fairleigh Dickinson University in New Jersey, have little choice. FDU requires its students to take at least one online course per year, according to the University's online coordinator.

The sector is booming even though online college courses have been dogged by complaints about poor quality and high prices. For example, the website of about-to-close Warren National University, which is not accredited by any federally approved agency, says it charged $9,000 for the course work of a master's degree. Unaccredited courses and degrees are generally not recognized by employers or other colleges.

But demand for online courses might soon jump even more as expanding ranks of traditional ivy-covered universities and Internet entrepreneurs introduce online programs that are just a few hundred dollars per course. Meanwhile, technological improvements, such as easier-to-use video cameras and software, are helping online schools make their courses more rigorous and more engaging. And some long-established online colleges may kick-start a race to raise quality by publishing indicators of their students' satisfaction and progress at a new website that is expected to launch this spring.

The competition and technological improvements add up to "a great thing" for anyone interested in learning, says Clayton Christensen, a Harvard Business School professor who studies the impact of technology on education. "What used to be expensive and inaccessible becomes convenient and accessible," he says. "You can see price competition coming." What's more, the best online courses, in many cases, now rival the quality of traditional classes, says Christensen, who recently virtually audited a Brigham Young University online accounting course. "Anything beyond the 10th row in a large lecture hall is distance learning anyway," he jokes.

Although some of the big, established online players charge more than $1,500 a course, many of the newer entrants and public universities charge significantly less. Colorado State University - Global, which started offering online classes in 2008, asked in-state students signing up for their first online course this spring for $797. In 2007, Lamar Institute in Beaumont, Texas, started offering graduate education courses for just $412.50 apiece, which means a student could get a master's for as little as $4,950 in 18 months. Next fall, the public university plans to launch undergraduate online courses for a tuition that school officials predict will very likely come in under $500 for a standard three-credit course - no matter where the student lives.

And several new Internet start-ups are promising even lower-cost courses, though they do not yet have the stamp of approval from government-approved accreditation agencies. The new nonprofit University of the People, which plans to start accepting students this spring, will offer totally free online courses and textbooks leading to business and computer technology bachelor's degrees. The new university will charge students only up to $50 for admission and $100 for each final exam. (Those in the developing world will pay less.) The university will accept 300 students from around the world for its first semester this fall but hopes to expand quickly. The University of the People is not currently accredited. But founder Shai Reshef, chairman of Cramster. com, is hopeful of eventual accreditation because he's using volunteer professors from major universities.

Another group of volunteer professors is putting the finishing touches on the free, online Peer-to-Peer University. Joel Thierstein, whose day job is as an associate provost of Rice University in Houston, says that by this summer, volunteers should be ready to present a few free online courses in subjects like economics, music theory, and writing. The website will also enable anyone to create any kind of free course for anyone else. These first courses, at least, will not be accredited.

Many major universities, including Yale, M.I.T., and Stanford, have been allowing webizens to virtually audit lectures on their websites or via iTunes U. While there's currently no way to take tests or earn credit, a for-profit website that started in January, Academic Earth, is gathering many of the free online college courses on one site to make it easier to peruse all the offerings. Eventually, 23-year-old founder Richard Ludlow hopes, the site will also offer free online textbooks and podcasts and opportunities for interaction among students. Eventually, Ludlow also hopes Academic Earth will make some money through advertising or promotion of other education-related content.

Of course, price is only part of the equation. Even free classes can waste precious time if the students don't learn. There's still plenty of skepticism about the quality of online classes. Indeed, some of online education's biggest boosters say that most virtual classes are designed for working adults and may not be a good fit for, say, 18-year-old freshmen with poor self-discipline and time-management skills. Those students, they say, might need peer pressure and in-person reminders from professors to meet homework deadlines.

Critics of online learning can be yet more damning. A recent survey of university and community college professors found that nearly half of those who had taught an online course felt that online students received an inferior education. Plenty of students also feel burned. Rosie Joseph, 20, of Cincinnati dropped out of her University of Phoenix finance courses last year after two of her four instructors failed to respond promptly enough to her E-mails asking for explanations. "They weren't helpful at all," she says. The clincher for her: She called up local employers to see if they would hire someone with an online degree, and at least one said, "We don't encourage it," Joseph says.

But her fiancé, 25-year-old Tim Scott, says he's sticking with his online University of Phoenix information technology courses. He says his instructors have been responsive, and while he says the classes are sometimes boring and comparatively easy, he feels he is improving his writing and computer skills. Besides, he says, "this is pretty much the only way I could get a college education," since he works nights as a clerk in a drugstore.

Analysts say the market and technological forces that are driving down prices will cause some schools to improve services and quality. In fact, many online colleges are responding to complaints like Joseph's. The University of Phoenix, the University of West Florida, and other online schools require instructors to respond to student queries quickly, typically within 24 hours. The schools usually check up on professors by surveying students. Some online schools, such as Tiffin Universities Ivy Bridge online two-year college, go even further, hiring "coaches" or "advisers" who call or E-mail students regularly to encourage them and resolve complaints. And some schools are trying to ensure quality by limiting online courses to about 20 students each.

To make their courses more convenient for working adult students, some schools are replacing job-unfriendly 13-week semesters with shorter, more intense courses. And some online universities, such as Capella, are trying to reduce frustration with online student collaboration by accepting only more mature students.

Many colleges are also ratcheting up the rigor of online schoolwork. Online courses now typically require students to post gradable comments about each week's assignment, which means that online students can't sit in the back of the class hoping the professor won't call on them. And several schools are cracking down on cheating. Some professors now require online students to collaborate on projects using software that shows who made what changes, so they'll know if any team members slacked off. Troy University in Alabama requires online students who want to take their tests at home to install software that locks down their Web browsers and a spy camera so that remote observers can make sure they don't cheat.

Colleges are also trying to make online courses more engaging by moving beyond simple reading assignments and videotaped lectures. Jeannette E. Riley, named the best online teacher for 2008 by the Sloan Consortium, uses and assigns podcasts and videos in her online English and women's studies classes at the University of Massachusetts-Dartmouth. Good online courses require more work on the part of instructors and students, which can pay off in more learning, she says. "I love online teaching because no one can hide. Every voice is heard."

All of these new changes are drawing in students like Linda Summers, a 51-year-old corporate trainer in Canton, Ga., who wanted to beef up her résumé and skills but didn't have the time to travel to a university campus. When she signed up for her first online graduate education course at Troy University, "I thought: 'What have I done?' I thought I had made the biggest mistake," because that course required about 20 hours a week on top of her 40-hour-a-week work schedule. But now, in her second course, Summers is comfortable with the homework and has been pleasantly surprised by how much she enjoys the online conversations with the other adult students. "Online courses are perfect for me," she says.

DISCUSSION

1. What is the thesis of the essay?
2. What factual evidence is provided to show the increase in online course enrollment?
3. What factual evidence is provided to show the affordability of online courses?
4. What criticisms of online learning are presented and how are they addressed?
5. What empirical evidence is provided to support the thesis, and how effectively is it used?
6. Based on your experience and observation, do you agree with

the thesis? How educationally effective do you think online course are, and what student population do they best serve?

The State of America's Health
By Michelle Andrews

President-elect Barack Obama's political opponents used to suggest that he's different from the average American. Indeed he is, though in ways that have nothing to do with his unusual name or upbringing. Just look at the man. He's lean. He goes to the gym every morning. When he hits the bottle, it's got water in it. Sure, he has admitted to lighting up the occasional cigarette. But compared with the typical pudgy, sedentary, fast-food-craving American's lifestyle, the president's healthful habits make him anything but average.

As the national conversation about healthcare reform continues, the new president has a chance to do much more than lead by example. Despite the continuing economic uncertainty and a host of competing priorities, Obama has pledged to keep his campaign promise to bring comprehensive reform to our ailing healthcare system. In contrast to the last big push for reform during the Clinton administration, this time there has been more agreement among insurers, employers, consumers, and lawmakers on the broad outlines for change. Although many specifics have yet to emerge, all parties agree that any plan must place a strong emphasis on encouraging healthful behaviors and preventing disease. Reform can't happen soon enough. Americans today are fatter and less active than ever. Two thirds of adults are either overweight or obese, and fewer than a third exercise at least three times a week. Twenty-four million people have diabetes, the vast majority of it related to lifestyle, and an additional 57 million are prediabetic. Despite decades of public anti-tobacco campaigns, 1 in 5 adults smokes. At the same time, nearly 46 million Americans, including 8 million children, lack health insurance.

The news isn't all bad, though. In recent years, we've made inroads against some of the most lethal illnesses: The death rate for heart disease, the No. 1 killer, has declined by 26 percent since 1999. Both the incidence of and death rate for cancer, the second most common killer, are in decline for the first time.

Our expanding girth is America's most visible health problem. Not only are most adults too heavy, but obesity rates for children have more than doubled in the past 30 years. Excess weight is a significant factor in four of the six leading causes of death: heart disease, cancer, stroke, and diabetes. Obesity has fueled a 45 percent rise in diabetes over the past 20 years; someone born in 2000 has a 1 in 3 chance of developing the disease. Unhealthful behaviors take a toll not only on individuals' lives but also on our already overburdened healthcare system.

The United States spent more than $2 trillion on healthcare in 2006. It accounts for a whopping 16 percent of our gross domestic product, and that's projected to rise to 20 percent by 2017. Much of this healthcare spending can be tied to preventable health problems. For example, obesity-related spending, chiefly to treat high blood pressure and diabetes, accounted for 27 percent of the increase in overall health spending between 1987 and 2001, according to a study by Kenneth Thorpe, a professor of health policy at Emory University. Overall, caring for people with chronic complications seems like a no-brainer. Indeed, politicians frequently extol the money-saving benefits of preventive medicine. In its section on reducing healthcare costs, for example, the Obama-Biden healthcare reform plan says the team will "improve access to prevention and proven disease management programs."

But here's where healthcare reformers run up against an awkward reality: Preventing health problems doesn't necessarily save money. Sure, eating sensibly is free, and so is walking or jogging. But many of the screening tests and other services aimed at early detection of medical conditions cast a large - and therefore expensive - net in order to identify the relatively small number of people who actually have breast cancer, for example, or HIV. The frequency of screening is also a factor; repeated screening may detect more problems earlier, but there's a trade-off in cost.

Researchers put a fair amount of energy into trying to figure out which preventive measures provide the most benefit for the money. One way they evaluate the cost-effectiveness of a particular preventive service is by determining the cost per year of life saved. Breast cancer screening, for example, costs $48,000 per year of life saved, according to estimates from the Partnership for Prevention, a policy and advocacy group. In other words, you have to do $48,000 worth of preventive mammography screening in order to extend one woman's life for one year. Colorectal cancer screening is more cost-efficient; it costs only $12,000 to extend a life for a year.

A few preventive services actually do save money. These include taking a daily aspirin to prevent heart disease with men over 40 and postmenopausal women; pneumococcal vaccination in adults over 65; and smoking cessation counseling. One of the very best buys is childhood immunization, which prevents children from developing a whole host of diseases for very little cost.

But cost is hardly the only consideration. "The reason to do prevention is to save lives, not to save money," says Ned Calonge, chairperson of the U.S. Preventive Services Task Force. The task force is a congressionally mandated, 16-member panel that reviews the scientific research supporting some 200 preventive services and makes recommendations about which services people should get and when. Members calculate the net benefit of a service - the improvement in morbidity or mortality minus the potential harm - and use that information to determine that screening, for example, should be strongly recommended for women who have been sexually active. Many providers and insurers rely on the task force's recommendations.

If everyone followed the task force's advice, about half of all deaths each year could be prevented, at least temporarily, according to Calonge (no one cheats death forever, of course). But in general, only a fraction of people who should get a particular preventive service do so. Fewer than half of adults age 50 or older have had a colonoscopy or other screening for colorectal cancer, for example, and just over a third of adults in the same age group get an annual flu shot. If 90 percent of people in those two groups got just those two preventive services, 26,000 lives would be saved annually, the Partnership for Prevention estimates.

Experts generally agree that certain screening tests improve the overall health of the population; blood pressure testing is one example. But there's controversy over the value of other tests. Screening can, paradoxically, "make the population less healthy because it leads to so many more diagnoses and to overtreatment," says H. Gilbert Welch, a professor of medicine at Dartmouth Medical School. He cites prostate cancer screening as an example. Since the prostate specific antigen test was introduced in the late 1980s, over a million men have been diagnosed with prostate cancer who otherwise would not have been, Welch says, and up to half suffer serious treatment-related side effects like impotence and incontinence. Prostate cancer deaths have declined since the introduction of the PSA test, but factors other than more aggressive diagnosis - improved treatments, for example - might be responsible for the decline. "We still don't know whether this test helps reduce prostate cancer mortality," Welch says.

An oft-cited reason for people not getting timely screenings and for poor management of chronic conditions is that the healthcare many people receive is fragmented. In recent years, policy experts and clinicians alike have embraced a "medical home" model of primary care that takes a back-to-the-future approach in which patients' primary-care doctors are responsible for managing their healthcare, not just the particular issues that arise in a brief office visit. Medical home practices often employ a team approach to managing care and keep close tabs on their patients with high-tech information technology.

Medical homes also strive to enhance access to care, and patients can often communicate with their doctors by E-mail or make same-day appointments. The American Academy of Family and other professional groups are also experimenting with the model. Geisinger Health System in Pennsylvania reduced hospital admissions by 20 percent and trimmed medical spending by 7 percent by using a medical home model of care, according to a study in the September/October 2008 issue of the journal *Health Affairs*. But such practices are still rare, and it's too soon to know how they might affect healthcare delivery or costs overall.

At Harbor of Health, a primary-care practice in Memphis that is one of the TransforMED demonstration sites, there are only four chairs in the waiting room. Everybody gets same-day appointments, and patients are whisked into the exam room within five minutes, according to Susan Nelson, one of the physicians there. Even though she spends more time one-on-one with her patients now, they are in and out of the office in just 45 minutes, compared with nearly an hour before. "It's labor-intensive, because you have to be a health coach, and people don't want to exercise or diet," says Nelson.

How we organize our communities and even our own homes may have as great an impact on our health as the way our healthcare system is structured. Communities without sidewalks or bike paths offer little encouragement for people to rely less on their cars. School cafeterias that serve french fries and sugary sodas tempt kids with unhealthful lunch choices.

Researchers are taking aim at our physical and social environments. "If we can start to shift our systems, it will go a lot farther than trying to reach 300 million people one-on-one," says Christina Economos, an assistant professor at the Friedman School of Nutrition Science and Policy at Tufts University. Economos led the "Somerville" study, a three-year CDC-funded childhood obesity intervention in which researchers worked with the city of Somerville, Mass., to make it easier for children to "eat right, play hard," as the study's slogan puts it. Over the course of two years, school cafeterias—and even local restaurants— changed menus to offer more fruits, grains, and vegetables. Fatty snacks and sugary drinks were eliminated from lunchrooms. Parents were encouraged to take televisions out of kids' bedrooms. Bike racks were installed at the schools, and trees were planted to create leafy shade over the sidewalks. The changes worked: The city's first through third graders gained a pound less during each of the two years than their peers in two control communities.

But the changes didn't end when the study finished in 2005. Somerville has continued to alter its environment to encourage people to eat smart and play hard, including extending bike paths, creating new parks, and opening farmers' markets "This is about social change," says Somerville Mayor Joseph Curtatone. "We're changing the culture and behavior of people to get them to move in another direction." The reality is, getting Americans to move at all would be a good first step toward health improvement. The nation's new health coach in chief, clearly, has his work cut out for him.

DISCUSSION

1. What is the thesis of the essay?
2. What factual evidence does the author provide to support the thesis? How effectively is it presented?
3. What impact, according to the essay, does obesity have on American's health problems and the high cost of healthcare? What evidence is provided to support that contention?
4. What specific solutions does the essay provide to improve the health of Americans and what evidence is presented to support them? How effective do you think the solutions are, and why?
5. Based on the negative health consequences associated with obesity, smoking, and lack of exercise, why do you think Americans are so resistant to change?

The Amazing Teen Brain
By Nancy Shute

Behold the American teenager, a lump in a hoodie who's capable of little more than playing "Grand Theft Auto," raiding the liquor cabinet, and denting the minivan, thanks to a brain so unformed that it's more like a kindergartner's than a grown-up's. That's the message that seemed to emerge from the past decade's neuroscientific discoveries: that the brain, once thought to be virtually complete by age 6, is very much a work in progress during adolescence and not to be trusted. But experts now are realizing that the popular parental response - to coddle teens in an attempt to shield them from every harm - actually may be counterproductive.

Yes, teenagers make woefully errant decisions that factor big in the 13,000 adolescent deaths each year. And yes, their unfinished brains appear to be uniquely vulnerable to substance abuse and addiction. But they also are capable of feats of learning and daring marvelous enough to make a grown-up weep with jealousy. How they exercise these capabilities, it now appears, helps shape the brain wiring they'll have as adults. "You have this power you're given," says Wilkie Wilson, co-director of DukeLEARN, a new program at Duke University designed to teach teenagers how to best deploy their brains. Far from coddling the kids, he says, Mom and Dad need to figure out how to allow enough "good" risk-taking to promote growth and prevent wasted talent - while also avoiding disaster.

It can be a nerve-racking exercise. "These kids are such a crazy mix of impulsiveness and shrewdness," says Marcia Harrington, a survey researcher in Silver Spring, Md. She recalls the time she thought her then 16-year-old daughter, Alexandra Plante, had sleepover plans, but the girl instead ditched school and flew to Chicago to visit an acquaintance she'd met briefly during a family trip. The scheme was revealed only because bad weather delayed the flight home. Alex returned unharmed and has never conceded that the escapade was too risky. "She's going to be a great adult someday," says Harrington. "But, boy, there are moments that are terrifying." Further along the road to adulthood now, Alex has applied her daring spirit to becoming an emergency medical technician and volunteer for the local fire department, and to heading off to college 2,500 miles from home.

While society has known since forever that adolescents can be impulsive risk-takers, it wasn't until the 1990s, when MRI scans became a common research tool, that scientists could peek into the teenage cranium and begin to sort out why. What they found astonished them. The brain's gray matter, which forms the bulk of its structure and processing capacity, grows gradually throughout childhood, peaks around age 12, and then furiously "prunes" underused neurons.

By scanning hundreds of children as they've grown up, neuroscientists at the National Institute of Mental Health have been able to show that the pruning starts at the back of the brain and moves forward during adolescence. Regions that control sensory and motor skills mature first, becoming more specialized and efficient. The prefrontal cortex, responsible for judgment and impulse control, matures last. Indeed, the prefrontal cortex isn't "done" until the early 20s—and sometimes even later in men. Meantime, the brain's white matter, which acts as the cabling connecting brain parts, becomes thicker and better able to transmit signals quickly. Recent research shows that this myelination process of white matter continues well past adolescence, perhaps even into middle age.

Today dozens of researchers are studying how all these changes might affect adolescent behavior and also shape adult skills and behavior, for good and for ill. The maturation lag between emotional and cognitive brain centers may help explain why teenagers get so easily upset when parents see no reason; teens seem to process input differently than do adults.

In one experiment, young teenagers trying to read the emotions on people's faces used parts of the brain designed to quickly recognize fear and alarm; adults used the more rational prefrontal cortex. Deborah Yurgelun-Todd, the researcher at McLean Hospital in Belmont, Mass., who led this work, believes young teens are prone to read emotion into their interactions and miss content. Therefore, parents may have better luck communicating with middle-schoolers if they avoid raising their voice and instead explain how they're feeling.

Other experiments shed light on why even book-smart teenagers come up short on judgment: Their brain parts aren't talking to each other. When Monique Ernst, a child psychiatrist and neurophysiologist at NIMH, uses functional MRI to watch teenage and adult brains engaged in playing a gambling game, she finds that the "reward" center lights up more in teens than in adults when players are winning, and the "avoidance" region is less activated in teens when they're losing. There's also less activity in teens' prefrontal cortex, which adults use to mediate the "yes" and "no" impulses from other brain regions. "The hypothesis is that there is this triumvirate of brain regions that needs to be in balance" in order to produce wise judgments, says Ernst, whether that's to wear a seat belt or use contraception.

Does an unfinished brain make for bad behavior? There is as yet no proven link between bright blobs on an MRI and real-life behavior, but researchers are hard at work trying to make that connection. In a 2005 study by Laurence Steinberg, a developmental psychologist at Temple University, teenagers in a simulated driving test were twice as likely to drive dangerously if they had two friends with them, and brain scans showed that the reward centers lit up more if teens were told that friends were watching. A savvy parent might conclude that what's needed in the teen years is more guidance, not less.

In fact, study after study has shown that one of the most powerful factors in preventing teen pregnancy, crime, drug and alcohol abuse, and other seriously bad outcomes is remarkably simple: time with responsible adults. "It doesn't have to be parents, necessarily," says Valerie Reyna, a professor of psychology at Cornell University. But it does mean that teenagers should be directly monitored by responsible adults so they have less time to get in trouble. Reyna thinks adults also need to teach what she calls "gist" thinking, or the ability to quickly grasp the bottom line. Instead, she says, teenagers often overthink but miss the mark. When Reyna asks adults if they'd play Russian roulette for $1 million, they almost universally say no. Half of teenagers say yes. "They'll tell you with a straight face that there's a whole lot of money, and they're probably not going to die. It's very logical on one level, but on another level, it's completely insane."

If it's any comfort, the evidence suggests that teenagers' loopy behavior and combativeness is hard-wired to push them out of the nest. Adolescent primates, rodents, and birds also hang out with their peers and fight with their parents, notes B. J. Casey, a teen brain researcher who directs the Sackler Institute at Weill Medical College of Cornell University in New York City. "You need to take risks to leave your family and village and find a mate."

The revved-up adolescent brain is also built to learn, the new research shows, and those teen experiences are crucial. Neurons, like muscles, operate on a "use it or lose it" basis; a teenager who studies piano three hours a day will end up with different brain wiring than someone who spends that same time shooting hoops or playing video games. A 16-year-old who learns to treat his girlfriend with care and compassion may well develop different emotional brain triggers than one who's thinking just about the sex.

Only in early childhood, it turns out, are people as receptive to new information as they are in adolescence. The human brain is designed to pay attention to things that are new and different, a process called salience. Add in the fact that emotion and passion also heighten attention and tamp down fear, and teenagerhood turns out to be the perfect time to master new challenges. "You are the owners of a very special stage of your brain development," Frances Jensen, a neurologist at Children's Hospital Boston, tells teenagers in her "Teen Brain 101" lectures at local high schools. "You can do things now that will set you up later in life with an enhanced skill set. Don't waste this opportunity."

Jordan Dickey is one teen who seized opportunity. As a 14-year-old high-school freshman, he asked his father for something unusual: a $26,000 loan to start a business. The Dickey family, of Ramer, Tenn., raised a few cattle, and Jordan had noticed that people paid a lot more for hay in square bales than for the same amount in less-convenient round bales. After doing a feasibility study as an agriculture class project, Jordan convinced his dad to give him a three-year loan to buy a rebaling machine. He worked nights and weekends, mowing, raking, and rebaling; paid friends $7 an hour to load the bales into a trailer; and hired drivers to deliver the hay to local feed marts, since he was too young to drive. "It taught me how to manage my own money," Jordan says. That's an understatement. Not only did he pay off the loan in one year, he made an additional $40,000. Now 17 and a senior, he has saved enough money to pay for a big chunk of college, much to his parents' delight. "He likes for the job to get done and get done right," says Perry Dickey, who owns an electroplating shop. "It was a big responsibility for him, and I'm glad he took the lines and produced."

Teens can apply the new findings to learn more without more

study, notes Wilson, whose DukeLEARN program will be tested in ninth-grade health classes next year. Key points:

- Brains need plenty of sleep because they consolidate memory during slumber.
- The brain's an energy hog and needs a consistent diet of healthful food to function well.
- Drugs and alcohol harm short and long-term memory.

Teens' predisposition to learn plays a critical role in the vexing issue of teenage drinking, smoking, and drug use. Neuroscientists have learned that addiction uses the same molecular pathways that are used in learning, most notably those involving the neurotransmitter dopamine. Repeated substance use permanently reshapes those pathways, researchers say. In fact, they now look at addiction as a form of learning. Adolescent rats are far more likely to become hooked than adults.

And epidemiological studies in humans suggest that the earlier someone starts using, the more likely he or she is to end up with big problems. Last month, a study tracking more than 1,000 people in New Zealand from age 3 to age 32 found that those who started drinking or using drugs before age 15 were far more likely to fail in school, be convicted of a crime, or have substance abuse problems as an adult. "You can really screw up your brain at this point," says Jensen. "You're more vulnerable than you think."

Jay Giedd, an NIMH neuroscientist who pioneered the early MRI research on teen brains, is fond of saying that "what's important is the journey." Researchers caution that they can't prove links between brain parts and behavior, or that tackling adult-size challenges will turn teenagers into better adults. But common sense suggests that Nature had a reason to give adolescents strong bodies, impulsive natures, and curious, flexible minds. "Our generation is ready for more," insists Alex Harris, 20, of Gresham, Ore., who, with his twin brother, Brett, writes a blog and has published a book urging teens to push themselves. Its title: "Do Hard Things."

DISCUSSION

1. What is the thesis of the essay?
2. What factual evidence does the essay provide to support its thesis, and what evidence do you find most compelling?
3. Based on what neurologists know of the adolescent brain, what advice does the essay give to parents of teenagers? In what ways does the advice appear contradictory?
4. What findings on the adolescent brain did you find most interesting and why?

5. What impact did the essay have on your thinking regarding teen behavior, or perhaps your own?

Writing About Writing

After the "Readings" section in each unit, you have the opportunity to write a critique of an essay, providing your analysis and evaluation of the essay and its impact on you as a reader. Critique writing helps to enhance your evaluative and writing skills, furthering your development as both writer and critical reader.

Writing the Critique

As you learned in the first unit, writing a critique begins with a close and critical reading of the essay you are critiquing. Review the suggestions on critical reading on page 52 to help you get the most from the essay you choose to write on.

Before writing your critique, also review the suggestions for critique writing on page 55 and reread the essay critiques on pages 46 ("The Case Against Quick-Fix Marriage") and 56.

Activity 2.18

Select an essay from the text (or an outside essay or article with your instructor's approval) to write a critique on. Select an essay that you find interesting and that makes an impact on you. Write your critique after reading the essay critically, perhaps more than once, and giving some thought to how you might proceed with your writing.

Unit Three
Logical Evidence

To support their opinions, writers often use logic or reason to influence their readers. They provide arguments that they feel would make the most sense to reasonable people. In doing so, they make the assumption that readers will most readily embrace an idea that appeals to their sense of logic. While this may not always be the case, it occurs frequently enough for writers to employ logical arguments whenever they are appropriate.

Scientific advancements have often been based on logical assumptions. For example, the psychological concept of *positive reinforcement* was based on the reasonable assumption that animals, including the human kind, would continue to perform a particular behavior for which they are rewarded. People work forty hours a week because they are rewarded with equitable pay, and logic suggested that they would work even more enthusiastically if they could work those forty hours within a four-day work week. Elementary students who hadn't developed a love of reading would read more books, it was reasoned, if they were rewarded with some form of recognition. That a person will do something that may not be intrinsically appealing to get something that *is* appealing makes logical sense, and writers often rely on the ability of readers to understand and embrace such logic.

Readers are most apt to agree with a particular opinion when they can say, "That really makes sense," or "I can see the logic in that," or "that seems the most reasonable option." Writers lead them to those conclusions by presenting the most effective line of reasoning available to support their opinions.

In writing your essay for this unit, you will include some logical evidence to support your opinion. If you can show readers that your opinion is the most reasonable, logical, and sensible, they are most likely to take it seriously.

Using Logical Evidence

To use logical evidence most effectively in your writing, consider the following suggestions.

1. **Think of the most logical arguments in support of your opinion.** For example, let's say that a writer believes that America should not continue waging war in Afghanistan. What logical arguments might she use to help make her case? First, American generals concur that war in Afghanistan could last a decade or more. Surveys have shown that Americans have a strong distaste for war and concern over the loss of American lives. Therefore, it is *logical* to think that most Americans would not support a long, drawn-out war.

    Second, the Soviet Union was mired in a war in Afghanistan for over ten years and gained nothing from it. It is *reasonable* to conclude that America could have a similar experience. Third, war in Afghanistan will add billions of dollars annually to the burgeoning national deficit. Given the drawn-out nature of the war and the questionable end results, many Americans may believe that pouring billions of dollars into an Afghani war *does not make much sense.*

2. **In considering the best logical arguments, keep in mind the impact of self interest on people's viewpoints.** For example, let's say a writer supports a state tax increase to reconfigure the state's water delivery system to ensure adequate irrigation water for the agriculture industry. Tax increases are not in most people's self interest and are frequently opposed. However, if the writer could show people how they would be negatively affected by a failing agricultural industry - e.g. short produce supplies in markets, decreasing property values, loss of jobs, plummeting state revenues leading to greater tax increases - they might see the *logic* in the tax increase as it applies to their self interest.

3. **Logical arguments often take the form of a *syllogism.*** A syllogism is a form of logical argument where a conclusion is drawn from a *major and a minor premise*, the major premise being *general* or *universal* and the minor premise *particular* or *specific*:

    Major premise: Children like eating at restaurants with special kids' meals.

    Minor premise: The new Green Onion restaurant has a special kids' menu.

Conclusion: Children will like eating at the Green Onion restaurant.

While logical arguments don't always take the shape of a classic Greek syllogism, they frequently include major and minor premises - statements whose validity is assumed - from which logical conclusions are drawn. For example, let's say a student writer opposes both the location and the usage restrictions proposed for a new on-campus library. She presents the following major and minor premises to reach her conclusion:

Major premise: Students frequent places on a campus that are in nearby walking distance.

Major premise: Many students prefer studying in a quiet, library-like setting.

Minor premise: The proposed library site is a long walk across campus for most students.

Minor premise: The proposed library restricts study areas to small conference rooms.

Conclusion: Many students will not use the library as it is proposed.

In using syllogisms effectively, it is important that readers agree with the premises from which the conclusion is drawn and that those premises are valid. For example, in the previous example on the Afghanistan war, one major premise was that Americans have a strong distaste for war. However, some readers may feel that while Americans may have a distaste for war, they will support a war if they feel it is necessary.

An influential premise in the support of capital punishment was that the death penalty would be a deterrent against murder. However, that premise has proven questionable since the implementation of the death penalty has not correlated with a reduction in the murder rate in America. When considering the premises from which to draw a logical conclusion, make sure that they are valid and that most readers would agree with them.

4. **Consider using logical arguments that would have the greatest impact on readers**. Ask yourself, "What arguments would make the greatest sense to the most people?" In trying to convince the American public of the need for a governmental stimulus package during the 2008 recession to help out the failing banks, one argument that Congressional spokespersons used went something like this:

Millions of Americans are always in the market to buy

a house, and they need bank loans to do it. However, banks are in no position to lend money if they are failing. Therefore, it is in the interest of most Americans that the banks don't fail, which can be accomplished with an infusion of Federal money.

The simple argument made sense to many people, and it showed how the bank stimulus could affect them personally in a positive way.

5. **Common-sense arguments are often the most effective.** A convincing logical argument does not always have to be the most cerebral or inspired. People often rely upon their common sense to make important decisions and judgments, and they can relate to arguments that appeal to their good judgment.

For example, while there were many arguments both for and against the busing of children to help implement school integration law in the 1970's, the strongest argument of those opposed to forced busing appealed to common sense: It makes little sense to bus children many miles across town to school when they have one in their neighborhood. Forced busing has not been widely successful as a school integration tool because logistically, it flew in the face of common sense.

Activity 3.1

Complete the following syllogisms to reach conclusions that support each thesis.

EXAMPLE

    Topic: Entrance fee for city's metropolitan museum
    Thesis: The fee should be kept as low as possible.
    Major premise: Museums should be accessible to all people in a city.
    Minor thesis: Expensive fees would deny entrance to many parents and children.
    Conclusion: The museum fee should be inexpensive so everyone has access.

1.   **Topic:** On-campus events center
    Thesis: The college should build an on-campus events center.
    Major premise:
    Minor premise: The downtown events center is a

long way from campus.
Conclusion: More students would attend events at an on-campus center.

2. **Topic:** Welfare-to-work programs
    Thesis: Welfare-to-work programs should include free child care for mothers.
    Major premise: Child care in America is very expensive.
    Minor premise: Most women in welfare-to-work programs have young children.
    Conclusion:

3. **Topic:** Health care jobs
    Thesis: Jobs in the health care industry are among the most plentiful in America.
    Major premise: America has an aging population that is living longer than ever.
    Minor premise:
    Conclusion:

4. **Topic:** Teacher education programs
    Thesis: Student teaching is an integral part of any teacher education program
    Major premise:
    Minor premise:
    Conclusion: All education majors should be required to perform at least one semester of monitored student teaching.

Activity 3.2

Decide on the best logical evidence you could use to support each of the following theses.

EXAMPLE
   Topic: gun control

   Thesis: Buying hand guns should be illegal in the U.S.
   Logical evidence:
   Hand guns are responsible for the vast majority of murders in the U.S. Most of those hand guns are purchased legally. Therefore, banning hand gun purchases would

greatly reduce the number of murders. Some people would still resort to purchasing hand guns illegally on the black market. The only handguns available would be illegally purchased. Therefore, confiscation of guns and prosecution of gun owners and sellers would be easier.

1. Topic: escalating cost of college tuition
    Thesis: Colleges will ultimately lose money if they continue raising tuition.
    Logical evidence:

2. Topic: art and music in elementary schools
    Thesis: Reducing or eliminating the time allotted for art and music in elementary schools hurts children.
    Logical evidence:

3. Topic: Drug addiction
    Thesis: Drug addiction should be treated as a medical rather than a criminal condition.
    Logical evidence:

4. Topic: online shopping
    Thesis: There should be a sales tax for online purchases just like there is for store purchases.
    Logical evidence:

5. Topic: Quality of public school education
    Thesis: Every public school should provide high quality education for all students.
    Logical evidence:

Activity 3.3

Read the following essay and evaluate the logical evidence provided by the writer. Consider the validity of the premises she uses and conclusions she draws, and whether her arguments seem reasonable and sensible.

Welfare-to-Work Programs

Welfare-to-work programs, mandated by Federal law to move welfare recipients into the work force, have varying success rates depending on different factors. Since the programs primarily target women with children, by far the largest segment of Americans on welfare, they are most successful when they are tailored to meet these women's needs.

Obviously, the number one criterion for success is that a woman must be better off working than she was while on welfare. If she makes the same or less money working than she was paid while on welfare, there is little incentive to work. Therefore, successful programs help place women in jobs where they can earn significantly more money than a combination of welfare checks and food stamps would provide.

Second, women need child care for their children when they leave the home to work. Since child care is expensive, and would devour any salary advantage of a work check over a welfare check, successful programs provide free or inexpensive child care for working mothers.

Finally, working and leaving their children at day care facilities is a huge change for women who have been stay-at-home welfare recipients. Successful programs recognize this monumental life change, breaking lifestyle patterns that most welfare mothers have known since their own childhoods, and provide regular counseling for new working mothers and long-term follow-up visitations. As with any persons trying to change their lives, welfare-to-work mothers are most successful when they have someone in their corner to provide continual encouragement and support.

Successful welfare-to-work programs provide a brighter future and greater self-esteem for millions of women, but they have an equally positive effect on the children of these women. The model of the stay-at-home welfare mother is replaced by the model of the productive working mother, and the children of the new working mothers are more likely stay off of welfare themselves and become productive members of society. Programs that help provide former welfare recipients with living wage jobs, affordable day care, and regular counseling are helping to break the welfare cycle for millions of women and children alike.

Prewriting

For your upcoming essay, you will present logical evidence, along with other support for your thesis, and acknowledge and respond to opposing viewpoints to help accomplish your purpose. During the prewriting phase, you may do a number of things, including deciding on your topic, determining a probable thesis, generating some supportive material, considering the types of logical evidence you might include, considering some opposing arguments to your thesis and how you might respond to them, and determining your writing purpose and audience. Use the prewriting suggestions in the text in ways that best prepare you to write the first draft.

In each unit, you continue to build on what you have learned in previous units. In the first unit, you developed your essay primarily through the use of empirical evidence: experiences and observations that helped to validate your arguments. In the second unit, you relied primarily on factual evidence to develop your essay. In both units, you wrote for particular audiences with a specific purpose in mind. In this unit, you draw primarily upon logical evidence, along with the other types of evidence, to develop your points and help accomplish your purpose.

Topic Selection

Once again, you will select a writing topic on which people's opinions differ. If the vast majority of readers believe the same as you on a particular topic, such as how terrible child abuse is or the value of a college education, there are few readers left to convince.

However, many topics are the subject of hot debate among readers: raising taxes to cover state budget shortfalls; colleges entering into commercial enterprises to generate income; "closed campus" policies in high schools; decriminalizing marijuana; lowering the drinking age to eighteen; outsourcing traditional American jobs to other countries; placing finance limits on political campaigns; legalizing same-sex marriages; America's foreign policy in the Middle East. There is never a shortage of issues on which readers line up on different sides.

To select a possible topic for your upcoming essay, consider the following suggestions:

1. **Select a topic on which people have differing opinions.** The issue may be local, state, national, or international in scope and may be from any field: health, environment, law, education, criminal justice, technology, economics, child

issues, gender issues, family/relationship issues, social issues, work-related issues, and so on.

2. **Select a topic that you are interested in and that would be of interest or concern to others.** The stronger your interest in a topic, the greater your enthusiasm for writing about it and the greater the likelihood of writing a compelling paper.

3. **Select a topic that is serious enough to engage readers' interest and that affects people's lives.** Ask yourself, "Is anyone affected seriously enough by this topic to take a strong interest in it?"

4. **Select a topic that is specific enough to cover effectively within the length parameters your instructor may set.** For example, the broad topic of America's South American foreign policy could fill a book. However, the narrower topic of how America can best deal with new socialist-leaning governments in Venezuela and Bolivia may work well for an essay.

5. **Select a topic for which you could use logical evidence to support your opinion.** In considering a particular topic, ask yourself, "What logical or common-sense arguments might be made to advance a particular thesis?"

Activity 3.4

Considering the suggestions presented, select a topic for your upcoming essay. You may want to do some reading and investigation of possible topics before making a decision.

EXAMPLE

> **Topic:** Limiting funding for state's pre-school education program

Thesis and Support

As you know, the *thesis* for your essay is your viewpoint on the topic, which is validated by the supportive evidence you provide. You may already have a strong opinion on your topic, or you may need to learn more about it before drawing any conclusions. Through your investigation, you may even end up changing your opinion and ultimately supporting a different thesis.

Thesis

To determine a thesis for your essay, considering these suggestions.

1. **Your thesis should reflect what you believe about the**

issue based on what you know or learn. The most effectively supported theses often come from writers who transmit their passion and enthusiasm for what they believe to their readers.

2. **Generate a thesis that is supported by the evidence.** If you discover that your thesis has little evidence to support it, you probably want to reconsider your thesis or your topic. For example, a writer may feel that the increase in the immigrant population in his city is costing local residents jobs, but his research may indicate otherwise. Or another writer who feels that the standardized testing emphasis in elementary schools is thwarting children's creativity may discover that a five-year study showed no negative correlation between the testing emphasis and student creativity. Sometimes when the evidence doesn't correspond to a writer's opinion, it may be best change that opinion or look for another topic.

3. **Ultimately, your thesis may have a *qualifying* aspect to it, one that recognizes people's different life circumstances or the role of compromise in influencing change.** For example, a writer who strongly supports a local two-cent sales tax increase for the city to continue providing basic services to residents *qualifies* her position by suggesting a two-year limit on the increase. Or a writer who supports increased police presence in a crime-ridden section of the city also recognizes the local residents' fear of racial profiling and calls for an external oversight body to monitor policing activity. Or a writer who favors rent control in housing around the college area also recognizes the increasing expenses of apartment owners and supports a gradual rental increase no greater than the Consumer Price Index annual inflation rate.

4. **Select a thesis that you can support with logical evidence.** Since the emphasis in this unit is on providing logical evidence, make sure that you select a thesis that you can show is reasonable, logical and makes the greatest sense.

Activity 3.5

Generate a possible thesis statement for your upcoming essay based on what you know and believe about the topic. If you are uncertain of your position, you may want to do some investigating before reaching a conclusion. Your initial thesis may also change as you learn more about your topic, and your ultimate thesis may be *qualified* based on your analysis of differing perspectives, the different life circumstances of those affected, and how you can best accomplish your purpose.

EXAMPLE

> **Topic:** Limiting funding for state's pre-school education program
>
> **Thesis:** Reducing funding for the state's pre-school education program hurts children and will ultimately hurt the state.

Support

How well a writer supports her thesis often determines the essay's impact on readers. No matter how adamant a writer feels about her position on a topic, skeptical readers will judge her thesis on the quality of its support.

The following questions will help you support your thesis convincingly:

1. **What are the reasons that I believe as I do about the topic?** What impact may each reason have on readers?
2. **What logical, common-sense arguments can I make to support my thesis?** What arguments will make the greatest impact on readers and appeal to their sense of reason?
3. **What other *evidence* can I provide to support each reason?** What facts do I have to support it? What personal experience or observations can I draw from that would help convince readers?
4. **Where can I find the best factual evidence to support my reasons?** What available sources of information would readers find most credible?

Activity 3.6

To consider support for your thesis, answer the four questions just provided.

EXAMPLE

> **Topic:** Limiting funding for state's pre-school education program
>
> **Thesis:** Reducing funding for the state's pre-school edu-

cation program hurts children and will ultimately hurt the state.

1. **Reasons:**
   a. Funding cut would limit access to children who need pre-school the most.
   b. Limiting access will hurt families financially.
   c. There is a correlation between pre-school education and student success.
   d. Students who don't succeed often end up costing the state money while students who do succeed contribute to the state's economy.
   e. Pre-school programs provide more than education.

2. **Logical evidence:**
   a. It makes sense that limited funding is going to have the greatest impact on poorer families, whose children need pre-school the most.
   b. It makes sense for the state to invest whatever is needed to fund pre-school to help students succeed and become productive members of society rather than paying considerably more later in welfare and prison costs.
   c. It makes sense that providing children with another full year of school prior to kindergarten can only help their chances of educational success.

3. **Other evidence:**
   a. Find out the number of students statewide who will be affected by cuts.
   b. Find out the number of parents who will have to pay for child care based on the cuts.
   c. Find studies showing how well students with pre-school education do in elementary school compared to students with no pre-school.
   d. Get figures for the percentage of adults on welfare programs who dropped out of school at some point. Contrast this with the much lower percentage of adults on welfare programs who at least graduated from high school.
   e. Find out additional benefits of pre-school, e.g. breakfast program, socialization, maturation, health, discipline.

f. Use empirical evidence of personal accounts comparing children who attended pre-school and children who didn't.

4. a. Get information from county agencies that manage state pre-school program.

b. Get some determination from county agencies, from pre-school sites, and from parents. Also use personal observation.

c. Check elementary education journals, look up pre-school education studies on line, check with college child development instructors for sources.

d. Get information from county welfare department.

e. Talk with pre-school instructors and administrators and also ask them for further sources.

Differing Perspectives

For your upcoming essay, you selected a topic on which people have differing viewpoints. There may be one differing viewpoint from your position on the issue, or there may be more than one. For example, with a two-candidate political contest or an "accept/reject" ballot initiative, there are two opposing sides: those in favor of one candidate or the other, or those in favor or against the ballot initiative. However, with complex issues such as gun control, there may be several contrasting viewpoints ranging from people who support a ban on the sale of all guns to those who reject a ban on the sale of any gun. In between, there are those who favor a ban on hand guns only or on assault weapons only, those who would restrict the sale of guns to "qualified" applicants only, and those who emphasize stricter enforcement of current gun laws. Considering where your readers may stand on a particular issue is important in responding to their concerns.

To identify and respond to viewpoints differing from your thesis, consider these questions.

1. **What viewpoint or viewpoints on the issue may exist that are contrary to my own?** Of these, what viewpoint or viewpoints are serious or widespread enough to address in my essay?

2. **What are the primary arguments supporting an opposing viewpoint?** What is the basis for each argument: factual information? misinformation? unsubstantiated claims? personal feelings? unfounded speculation? self-interest?

3. **What is the best way to respond to each argument in a manner that supports my thesis and could influence**

readers? How can I undermine opposing arguments without alienating readers who agree with them?

4. **Who are the readers who may hold an opposing viewpoint and what is the best way to move them off of their position?** Showing an understanding and some sensitivity towards your readers' position on an issue may serve your purpose better than lambasting their belief.

Activity 3.7

Read the following essay and note how the writer deals with different perspectives, responds to opposing arguments, and connects with readers. Also note the reasons he uses to support his thesis, the evidence he provides, including logical evidence, and the source acknowledgments for each piece of factual evidence. Determine how clearly he reveals his purpose and evaluate the effectiveness of the essay.

Plight of Part-time Instructors
(audience: students, instructors, administrators, trustees)

A not-so-funny joke goes like this. How do you tell a part-time instructor from a full-time instructor? Answer: by the car he drives. Part-timers drive the beat up Volkswagons while full-timers drive the new sedans, evidence of their very different economic situations. While it is often difficult to distinguish part-time from full-time faculty regarding the quality of instruction or dedication to teaching, the great disparity between their salaries and benefits is striking. Part-time instructors are not compensated fairly for the teaching contribution they make to two-year and four-year colleges, and the situation needs to change.

According to the Wolfe State faculty handbook, part-time faculty are required to have the same degrees, exhibit the same level of competency, and do the same class preparation and student evaluation that full-time faculty do. They have full responsibility for their classes, the same liability risks, and are evaluated in a similar manner to full-timers. At the same time, full-time and part-time faculty salary schedules at Wolfe reveal a major pay discrepancy. On average, full-time faculty make more than twice as much as part-time faculty. On top of that, while full-time faculty receive paid medical benefits as part of their negotiated contract with the college, part-time faculty must *buy in* to the medical plan if they want coverage, further diminishing their already meager salaries. Does it make any sense to treat two groups of similar employees so differently?

Wolfe State's treatment of part-time faculty reflects what is going on around the country. According to a 2008 article in *Higher Education*, part-time faculty are on different and significantly inferior salary schedules in most two-year and four-year colleges. In addition, college-paid medical insurance for part-time faculty is the exception rather than the rule. To make ends meet, part-timers often have to teach at two or three different institutions and carry larger-than-normal teaching loads. In California, they have been nicknamed "freeway flyers" for all of the freeway miles they log between teaching assignments.

If part-time faculty have the same teaching requirements and responsibilities as full-time faculty, why are they paid so differently? The answer is simple: economics. Colleges can save money by hiring cheaply paid part-time instructors, so they do just that. According to a State Chancellor's Office Load Report, part-time instructors make up over 60% of state college faculty and teach over 40% of the classes offered. When paid less than half of what full-time faculty make, you can see the savings to a college by using part-timers. So colleges become dependent on part-time faculty to balance their budgets and find ways to justify their mistreatment.

"Part-time faculty have full-time jobs elsewhere, so they don't need the same salaries as full-time faculty," say defenders of the status quo. However, a survey of Wolfe's part-time instructors, as well as similar surveys at other colleges, reveals otherwise. While thirty years ago part-time college faculty may have been moonlighting high school teachers and business people, the majority of today's part-time faculty have no other jobs. College teaching is what they do, and they keep on with the hopes of someday landing a full-time position. They are completely dependent on their inadequate college income.

Defenders of the status quo also point out that part-time instructors *don't* have the same responsibilities as full-time instructors, so they shouldn't be paid the same. They allude to full-time faculty's work on hiring committees, curriculum, and faculty senates. In reality, part-time faculty *are* doing more of the things that were once the domain of full-timers, and part-time faculty at Wolfe, according to several faculty department chairs, *do* develop curriculum, serve on the senate, and attend department meetings regularly. They can't be *required* to do these things for a simple reason: they don't get paid for their time like full-time faculty.

Some college administrators and trustees at Wolfe have said on record that part-time faculty deserve to be paid better but that the college's budgetary situation makes it difficult. At board meetings, trustees have also lauded the contributions of part-time instructors and the indispensable role they play at Wolfe. No doubt they are sincere, but the way that part-timers are exploited for financial purposes sends a much louder message. Underpaying employees to save money simply isn't justifiable, particularly in colleges, which should provide an exemplary employment model for students. It is only fair that two faculty, one full-time and one part-time, teaching the same courses in side-by-side classrooms be compensated the same.

Some colleges have made headway in paying part-time instructors more equitably. State colleges such as Monroe and Hemstead now have a single salary schedule for part-time and full-time faculty, and other colleges have increased their part-timer pay to 70%-90% of what full-time faculty make, according to the Chancellor's Office 2008 Salary and Benefits Study. Wolfe, however, still lags far behind, as do many other colleges in the state. Since salary schedules are set college-by-college through local negotiations, Wolfe is in control of its own fate, and it needs to look at the colleges who have made progress to see how they are balancing their budgets and paying their part-time employees fairly at the same time. It obviously can be done, and it needs to be done at Wolfe.

The student newspaper's annual evaluation survey of faculty always finds several part-time faculty among the college's top thirty instructors. Logic and fairness dictate, then, that they should also be among the best paid.

Activity 3.8

Consider the viewpoint or viewpoints in opposition to your thesis, the readers who hold them, the arguments that support each viewpoint, the basis for each argument, and how you might respond to it in a way that has the greatest effect on readers and accomplishes your writing purpose.

EXAMPLE

Topic: Limiting funding for state's pre-school education program

Thesis: Reducing funding for the state's pre-school education program hurts children and will ultimately hurt the state.

Opposing viewpoint: Reducing the funding is a necessity given the state's budget picture.

Readers who oppose: Primarily legislators who are implementing the cuts and special interest groups who are concerned about their own programs.

Opposing arguments:
1. With the revenue deficit, all state programs need to bear the brunt of the cuts.
2. Making cuts in pre-school ed is not as critical as cuts in regular education.
3. Pre-school is not a traditional or required part of the state's educational role.
4. Pre-school has not proven to be critical for the educational success of children.

Responding to opposing arguments:
1. All state programs are not equal in importance or value, and pre-school education is a program that needs to be protected because of its great value.
2. Pre-school cuts are just as critical as any educational cuts since pre-schools provide the foundation for the success of many students.
3. Pre-school *should* be a part of the state's educational role knowing what we know about its importance to a child's educational success.
4. All studies show that pre-school *has* proven to make a difference in a child's educational success.

Audience and Purpose

For your upcoming essay, your primary reading audience are people who hold differing viewpoints from your own on the topic. Whatever your purpose may be - to move readers to action, to persuade them *not* to act, to open their minds to a different perspective -, it can only be accomplished if readers begin thinking differently about the topic after reading your essay.

For example, one of the most difficult things to do in tough economic times is to raise money for worthwhile causes. Citizens trying to raise money in a community for a senior center knew that they had to tap in to all ages of adults, most of whom weren't seniors themselves.

To find a common denominator among potential contributors, the citizens' group hit upon a unifying theme for their communications: "We are *all* senior citizens." In other words, from the youngest to the oldest of contributors, in time everyone would benefit from having a center in the community. The "We are all senior citizens" theme resonated well enough that within two years, the money was raised to break ground on a new center. Uniting all potential contributors with a common thread showed the committee's understanding of their audience and ability to influence them. Understanding your reading audience may pay similar dividends.

Audience

Discovering what may work to move a particular group of readers is not easy, but there are a few things that we know:

1. **Most people like to think they are doing the right thing.** If readers can believe that by taking a certain action they are on the side of "right," they will be most inclined to go along.
2. **Most people like to feel they are helping others.** If readers can believe that what you are promoting will help people, they may want to be a part of it.
3. **Most people don't like to feel they are being attacked or criticized.** If you can point out the problem in an opposing viewpoint in a way that doesn't offend readers who hold that position, you have the best chance of their listening.
4. **Most people like to have their concerns acknowledged.** When you can convince readers that you respect their viewpoint and understand their concerns, they are most likely to keep their minds open.
5. **Most people like to feel like they have not forsaken their principals to accept another viewpoint.** For example, anti-tax citizens who were against a local two-cent sales tax increase to make up for city revenue losses may have seen in the writer's proposal to "sunset" the tax increase after two years a way to support the increase without compromising their basic belief.

Activity 3.9

For your upcoming essay, decide on an audience of readers who hold differing viewpoints from your thesis or who may have no clear viewpoint. Consider an audience that can make an impact on the issue based on what they may or may not do.

Next, consider the five preceding thoughts on reading audiences and how you might employ some of them to make the greatest impact on your readers.

EXAMPLE

> **Topic:** Limiting funding for state's pre-school education program
>
> **Thesis:** Reducing funding for the state's pre-school edu-

cation program hurts children and will ultimately hurt the state.

Audience: State legislators and governor

Audience considerations:
These are mainly intelligent people who may not be particularly knowledgeable about pre-school education and its impact on children. They need to be "educated" on the subject but not in a condescending way. Education is an issue that most legislators want to support since it is the parents of children who elect them, so appealing to their support for education, and pre-school education in particular, is important. These are some of the people who originally created the state's pre-school education program, and they should be commended for it, pointing out that they are helping to save their own program. The common bond to emphasize between writer and readers is wanting to do what is best for the state's children, which in this case is not cutting pre-school funding.

Purpose

Your *purpose* in writing a particular essay influences everything that you write. Not only do you have to provide significant support for your thesis to influence readers, you need to do so in ways that will help accomplish your purpose. Readers are affected both by *what* a writer has to say and *how* she says it. A writer may "win the battle but lose the war" by presenting excellent support for her thesis but in a way that turns off readers, such as giving the impression that she is clearly better informed than they are.

To determine your purpose for the upcoming essay and how to accomplish it best, consider these questions.

1. **What impact do I want to make on readers?** What do you want them to think, believe, and do as a result of reading your essay?
2. **What can I realistically accomplish with this particular reading audience?** If your purpose is unrealistic and unattainable, such as getting an audience of National Rifle Association members to support a ban on the sale of guns, you may miss out on accomplishing something more attainable, like changing some minds on the banning of assault weapons.
3. **How can I best accomplish my purpose?** What combina-

tion of support for your thesis, acknowledgment and response to opposing viewpoints, consideration of your audience, and appropriate *tone* will give you the best chance of moving readers?

4. **What do I need to know and keep in mind about my readers to help accomplish my purpose?**   How can you use your reader's knowledge, or lack of knowledge, on the topic, their attitudes towards it, the cause of those attitudes, and how they are affected by it to your writing advantage?

Activity 3.10

Answer the four preceding questions to help prepare for your upcoming essay.

EXAMPLE

> **Topic:** Limiting funding for state's pre-school education program
>
> **Thesis:** Reducing funding for the state's pre-school education program hurts children and will ultimately hurt the state.
>
> **Audience:** State legislators and governor

1. I want them to delete the proposed cuts in the pre-school education program in the state budget for the upcoming year. I want them to understand and believe in the value of the program and the importance of keeping it strong.
2. Realistically, all state programs may take a hit given the huge shortfall in revenues. However, by pushing for a continuation of regular funding, there may be a compromise where the only loss would be the annual inflationary increase in funding, meaning schools would have to stay within their previous-year's budget.
3. The studies showing how well children with a pre-school education do in elementary school compared to other children is my strongest evidence. It will appeal to readers' sense of logic. Equally important is to show what will happen to children as a result of the proposed cuts. I need to undercut the belief by

some that pre-school education is not that important and indispensable to a child's education. Appealing to most legislators' strong support for education and children's issues is important. Acknowledging the difficult position that legislators are in and the tough choices they have to make will show some understanding of their plight.

4. These are basically intelligent men and women who want to do the right thing for children. I will appeal to them on that basis. They are also politicians who want to be re-elected, so it makes sense to bring in the voting parents in the essay. They are also under great pressure from many sides not to cut this program or that, so it is important to acknowledge the tough position they are in without weakening the position that pre-school funding shouldn't be cut.

Drafting

Your prewriting preparation for the upcoming essay has been substantial, and no doubt you are more than ready to get started. The purpose of your first draft is to get your ideas on paper within a general organizational framework. Once you have done that, you can see what you have done well, what needs improving, and what specific changes you can make to strengthen your essay and help accomplish your writing purpose.

Drafting Guidelines

Consider the following suggestions as you work through your first draft.

1. **In your opening paragraph or paragraphs, introduce your topic, create interest for readers, and include your thesis statement**. As an option, you might save your thesis for the conclusion, presenting it after you have built your case in the middle paragraphs that leads inexorably to one logical conclusion.

2. **In the middle paragraphs, present your reasons in support of your thesis in the most effective order.** For each reason, develop the paragraph with logical, factual, and/or empirical evidence that validates it. Present your source information primarily in your own words (*paraphrasing*), and when you use a direct quotation, introduce its source and enclose it in quotation marks. In addition, if you feel readers need some background or explanatory information to understand the topic or its importance better, provide that information at the beginning of the middle paragraphs.

3. **As you present each piece of factual evidence, acknowledge the *source* of that evidence to lend it credibility and distinguish the source material from your own thoughts and responses.** Provide source introductions such as, According to a May 2008 article in *Science Digest*, A recent research study by the State Department on violent crimes in small rural towns suggests, The college Admission's Office confirmed that, Highly respected oceanographer Dr. Florence Griffin has concluded, A May 2009 student survey by the college newspaper indicates, and so on.

4. **Towards the end of the middle paragraphs, acknowledge and respond to opposing arguments in the best way to accomplish your purpose.** This may include providing

logical, factual or empirical evidence to help refute or discredit a particular argument. Sometimes a writer will lead off the middle paragraphs by addressing a critical opposing viewpoint rather than waiting towards the end if she feels the majority of readers favor that viewpoint and wants to get it out in the open immediately. That is an organizational option to consider.

5. **Conclude your draft in a manner that reinforces (or introduces) your thesis statement, clarifies and emphasizes your purpose, and leaves readers with something new to consider.** Writers sometimes "skimp" on their endings, having expended great energy on making their case in the middle paragraphs. As important as the ending can be in influencing readers and accomplishing your purpose, you may want to take some time to re-energize and refocus before writing it.

6. **Keep your readers in mind as you write, and connect with them in ways that will help accomplish your writing purpose.** To connect with readers, you might show an understanding of their perspective and concerns, reveal a common bond between writer and readers, *qualify* your thesis to address their concerns without weakening your purpose, or use a respectful writing tone.

7. **Since this is a first draft, don't worry about writing a perfect paper.** Any concerns with wording, organization, or content can best be addressed after you have completed the draft and can evaluate it as a whole.

Activity 3.11

Read the following sample draft, noting how the writer introduces her topic and thesis, provides some explanatory and background information, presents her reasons in support of her thesis, including the logical, factual and empirical evidence that validates them, provides source introductions for all "borrowed" material, acknowledges and addresses opposing arguments, and concludes by connecting with readers, emphasizing her purpose, and tying her ending to her beginning.

Then write the first draft of your essay.

Sample First Draft

Keeping Pre-School Education Strong (audience: legislators and governor)

Natalie Gomez is looking forward to attending the same pre-school that her brother Ralph attended two years ago. Ralph is now a second grader and doing very well, thanks in part to his two-year pre-school experience. Natalie and her parents, however, may get a rude shock come August when her neighborhood pre-school may be closed and along with it, the educational opportunity that could make the difference between her success and failure in school and beyond.

According to the state's pre-school education office, if the currently proposed budget cuts to the state's pre-school program are enacted, many pre-schools will have to close down, and those that remain open will have to reduce their hours of instruction or charge a fee. These cuts will have a devastating educational effect on millions of the state's children, and in particular those from low-income families and those who are non-native speakers. No matter how troubled the state's short-term financial situation may be, it can ill-afford to deprive its children of an opportunity that can benefit them for the rest of their lives.

The state's pre-school education program began in 2005, created through the support of the legislature and governor. Today, according the state's pre-school education office, over five million children ages three and a half to five attend a state-financed pre-school. Pre-schoolers are taught by credentialed pre-school teachers assisted by student aids, and class sizes are held to a maximum of fifteen children. "State-sponsored pre-schools provide an excellent environment for young children to learn and develop in," says State Education Superintendent Lorraine Tiller. "They are a tremendous asset to our public school system."

There is no question that attending pre-school enhances a child's chances of succeeding in elementary school. Studies by independent educational research foundations in three different states with pre-school programs all reached the same conclusion: children who attend pre-school do significantly better in elementary school than children of similar backgrounds who do not attend, meaning better grades and better test scores. This makes sense when you look at educational standards for students in the state's pre-school handbook, which include development of listening and attention skills, reading and math readiness skills, social skills, motor skills, and creative skills, and appropriate classroom behavior and self-control. What would not make sense is if children who attended pre-school for one-to-two years did *not* outperform children who received none of this instruction.

For children from lower economic situations or for non-native speaking children, pre-school is particularly critical to their educational development. Children from middle-class backgrounds with well-educated parents have definite advantages over other children, according to a June 2007 article in the *Pre-school Journal*, and learn many things in their homes that are taught in pre-school. However, according to the article, pre-school helps to bridge the gap between children of different economic backgrounds and is critical to children who need to learn English before they can be fully immersed in the elementary curriculum. If pre-school fees have to be charged for the first time to keep pre-school doors open, it is only logical that children from poorer families are going to see those doors close.

Common sense would suggest that the success that children who attended pre-school have in elementary school does not end there. Longitudinal studies by the state's Department of Education clearly show that children who do well in elementary school continue to do well in middle school and high school, and are more likely to attend college. Conversely, children who struggle in elementary school continue to struggle in middle school and high school, and constitute the majority of high school drop outs. The seeds that are first sown in pre-school reap rewards throughout a child's educational experience, and when those seeds are not sown, that experience can prove devastating.

Legislators today are facing difficult choices given the current economic conditions in the State. Some are calling for across-the-board cuts to all state programs, which they consider the fairest way to deal with the revenue shortfall. However, all programs are not equal in value to the state or its residents, and a program that literally saves millions of children from educational failure and its devastating consequences is of the greatest value.

The argument that fully funding our pre-schools will in the long run save the State billions of dollars and generate billions of dollars in revenue is not far-fetched. On the one hand, according to an article in National Educational Journal in 2009, you have pre-school-educated children who succeed in school, eventually get jobs, and contribute to the economy. On the other hand, you have children without pre-school education who fail in school, aren't employable, and often end up on welfare rolls or in prison. Certainly there are exceptions, but it is common knowledge that our prisons and welfare programs aren't being filled with high school and college graduates. Is it more reasonable for the state to invest initially in a child's future success or pay for his lack of success for the rest of his life?

In 2000, the legislature and governor did a great thing by creating the state-funded pre-school education program. It has become an integral part of the public education program, not an add-on or dispensable supplement that some people who do not know the facts may think. It has helped get millions of children out of the cycle of poverty that educational failure often condemns them to, and the state is better for it. Certainly every state program has its value, but the commitment that the legislature made to our children's welfare through the creation the pre-school educational program must not be broken. It makes no sense to enact a wonderfully successful educational program and then dismantle it when the fiscal situation gets a little tough.

Reducing funding for the pre-school program means limiting the chances for the state's neediest children to succeed in school and in life. Nothing could be less fair, and clearly no legislator wants to do that; no matter what it takes to keep the program whole, it must be done. Come August, Natalie Gomez and her parents will find out whether she has a pre-school to go to or not. I can't think of anyone who would not hope that Natalie finds the door to her pre-school and to her future wide open. This much we owe to every child in the state.

Once you have completed your first draft, you are ready to evaluate its content, wording, and organization and make any changes you feel will improve the essay and help accomplish your purpose. Nothing is sacred in a first draft, and often the revisions that a writer makes lead to a significantly better paper.

As previously mentioned, setting aside your draft for a while before revising it often helps you evaluate it more objectively. Things that you may not notice as you write your draft often jump from the page when you read it later: a particularly wordy or awkward sentence, a paragraph that seems out of place in its current location, a harsher tone in the conclusion than you had intended. In addition, you may discover new things to add to your draft - a new supporting reason, some additional factual or empirical evidence, a concluding point - that you hadn't previously considered. Much of the improvement that you make to an essay cannot occur until you have your ideas on paper to evaluate. That is why the revision process is so important to most writers.

Of course, knowing what to look for in evaluating a draft is helpful, and each "Revision" section provides you with some guidelines. In general, you revise a draft to make your ideas clearer, to organize them most effectively, to engage your readers' interest more intently, and to give yourself the best chance of accomplishing your purpose.

To do these things most effectively, it helps to view your draft through the eyes of readers and ask yourself, "How might they react to this idea?" or "How might they respond to this line of reasoning?" or "How might they react to this piece of empirical evidence?" As you move from first to second draft, you move from the "personal" draft which is for your eyes only to the "public" draft which is for your readers to judge.

Logical Fallacies

Since the evidentiary emphasis in this unit is on providing logical support, it is useful to be aware of some of the most common *logical fallacies* that appear in writing: errors in reasoning that tend to mislead rather than enlighten readers. Being aware of logical fallacies helps you avoid them in your own writing and identify and dismiss them in the writings of others.

The following are some of the most common logical fallacies, which you can usually find every day in your local newspaper's "letters to the editor" section:

1. **Deductive fallacy.** In a deductive fallacy, the conclusion

doesn't logically follow the premises from which it is drawn. For example, someone may write that the roads on any mountain pass are slippery when covered with a thin layer of ice, that the previous night's storm created an icy cover on Grover Pass road, and that drivers don't need to worry about having tire chains. The conclusion - that tire chains aren't necessary- appears to be a faulty deduction based on the premises provided. Make sure that the conclusions that you draw in writing follow logically from their premises, and require the same from the writings of others.

2. **Hasty Conclusion.** When a writer draws a conclusion from insufficient evidence, he has drawn a *hasty conclusion*. For example, if someone writes that there is no global warming because her section of the country experienced one of its coldest weeks on record, she has drawn a conclusion based on one small piece of evidence which is contradicted by years of world-wide evidence to the contrary. Or if a writer concludes that diets don't work because he has gone on different diets and always regains the weight he loses, his limited empirical evidence is not adequate to draw a general conclusion that applies to everyone and every diet.

3. **Post Hoc.** A *post hoc* fallacy assumes a cause and effect relationship that doesn't exist. For example, in the famous "Twinkie defense" trial of 1979, defense lawyers argued that Dan White had killed San Francisco mayor George Moscone and councilman Harvey Milk in part because of a mood swing brought about by the consumption of high-sugar foods. In other words, White had experienced a "sugar rush" which caused him to explode and commit the violent acts. The prosecution, of course, attacked the faulty cause-effect relationship, pointing out that most people don't go out and kill people after drinking a Coke or eating a Twinkie.

4. **Slippery Slope.** The "slippery slope" fallacy argues that if one thing occurs, it will undoubtedly lead to more dire consequences when there is no evidence to support the conclusion. For example, opponents of the "public option" for health care reform, which would provide a Federal health care option to private insurance, argue that the public option would be the first step towards socializing all aspects of American business and ending private enterprise. There is absolutely no evidence to support such a conclusion, and most industrialized countries have government-run health programs, which hasn't lead to a government take-over of private enterprise.

5. **Weak Analogy.** Writers often use analogies - comparisons between situations that have some similarities - to make a point. However, when the analogy is flawed, it doesn't further the writer's argument. For example, proponents of drug legalization make the analogy that the war on drugs is like the alcohol prohibition era of the 30's: prohibition didn't keep people from drinking, and was eventually lifted, and the war on drugs is equally ineffective. However, significant differences in the two situations weaken the analogy. First, alcohol was legal prior to prohibition, which made prohibition difficult, while illicit drugs don't have a legal history. Second, while prohibition did little to change people's drinking habits, the illegality of drugs has kept millions of people from risking drug use. Finally, while alcohol and hard drugs are both addictive, it can be argued that while millions of Americans consume moderate amounts of alcohol with little ill effects, hard drugs are much more devastating and destructive. The differences between alcohol prohibition and the war on drugs weaken the impact of the analogy.

6. **Ad hominem.** When a writer attacks and tries to discredit a person rather than attacking the position the person supports, he is committing an *ad hominem* fallacy. For example, let's say a writer opposes the city mayor's position of providing city funds to help save the financially troubled, privately operated metropolitan museum. Instead of providing arguments against the city's involvement, the writer attacks the mayor: "Mayor Stephenson has had personal financial problems herself and has been audited by the IRS, so her position on funding the museum should be discounted." Rather than providing arguments against city funding for a private institution, the writer attempts to discredit the mayor, whose personal finances have nothing to do with the issue at hand.

7. **Overgeneralization.** When a writer makes statements like, "*Everyone* agrees that Americans pay too much in taxes," or, "*Any clear-thinking person* understands that overpopulation is the world's biggest problem," or "*All women* are united on the equal- pay-for-equal-work initiative," she is overgeneralizing. The writer's purpose is to make readers feel that her position is universally accepted, but she obviously doesn't speak for all people, and her inclusive statements simply aren't true. Writers use qualifiers such as "Most people," or "The majority of women" or "Many international scientists" to avoid overgeneralizations.

8. **Guilt by Association.** When a writer tries to discredit a person or an issue by linking the person or issue to a negative association, he is using *guilt by association*. For example, during President Obama's candidacy for president, he was linked by the opposition to former 1960's political radical Bill Ayers, today a professor at the University of Illinois and respected civic leader in Chicago. Since Ayers was an Obama supporter, Obama had a "terrorist friend," and how could anyone who associated with terrorists lead America in its war against terrorism? Of course, Ayers was one of millions of Obama supporters and contributors, and his link to Obama was as a civic leader and educator. Nonetheless, some opponents attempted to use *guilt by association* to mislead potential voters and discredit Obama.

Activity 3.12

The following essay contains some logical fallacies. Identify each fallacy and indicate in what way(s) it misleads readers.

Involvement in Student Government

Most students on campus have little interest in student government. Less than ten per cent of the student body votes in student elections, and it is sometimes difficult to find candidates for some offices while candidates for other offices run unopposed. If student government disappeared tomorrow, no student would even notice it, at least for a while.

However, there is a definite purpose for student government at any college, and students need to be more aware of what they would lose if it vanished. Students need to support their student government, vote in elections, and become more involved in the process.

If student government disappeared, students would have absolutely no say in the decision-making for the college. Without the student voice, the college would do everything it could to save money: increase class sizes dramatically, hire only part-time, non-tenure track instructors, increase tuition, health, and parking fees, and eliminate all sports that don't generate income. If student government disappeared, it would be the equivalent of a democratic country being taken over by a fascist regime. Students' freedom of speech and assembly, which is often exercised through student government, would be lost.

A nearby college gave up its student government a year ago due to lack of participation, and with little complaint from students. Today, that college has experienced a decline in daytime enrollment and an increase in night enrollment, due largely to the lack of a student government. No students want to go to school at night if they can get the day classes they want.

Once a school loses its student government, it is almost impossible to get it reinstated. Mia Jung, a former student vice-president at the neighboring college, approached the school's board of trustees about the possibility of reinstating student government, and her efforts were rebuffed. Of course, two of the five board members are local businessmen who aren't used to sharing power or decision-making with anyone in their companies, so it isn't surprising that they aren't favorable to reinstating student government. Other board members are friends and supporters of the local mayor, who runs an autocratic city government, so it is obvious where they get their opinions.

Is our school at risk of losing its student government, and should anyone care? If you believe that a college is here for its students, and that the decisions made by the college should be in the best interests of the students and their educational pursuit, you should care deeply about student government. While few students attend board meetings and see the student representatives work to ensure that tuition and other fees are kept as low as possible, that the cafeteria serves healthy, reasonably priced food, that the bookstore keeps its profit margin to the minimum, and that the dormitories provide a safe, quiet environment for serious students, all students benefit from the strong student voice. With only ten per cent of students voting and the difficulties finding students to run for offices, the college isn't going to consider getting rid of student government at this time. But there is no guarantee for the future.

The next student election that comes up, take the time to vote, or even run for an office yourself. If you believe in the democratic process, if you don't want your life controlled by college bean counters, if you don't want your tuition doubled, and if you don't want poorly prepared, undereducated instructors, you need to support student government. All students want the best education they can possibly get, and without student government, that isn't possible.

Revision Checklist

As you revise your draft, it helps to be aware of the different elements of the draft that may need revision. The following checklist provides some specific aspects to consider for revision, which you may want to look at one at a time as you revise.

1. **Opening**: Read your opening to see how well you have introduced your topic, created interest for readers, and pre-

sented your thesis statement. What can you add or change to strengthen your opening?

2. **Explanatory information**: Based on you readers' familiarity with the topic, did you include any explanatory or background information at the beginning of your middle paragraphs that would help them understand the topic better? What might you add to assure that readers understand the topic well enough to evaluate your thesis and support most intelligently?

3. **Support:** In the middle paragraphs, evaluate your reasons in support of your thesis to determine whether each would help convince readers of the thesis' validity. How might you reword a particular reason to make it clearer or more impressive, and what might you add (or delete) to strengthen your support?

4. **Evidence:** Evaluate the logical, factual or empirical evidence you provide to support or verify each reason, with a particular emphasis on logical evidence. Check your paper for any *logical fallacies* that need deleting or revising. What might you add or change to make your evidence more convincing to readers? Make sure that you have put most of the factual evidence into your own words (*paraphrasing*) and put quotation marks around directly quoted material.

5. **Source acknowledgment:** Check to make sure that you have included a source acknowledgment for each piece of factual evidence: According to botanist Eugene Smeds , A study by the Asthma Institute of UC San Francisco indicates, In a 2008 article in *Atlantic Monthly*, The majority of health care professionals at the state health symposium agreed, and so on. Add a source acknowledgment to any piece of evidence that is not clearly identified.

6. **Opposing viewpoints:** Check to make sure that you have acknowledged and responded to the major arguments of readers holding an opposing viewpoint to your own. Evaluate how effectively you have addressed each argument, how readers may react to your response, and what you might change or add to elicit the desired reaction.

7. **Organization**: Read your middle paragraphs and evaluate how effectively you have ordered your supportive reasons. If necessary, reorder them so that the strongest arguments clearly stand out. In addition, determine whether you have placed your response to opposing arguments in the most effective location.

Finally, check to see whether a particular paragraph or sentence within a paragraph seems out of place in its current location. If so, move the paragraph or sentence to a place where it fits most logically.

8. **Paragraphing**: Check your paragraphs to make sure that, for the most part, you have presented one main idea in each paragraph and that all sentences within the paragraph are related to that idea. Also make sure that you have changed paragraphs each time you move to something new in the essay.

   In addition, check to see whether you have any overly long paragraphs that need dividing into two or any pairs or groups of short successive paragraphs (one or two sentences) that need to be combined or developed further.

9. **Wording**: Read each sentence carefully and improve wording by eliminating unnecessary words or phrases, rewording awkward sentences, replacing questionable word choices, and clarifying vague sentences. In the end, each sentence should read exactly the way you want, and each word should be indispensable to complete the sentence's meaning.

10. **Conclusion**: Read your conclusion to see whether it reinforces your thesis statement, makes your purpose clear to readers, leaves them with something new to consider, and is a compelling part of your paper. Since your ending is the last thing that readers read, what can you add or change to make the most lasting impression on them?

11. **Audience connection**: How have you connected with the reading audience in ways that will help them to consider your ideas most seriously? What might you do to create a stronger connection that may help you accomplish your purpose?

12. **Purpose**: Reread your entire draft with one question in mind: how well am I accomplishing my writing purpose? What might you change or add in any place to help your purpose resonate with readers: a stronger, firmer tone? greater emphasis on the importance of the issue? a warning of the consequences if your purpose is *not* accomplished? Stronger evidence to support your alleged facts? a more engaging opening or powerful ending?

Activity 3.12

Read the following first draft and apply the revision considerations just presented. What suggestions might you make to the writer for improving different aspects of his draft and for strengthening its overall impact?

Sample First Draft

Neighborhood Parking Problem (reading audience: city council and mayor)

Looking down Avenida Los Mares mid-morning on a Saturday, the residential street resembles a parking lot. Cars are parked front-to-end on both sides of the street from one end of the block to the other. The majority of the vehicles are big - SUVs, two-seater trucks, and vans -, and all of the road that is left visible is a narrow strip in the middle wide enough for one vehicle to go through. Los Mares, however, is a two-way street.

The on-street parking congestion on Avenida Los Mares and its unsafe consequences are a cause of concern for the street's residents as well as other motorists passing through to other streets. The city of Lanare needs to take a good look at the problem and do something about it.

Driving up or down Los Mares is a real problem. Since two cars cannot pass one another on the street since it is so narrow with all of the cars parked on both sides, drivers have to pull to the side of the road to let another vehicle pass by. This is enough of a problem in itself, but with cars parked front-to-end on both sides of the street, often there is no space to pull into to let another car pass. As a result, cars sometimes have to pull into someone's driveway to get out of the way, something I have done several times. Of course, the people living in the house don't appreciate it, and some have even put in signs reading, "Private driveway: No trespassing." In addition, since there is not always a handy driveway to pull into, I have seen cars have to back up a considerable distance just to find a place to get out of the way of an oncoming car. I as well as others in the neighborhood have witnessed bottlenecks on the street where one car backing up forces another car or two behind him to do the same while oncoming cars back up and wait. There are also the occasional shouting matches when neither driver approaching the other wants to be the one to "yield" and the two cars face off in the street like combatants, sometimes requiring a third party from the neighborhood to intervene and get traffic moving again.

Los Mares, according to the city's public works department, is one of the narrower residential streets in the city, which is a part of the problem that is not solvable since the houses are not far enough from the road to widen it. Thirty or forty years ago the street was passable since vehicles were not as large as the current SUVs and trucks, and residents in general owned fewer cars than today, according to the city's superintendent of public works. The street simply was not built for today's larger vehicles and three-car families, but somehow residents have to make do.

Safety is a big issue with the current parking situation. With cars approaching one another on what amounts to a one-lane road with no right-of-way, with cars having to move into small spaces to get out of the way of oncoming cars, and with cars sometimes having to back up to find a space, it is not surprising that fender-bender accidents and scraped parked cars occur with some regularity.

The safety of the many children living on the block is a bigger concern. With all of the large vehicles parked on both sides of the road, it is very difficult to see a child dart into the street to retrieve a ball and equally difficult for children to see an approaching car. Two children were hit on the street in the past year, as confirmed by police reports for each incident, and fortunately no child was killed. However, that is more accidents involving children and vehicles on Los Mares than on any other residential street for the same period of time, according to police accident records for the city. It is not surprising that residents of Los Mares petitioned the city last March to do something to improve the situation, but as of yet, nothing has been done.

A final problem is simply finding a place to park at your house. Not only are there the regular cars of residents parked on the street, there are also other vehicles vying for parking space: gardeners, repairmen, plumbers, cleaning women, and so forth. It's first-come-first serve parking since the street area in front of one's house is public property, and I've come home many times to find all of the parking space in front of our house filled with three cars, some of which I don't recognize. It is not uncommon to find a resident's vehicle parked several houses down from his own, which probably sounds unbelievable to most residents of the city.

Since the street can't be widened and since the city can't tell residents what kind of vehicles to buy or how many, the solution must lie elsewhere. For the sake of safety, the intent is obvious: to have significantly fewer vehicles parked on the street. This would provide more room for cars to pass one another, better street visibility for drivers and for children, and a safer street. For Avenida Los Mares, the city needs to do what is being done in some of the gated communities within the city whose streets are controlled by resident associations, and that is to restrict the number of vehicles parked on the street. Some gated residential neighborhoods do not allow residents to park on the street at all. While this may be impossible to duplicate on Los Mares, given the limited driveway and garage parking space that many residents have, a restriction can still be placed on the number of vehicles. If the city passed an ordinance allowing residents no more than one vehicle to be parked on the street, that would help the situation tremendously, given that many residents park two or three vehicles on the street. Many residents would be forced to fill their garages and driveways with vehicles, but that is a small price to pay to get our street back and make it safe for children and motorists.

How can the city restrict parking on Los Mares and not on other streets, a number of people have argued. Los Mares is, after all, a public street like any city street, so the same public usage ordinance should apply. The problem with that viewpoint, which some small-minded city council members have hidden behind, is that it does nothing to solve a serious problem. Some city council members seem to feel that since they don't live on the street, or have to drive on it, that it isn't their problem. So they simply say they'll "review" the situation, which has meant doing nothing while two children were hurt in accidents on the street due to the council's neglect.

Language for a new city ordinance that would affect residential streets the width of Los Mares is simple: on residential streets of a certain width or narrower, that width determined by whether the street can accommodate two-way traffic given its current parking situation, residents are restricted to parking one vehicle on the street, the ordinance to be enforced by the parking division of the city police. Ninety per cent of the streets and residents of the city wouldn't be affected, according to the city's public works department, since they are wide enough to accommodate two-way traffic without on-street parking restrictions. However, the other ten per cent of the streets would get a solution to a serious safety and convenience problem for their residents.

Another proposal that has been raised is to make Los Mares a one-way street, but that would create as many problems as it solves, forcing residents to drive in one direction when they often want to go in the other. Currently there are no one-way residential streets in the city, according to the public works department, and the reason is simple: they create huge inconveniences for residents. Besides, turning Los Mares into a one-way street would not solve the safety problem for children since there would still be the same number of cars parked on the street and the same limited visibility.

Finally, the city has a large liability problem on its hands that it is closing its eyes to. Los Mares is a two-way street that does not allow two-way traffic. It is surprising that no motorist involved in an accident on Los Mares hasn't sued the city, but that day will surely come. If the council does nothing to solve the problem, the day will also come when council members have the blood of a dead child on their hands, killed by a motorist who couldn't see her dart into the street until it was too late. It is not too late for the council to do something to solve the Los Mares street problem, but that child could dart out into the street tomorrow or the next day. This is not an issue for further review. It is time for action.

Sentence Wording

A significant part of the revision process for most writers is rewording their first-draft sentences to make them as clear and well-written as possible. When a writer first puts her thoughts on paper, they seldom appear in perfectly worded form. That is the reason that for most writers, writing good sentences is a two-step process: first, getting the idea on paper and second, wording it in the best way possible.

For example, a writer wrote the following first draft sentence:

The actual time that it takes for people to apply for unemployment insurance, given the hours of waiting in long lines, along with the laborious interview process and tedious paperwork involved, discourages many people from following through and getting insurance.

Obviously, this is a rather lengthy sentence, with a lot of stopping and starting for readers. As with any sentence, there are various ways to revise and improve it, including smoothing out the single sentence or dividing it into two sentences. Here is one example of each option:

One sentence:
The hours required for people to apply for unemployment insurance, given the long waiting lines, lengthy interview process, and tedious paperwork, discourages many people from getting insurance.

Two sentences:
Applying for unemployment insurance involves waiting in long lines, going through a lengthy interview, and doing tedious paperwork. This process takes many hours and discourages people from getting insurance.

Activity 3.11

Revise the following first draft sentences by eliminating unnecessary words, smoothing out awkward sentences, replacing questionable word choices, and moving words and phrases around to create the most readable sentences.

EXAMPLE

It isn't so much that state residents hate to have their taxes raised, they have too often seen them raised and seen no positive results from the increase.

Revised:
State residents only hate to have their taxes raised when they see no positive results.

1. The majority of the vehicles are big - SUVs, two-seater trucks, and vans -, and all of the road that is left visible is a narrow strip in the middle wide enough for one vehicle to go through.
2. The on-street parking congestion on Avenida Los Mares and its unsafe consequences are a cause of concern for the street's residents as well as other motorists passing through to other streets.
3. Los Mares, according to the city's public works department, is one of the narrower residential streets in the city, which is a part of the problem that is not solvable since the houses are not far enough from the road to widen it.
4. Since two cars cannot pass one another on the street since it is so narrow with all of the cars parked on both sides, drivers have to pull to the side of the road to let another vehicle pass by.

5. Language for a new city ordinance that would affect residential streets the width of Los Mares is simple: on residential streets of a certain width or narrower, that width determined by whether the street can accommodate two-way traffic given its current parking situation, residents are restricted to parking one vehicle on the street, the ordinance to be enforced by the parking division of the city police.

6. Los Mares, according to the city's public works department, is one of the narrower residential streets in the city, which is a part of the problem that is not solvable since the houses are not far enough from the road to widen it.

Activity 3.12

Revise the first draft of your essay, keeping in mind the suggestions presented in the "Revision Checklist." For the most effective revision, writers often cover one aspect of their draft at a time - the opening or conclusion, overall organization, source acknowledgments, sentence wording - before moving to the next. In that way, nothing gets lost in the evaluation process.

Editing

Editing your paper for errors in usually the final step of the writing process. It makes little sense to do a careful proofreading of a paper when you are still revising the content and wording of your sentences. You want to proofread your paper when you are looking at your sentences in final form.

Of course, whenever you discover an error at any point in your writing, the natural and best response is to correct it then and there. It might be an error that escapes your detection during the final editing phase. There is no "wrong" time to correct an error, but when it comes to concentrating exclusively on error correction, for most writers the best time is at the end of the process.

In this section, you are introduced to a new editing consideration: *active and passive sentences.* You will see that active sentences are generally preferable to their passive form, and you will learn how to change passive sentences to active ones. While using the passive voice, like writing non-parallel sentences, is not an "error" such as incorrect spelling or punctuation, it is an editing concern because it can produce weak sentences that may have little impact on readers.

Editing Checklist

The following checklist will ensure that you cover every aspect of grammar usage, punctuation, and spelling as you proofread your paper for errors.

1. **Spelling.** Use the spell check on your word processor and also proofread your paper for spelling errors.

2. **Punctuation**. Check to make sure you used the following correctly:
    End marks (periods, question marks, exclamation marks) to designate the end of each sentence. As you read your sentences, look for any *run-on sentences, comma splices, or sentence fragments,* and punctuate them correctly to eliminate the problems.

    Commas to separate words or phrases in a series; after introductory dependent clauses and preposition, participial, and gerund phrases; after conjunctions in a compound sentence; after "interrupters" such as "by the way," "incidentally," or "of course" at the beginning or within a sentences; before and after appositives or unrestricted relative clauses; to set off ending participial phrases, or at a point in a sentence where a pause is essential for the sentence to be read and understood correctly.

Semi-colons to connect two closely related sentences or to separate phrases within a series that also contain commas within the phrases.

Colons to set off a summary, series, or example following a main clause.

Dashes to set off a summary, series, or example *within* a sentence: The most difficult part of helping a child with school work - letting her learn from her own mistakes - is also one of the most important.

Apostrophes to identify possessive words and contractions.

Quotation marks to set off direct quotations.

3. **Grammar.** Check to make sure that your verbs agree with their subjects, pronouns agree with their antecedents, the correct pronoun subject and object forms are used, the correct comparative and superlative adjective forms are used, the correct adverb forms are used, and the correct irregular past tense verb forms are used.

4. **Parallelism**. Make sure that in sentences that contain a series of two or more words, phrases, or clauses, frequently joined by "and" or "or," all parts of the series are *parallel* in construction.

5. **Active/Passive Voice**. Make sure that most of your sentences are in the active voice, and use the passive voice only for special emphasis. (See the following section on "Active and Passive Voice.")

Active and Passive Voice

Sentences are written in the *active* or *passive* voice, depending on whether the subject *performs* the action or *receives* the action in the sentence. For example, the sentence, "Ralph passed his bar exam on the fifth try," is written in the *active* voice: the subject "Ralph" performs the action of passing the exam. The sentence, "The bar exam was passed by Ralph on his fifth try," is written in the *passive* voice: the subject "exam" *receives* the action, and "Ralph" becomes the object of the preposition "by."

The following are examples of sentences written in the active and passive voice. Notice that in the passive voice, the verb "is," "are," "was," or "were" is present, and the preposition "by" precedes the person or thing that performs the act.

Active: The CIA engaged in covert operations in Nicaragua in the 1970's.

Passive: Covert operations were engaged in by the CIA in Nicaragua in the 1970's.

Active: Mildred enjoys playing chess on her computer late into the evening.

Passive: Playing chess on her computer is enjoyed by Mildred late into the evening.

Active: The news of the stock market crash stunned the nation.

Passive: The nation was stunned by the news of the stock market crash.

Active: An Egyptian mediator proposed an intriguing settlement to the Israeli-Palestinian conflict.

Passive: An intriguing settlement to the Israeli-Palestinian conflict was proposed by an Egyptian mediator.

Active: The jury acquitted the defendant on charges of embezzling funds from the insurance company he worked for.

Passive: The defendant was acquitted by the jury on charges of embezzling funds from the insurance company he worked for.

In most writing situations, the active voice is preferred over the passive voice. It is more vivid and interesting because it *shows* the action to readers: "The dog bit the intruder on the buttocks." The passive voice, on the other hand, is generally less interesting because it *doesn't* directly show the action: "The intruder was bitten on the buttocks by the dog." In addition, sentences in the passive voice are usually wordier than sentences in the active voice. Notice in the ten example sentences that the passive sentence is always longer than the active sentence. Finally, a sentence written in the passive voice can be rather awkward, such as the example sentence, "Playing chess on her computer is enjoyed by Mildred late into the evening."

There are some situations, however, when the passive voice is more effective than the active voice. For example, if the person committing the action is not as important as the thing receiving the action (the direct object in an active-voice sentence), the passive voice moves the more important element to the forefront. For example, in the passive sentence, "An intriguing settlement to the Israeli-Palestinian conflict was proposed by an Egyptian mediator," the "intriguing settlement" may be more noteworthy than the person proposing the settlement. In the passive sentence, "The defendant was acquitted by the jury on charges of embezzling funds from the insurance company he worked for," that the defendant was acquitted may be the most noteworthy element in the sentence.

The following suggestions will help you use the active and passive voices effectively in your sentences.

1. **Write your sentences primarily using the active voice**. In general, active sentences are the most interesting for readers and convey what you have to say most vividly and concisely.

2. **Use the passive voice when you wish to emphasize the thing receiving the action rather than the person committing the action**. For example, the passive sentence, "A study of environmental effects on asthma sufferers conducted by University of California researchers concluded that city dwellers endure the worst conditions" highlights the important study rather than the people who conducted it.

3. **In editing your paper, check to see whether sentences are in the active or passive voice, and change passive sentences to active sentences *unless the passive sentence emphasizes the more important element*.** If a particular active sentence emphasizes a less important element, change the sentence to the passive voice to highlight what is most important.

   To change the passive voice to active, move the person or thing committing the action to the front of the sentence as the *subject* and put the current subject after the verb as the direct object:

Passive: The sky was darkened by soot from the belching volcano.
Active: Soot from the belching volcano darkened the sky.

To change the active voice to passive, move the direct object to the subject position, put the current subject preceded by the word "by" after the verb, and add "is," "are," "was," or "were" before the verb:

Active: Fleming reeled in the largest trout ever caught in Lake Elsinore.

Passive: The largest trout ever caught in Lake Elsinore was reeled in by Fleming.

Activity 3.13

Change the following sentences written in the passive voice to active sentences, and change sentences written in the active voice to passive sentences.

EXAMPLE

> Bottles were hurled at the police by the angry crowd, who launched smoke bomb canisters in return. (passive)

> The angry crowd hurled bottles at the police, who launched smoke bomb canisters in return. (active)

1. The narrow, treacherous strait was navigated by the young man in his sailboat like a seasoned sailor.
2. It was concluded by a majority of the Supreme Court that the plaintiffs' constitutional right to assemble was violated by the Philadelphia police who dispersed the crowd.
3. Researchers from Southern Methodist University discovered an intriguing new specie of fossilized snake with legs in a limestone quarry outside of Jerusalem.
4. When the crime scene investigation was completed by detectives, they were certain that what initially looked like a robbery had been staged.
5. Yuri Fialko, a geologist at the University of California, Berkeley, predicted an eminent earthquake of a 7.0 magnitude or greater due to the current stress level of the San Andreas fault.
6. General Motors was bombarded by urgent requests from the across the country for more information on its new Chevrolet hybrid model that purportedly gets fifty miles per gallon of gasoline.
7. U.S. geologists hit the country's maximum oil discovery rate in 1957, with the rate dropping annually since that time.
8. The poor voter turn-out for the gubernatorial election in New Jersey was caused by snowstorms that discouraged people from leaving their homes.
9. A northern section of Bagdad was evacuated by thou-

sands of Iraqis when news of a possible bombing attack spread through the area.

10. Medical researchers in France conducted a study on the effects of a new cancer-treatment alternative to chemotherapy.

Activity 3.14

The following paragraphs contain some passive sentences that would be more effective in the active voice and an active sentence or two that would be more effective in the passive voice. Change passive sentences to active and active sentences to passive when they would improve the paragraph.

EXAMPLE

> Student government offices were not run for by enough students to hold an election. A lack of power by students to influence educational decisions was being protested by the student body. (Both sentences are passive.)

> **Revised:**
> Not enough students ran for student government offices to hold an election. The student body was protesting the lack of power by students to influence educational decisions. (Both sentences are active.)

> Criminal activity on campus has increased in the past two years. The campus is frequented by more non-students, according to police, which contributes to the problem. Adults who don't attend the college committed over sixty per cent of the crimes on campus last year. The crimes included drug-related violence, assault, vandalism, and theft. The rising crime rate in the area, where gang-related crime is on the rise, is mirrored by the increase in criminal activity on campus.
> The presence of neighborhood patrols in the area has been increased by the police department. A similar increase by the college in its campus security force is certainly warranted. The college also needs to work with the police department to help identify known gang members who appear on campus. The college's list of priorities must be topped by the safety of every student on campus. If the

school cannot provide a safe environment, students are going to go elsewhere.

Activity 3.15

Proofread your draft for spelling, grammar, or punctuation errors and make the necessary corrections. In addition, correct any sentence with non-parallel elements to make them parallel, and change weak passive sentences to their active forms.

Back to Eighteen? Time to Re-examine the Drinking Law
By Radley Balco

It's been 20 years that America has had a minimum federal drinking age. The policy began to gain momentum in the early 1980s, when the increasingly influential Mothers Against Drunk Driving added the federal minimum drinking age to its legislative agenda. By 1984, it had won over a majority of the Congress.

President Reagan initially opposed the law on federalism grounds but eventually was persuaded by his transportation secretary at the time, Elizabeth Dole. Over the next three years every state had to choose between adopting the standard or forgoing federal highway funding; most complied. A few held out until the deadline, including Vermont, which fought the law all the way to the U.S. Supreme Court, and lost.

Twenty years later, the drawbacks of the legislation are the same as they were when it was passed. The first is that the age set by the legislation is basically arbitrary. The U.S. has the highest drinking age in the world (a title it shares with Indonesia, Mongolia, Palau). The vast majority of the rest of the world sets the minimum age at 17 or 16 or has no minimum age at all.

Supporters of the federal minimum argue that the human brain continues developing until at least the age of 21. Alcohol expert Dr. David Hanson of the State University of New York at Potsdam argues such assertions reek of junk science. They're extrapolated from a study on lab mice, he explains, as well as from a small sample of actual humans already dependent on alcohol or drugs. Neither is enough to make broad proclamations about the entire population. If the research on brain development is true, the U.S. seems to be the only country to have caught on to it.

Oddly enough, high school students in much of the rest of the developed world - where lower drinking ages and laxer enforcement reign - do considerably better than U.S. students on standardized tests. While their better test scores probably aren't caused by their legalized drinking, apparently it doesn't hurt.

The second drawback of the federal drinking age is that it sets the stage for tying federal mandates to highway funds, enabling Congress to meddle in all sorts of state and local affairs it has no business attempting to regulate - so long as it can make a tortured argument about highway safety. Efforts to set national speed limits, seat belt laws, motorcycle helmet laws and set a national blood-alcohol standard for DWI cases have rested on the premise that the federal government can blackmail the states with threats to cut off funding.

The final drawback is pretty straightforward: It makes little sense that America considers an 18-year-old mature enough to marry, to sign a contract, to vote, to have sexual relations, and to fight and die for his or her country, but not mature enough to decide whether or not to have a beer.

So for all of those drawbacks, has the law worked? Supporters seem to think so. Their primary argument is the dramatic drop in the number of alcohol-related traffic fatalities since the minimum age first passed Congress in 1984. They also cite relative drops in the percentage of underage drinkers before and after the law went into effect.

But a new chorus is emerging to challenge the conventional wisdom. The most vocal of these critics is John McCardell Jr., the former president of Middlebury College in Vermont. McCardell's experience in higher education revealed to him that the federal age simply wasn't working. It may have negligibly reduced total underage consumption, but according to McCardell, those who did consume were much more likely to do so behind closed doors and to drink to excess in the short time they had access to alcohol. McCardell recently started the organization Choose Responsibly, which advocates moving the drinking age back to 18. McCardell explains that the drop in highway fatalities often cited by supporters of the 21 minimum age actually began in the late 1970s, well before the federal drinking age set in. What's more, he recently explained in an online chat for the "Chronicle of Higher Education" that the drop is better explained by safer and better built cars, increased seat belt use, and increasing awareness of the dangers of drunken driving than in a federal standard. The age at highest risk for an alcohol-related auto fatality is 21, followed by 22 and 23, an indication that delaying first exposure to alcohol until young adults are away from home may not be the best way to introduce them to drinking.

McCardell isn't alone. Kenyon College President S. Georgia has expressed frustration with the law, particularly in 2005 after the alcohol-related death of a Kenyon student. And former *Time* magazine editor and higher ed reporter Barrett Seaman echoed McCardell's concerns in 2005. The period since the 21 minimum drinking age took effect has been "marked by a shift from beer to hard liquor," Seaman wrote in *Time*, "consumed not in large social settings, since that was now illegal, but furtively and dangerously in students' residences. In my reporting at colleges around the country, I did not meet any presidents or deans who felt the 21-year age minimum helps their efforts to curb the abuse of alcohol on their campuses."

The federal drinking age has become somewhat sacrosanct among public health activists, who've consistently relied on the accident data to quell debate over the law's merits. They've moved on to other battles, such as scolding parents for giving their own kids a taste of alcohol before the age of 21 or attacking the alcohol industry for advertising during sporting events or in magazines that are often read by people under the age of 21.

But after 20 years, perhaps it's time to take a second look - a sound, sober (pardon the pun), science-based look - at the law's costs and benefits, as well as the sound philosophical objections to it. McCardell provides a welcome voice in a debate too often dominated by hysterics. But beyond McCardell, Congress should really consider abandoning the federal minimum altogether, or at least the federal funding blackmail that gives it teeth. State and local governments are far better at passing laws that reflect the values, morals and habits of their communities.

DISCUSSION

1. What is the thesis of the essay?
2. What logical evidence does the essay provide in support of the thesis? How convincing do you find it?
3. What other evidence - factual or empirical - is provided, and how effectively is it presented?
4. What opposing arguments to the thesis are presented, and how effectively are they addressed?
5. What, if anything, is left out of the essay that is relative to the topic?
6. Do you agree with the essay's position on the drinking age, and why? How effectively is that position presented and supported in the essay?

Marked for Mayhem
By Chuck Hustmyre and Jay Dixit

Midnight in New Orleans. Lisa Z. was walking home from the French-Quarter hotel where she works when three men stepped around a corner and stopped in front of her. When she tried to cross the street to get away, the men charged after her. "One guy clotheslined me," she recalls, "then choked me, threw me on the sidewalk, and jammed a chrome, snub-nosed .38 revolver against my cheekbone." Lisa was kicked, robbed, and then told not to move or she'd be shot in the face. The men who robbed her likely chose Lisa because she unknowingly sent out signals that marked her as a "soft" target. Alone and encumbered by a backpack, she appeared to be a vulnerable person who could be easily controlled. "Some of these guys concentrate on people who are easy to overcome," says Volkan Topalli, a psychologist and criminologist at Georgia State University. "They'll target females, they'll target older people, but they're also looking for cues of weakness or fear."

Criminals, like their victims, come in all varieties, but researchers have found that they don't choose their victims randomly. There's a reason FBI agents begin crime investigations by creating profiles of victims. It's because the identity of victims - particularly if there are several victims with differing characteristics - helps investigators determine whether a criminal is targeting a specific kind of person. Criminals prey on people who appear to be the most vulnerable, and the signals a person sends out may either attract or deter a lurking assailant.

In the field of victimology, one of the central concepts is that of the "risk continuum" - the degrees of risk that you may be a victim based on your career, lifestyle, relationships, movements, and even personality, aspects manifested in your behavior and demeanor. Some factors that make people potential victims are obvious - flashing wads of cash, wearing expensive jewelry, walking alone on back streets. Others are subtler, including posture, walking style, even the ability to read facial expressions.

The cues add up to what David Buss terms "exploitability." An evolutionary psychologist at the University of Texas, Buss is examining a catalogue of traits that seem to invite some people to exploit others. There's cheatability (cues you can be duped in social exchange), sexual-exploitability (cues you can be sexually manipulated), as well as mugability, robability, killability, stalkability, and even sexual-assaultability. "As adaptations for exploitation evolved, so did defenses to prevent being exploited - wariness toward strangers, cheater-detection sensitivities, and possibly anti-rape defenses," explains Buss. "These defenses, in turn, created pressure for additional adaptations for exploitation designed to circumvent victim defenses. This co-evolutionary arms race can continue indefinitely."

Nowhere does victimology imply that people who stand out as easy targets are to blame for becoming victims. Predators bear sole responsibility for the crimes they commit and should be held accountable and punished accordingly. Moreover, many attacks are random, and no amount of vigilance could deter them. Whether victims are selected randomly or targeted because of specific characteristics, they bear no responsibility for crimes against them. But by being aware of which cues criminals look for, we can reduce the risk of becoming targets ourselves.

In a classic study, researchers Betty Grayson and Morris I. Stein asked convicted criminals to view a video of pedestrians walking down a busy New York City sidewalk, unaware they were being taped. The convicts had been to prison for violent offenses such as armed robbery, rape, and murder.

Within a few seconds, the convicts identified which pedestrians they would have been likely to target. What startled the researchers was that there was a clear consensus among the criminals about whom they would have picked as victims, and their choices were not based on gender, race, or age. Some petite, physically slight women were not selected as potential victims, while some large men were.

The researchers realized the criminals were assessing the ease with which they could overpower the targets based on several nonverbal signals - posture, body language, pace of walking, length of stride, and awareness of environment. Neither criminals nor victims were consciously aware of these cues. They are what psychologists call "precipitators," personal attributes that increase a person's likelihood of being criminally victimized.

The researchers analyzed the body language of the people on the tape, and identified several aspects of demeanor that marked potential victims as good targets. One of the main precipitators is a walking style that lacks "interactional synchrony" and "wholeness." Perpetrators notice a person whose walk lacks organized movement and flowing motion. Criminals view such people as less self-confident - perhaps because their walk suggests they are less athletic and fit - and are much more likely to exploit them. Just like predators in the wild, armed robbers often attack the slowest in the herd. People who drag their feet, shuffle along, or exhibit other unusual gaits are targeted more often than people who walk fast and fluidly. That criminals are attuned to cues of vulnerability makes sense given that most criminals, especially murderers, are looking for people who will be easy to control. Even rape is motivated less by sex and more by the desire for control and power.

Sexual predators in particular look for people they can easily overpower. "The rapist is going to go after somebody who's not paying attention, who looks like they're not going to put up a fight, who's in a location that's going to make this more convenient," says Tod Burke, a criminologist at Radford University in Virginia.

"If I had the slightest inkling that a woman wasn't someone I could easily handle, then I would pass right on by. Or if I thought I couldn't control the situation, then I wouldn't even mess with the house, much less attempt a rape there," says Brad Morrison, a convicted sex offender who raped 75 women in 11 states and is quoted in *Predators: Who They Are and How to Stop Them*, by Gregory M. Cooper, Michael R. King, and Thomas McHoes. "Like, if they had a dog, then forget it. Even a small one makes too much noise. If I saw a pair of construction boots, for example, out on the porch or on the landing, I walked right on by. In fact, I think if women who live alone would put a pair of old construction boots—or something that makes it look like a physically fit manly-type of guy lives with them—out in front of their door, most rapists or even burglars wouldn't even think about trying to get into their home."

Distraction is another cue criminals look for. Some people think talking on a cell phone enhances their safety because the other person can always summon help if there's trouble, but experts disagree. Talking on a phone or listening to an iPod is a distraction, and armed robbers are casting about for distracted victims. "Not paying attention, looking like a tourist - having the map out, looking confused - absolutely makes people more vulnerable," Burke says.

Being aware of your surroundings, however, may not help much if you don't know what to pay attention to. James Giannini of Ohio State University discovered something shocking: Women who are the victims of rape tend to be less able than average to interpret nonverbal facial cues - which may render them oblivious to the warning signs of hostile intent and more likely to enter or stay in dangerous situations. The same team also found that rapists tend to be more able than average to interpret facial cues, such as a downward gaze or a fearful expression. It's possible this skill makes rapists especially able to spot passive, submissive women. One study even showed that rapists are more empathetic toward women than other criminals—although they have a distinct empathy gap when it comes to their own victims. A highly attuned rapist and a woman who's oblivious to hostile body language make a dangerous combination.

Even personality plays a role. Conventional wisdom holds that women who dress provocatively draw attention and put themselves at risk of sexual assault. But studies show that it is women with passive, submissive personalities who are most likely to be raped, and that they tend to wear body-concealing clothing, such as high necklines, long pants and sleeves, and multiple layers. Predatory men can accurately identify submissive women just by their style of dress and other aspects of appearance. The hallmarks of submissive body language, such as downward gaze and slumped posture, may even be misinterpreted by rapists as flirtation.

Drinking and drug use, not surprisingly, also mark a person as a potential victim. "It's a robber's dream to knock a drunk down and take what they've got," says former Ohio detective Stacy Dittrich. That goes double for sexual assault. Drunken people not only appear more vulnerable, they're also especially likely to place themselves in dangerous situations. Alcohol decreases people's ability to evaluate the consequences of their actions and distorts their ability to predict how others perceive them. And women who are intoxicated, studies show, tend to be animated, giving off signals sexual offenders may misinterpret as sexual interest.

Many armed robbers have a chip on their shoulders and view life as inherently unfair, says criminologist Richard Wright, a professor at the University of Missouri at St. Louis and co-author of *Armed Robbers in Action: Stickups and Street Culture*. As a result, they often see someone else's success as a reminder of their own failure and inferiority. Worse still, they interpret outward signs of another's prosperity as a personal affront. "When they see people flaunting their wealth or driving fancy cars, they see this as an attempt to put them down."

Grayson, co-author of the classic study on body language and exploitability, believes people can be taught how to walk in a confident way that reduces their risk of assault. To reduce the chances of becoming a victim, you can't look like a victim. "Walk in an alert fashion, walk with purpose, with your shoulders held back," advises Topalli.

Even better, avoid placing yourself in dangerous situations and stay aware of your surroundings at all times. Location is a key factor in street crime, particularly in cases of sexual assault. Criminals prefer sites that are likely to serve up few witnesses and little chance of being caught. Plan routes that avoid such locations.

And while you're at it, don't even talk to strangers on the street in isolated locations. One warning sign that you may be about to be robbed or attacked is the approach of a stranger on the street. The person may try to engage you in conversation. He may ask for the time, directions, bus fare, or try to tell you about a nice club or restaurant just around the corner.

Calvin Donaldson, who's been in prison in Louisiana for the last 28 years after robbing a couple in the French Quarter who asked him for directions, offers some advice: "Once you stop and let this guy engage you in conversation, you're opening yourself up," he says. "Some people you don't talk to. You just keep going."

How do you survive unharmed if you find yourself targeted? Cooperate. "They're not going to hurt you unless they need to," says New Orleans Police Department psychologist James Arey. Convicted armed robber Darryl Falls, who admits to committing more than 100 robberies, agrees. "The quicker you comply and give them your goods," he says, "the quicker they're out of your face." Some of Falls' victims tried to conceal jewelry to which they had an emotional attachment—wedding rings, for example. "I understand the sentimental value," he says. "But you can get that back. You can't get your life back."

DISCUSSION

1. What is the thesis of the essay?
2. What logical evidence is provided to support the thesis? How convincing is the evidence?
3. What other types of evidence - empirical and factual - are presented, and how effectively are they used?
4. What recommendations were provided to decrease one's chances of being a victim, and how logical do they sound?
5. What, if anything, did you learn that you didn't already know about why predators prey on certain victims? How might that alter your own behavior?

The Pursuit of Happiness
by Carlin Flora

Welcome to the happiness frenzy, now peaking at a Barnes & Noble near you. In 2008 4,000 books were published on happiness, while a mere 50 books on the topic were released in 2000. The most popular class at Harvard University is about positive psychology, and at least 100 other universities offer similar courses. Happiness workshops for the post-collegiate set abound, and each day "life coaches" promising bliss to potential clients hang out their shingles.

In the late 1990s, psychologist Martin Seligman of the University of Pennsylvania exhorted colleagues to scrutinize optimal moods with the same intensity with which they had for so long studied pathologies. A new generation of psychologists built up a respectable body of research on positive character traits and happiness-boosting practices. At the same time, developments in neuroscience provided new clues to what makes us happy and what that looks like in the brain. Not to be outdone, behavioral economists piled on research subverting the classical premise that people always make rational choices that increase their well-being. We're lousy at predicting what makes us happy, they found.

It wasn't enough that an array of academic strands came together, sparking a slew of insights into the sunny side of life. Self-appointed experts jumped on the happiness bandwagon. A shallow sea of smiley faces, self-help gurus, and purveyors of kitchen-table wisdom have strip-mined the science, extracted a lot of fool's gold, and stormed the marketplace with guarantees to annihilate your worry, stress, anguish, dejection, and even ennui once and for all!

But all is not necessarily well. According to some measures, as a nation we've grown sadder and more anxious during the same years that the happiness movement has flourished; perhaps that's why we've eagerly bought up its offerings. It may be that college students sign up for positive psychology lessons in droves because a full 15 percent of them report being clinically depressed.

There are those who see in the happiness brigade a glib and even dispiriting Pollyanna gloss. So it's not surprising that the happiness movement has unleashed a counterforce, led by a troika of academics. Jerome Wakefield of New York University and Allan Horwitz of Rutgers have penned *The Loss of Sadness: How Psychiatry Transformed Normal Sorrow into Depressive Disorder*," and Wake Forest University's Eric Wilson has written a defense of melancholy in *Against Happiness*. They observe that our preoccupation with happiness has come at the cost of sadness, an important feeling that we've tried to banish from our emotional repertoire.

Horwitz laments that young people who are naturally weepy after breakups are often urged to medicate themselves instead of working through their sadness. Wilson fumes that our obsession with happiness amounts to a "craven disregard" for the melancholic perspective that has given rise to our greatest works of art. "The happy man," he writes, "is a hollow man."

Both the happiness and anti-happiness forces actually agree on something important - that we Americans tend to grab superficial quick fixes such as extravagant purchases and fatty foods to subdue any negative feelings that overcome us. Such measures seem to hinge on a belief that constant happiness is somehow our birthright. Indeed, a body of research shows instant indulgences do calm us down - for a few moments. But they leave us poorer, physically unhealthy, and generally more miserable in the long run, and lacking in the real skills to get us out of our rut.

Happiness is not about smiling all of the time. It's not about eliminating bad moods, or trading your Tolstoy-inspired ambivalence toward people and situations for cheery pronouncements devoid of critical judgment. While the veritable experts lie in different camps and sometimes challenge one another, over the past decade they've together assembled big chunks of the happiness puzzle.

What is happiness? The most useful definition - and one agreed upon by neuroscientists, psychiatrists, behavioral economists, positive psychologists, and Buddhist monks - is being satisfied or content rather than "happy" in its strict bursting-with-glee sense. It has depth and deliberation to it. It encompasses living a meaningful life, utilizing your gifts and your time, living with thought and purpose.

Some lucky souls really are born with brighter outlooks than others; they simply see beauty and opportunity where others hone in on flaws and dangers. But those with a more ominous orientation can alter their outlook, at least to a point. They can learn to internally challenge their fearful thoughts and negative assumptions - "she thinks I'm an idiot," "I'm going to get fired," "I'll never be a good mom" - if not eliminate them altogether. Engaging in positive internal dialogue is actually a mark of the mentally healthy.

You think happiness would arrive if you were to win the lottery, or would forever fade away if your home were destroyed in a flood. But human beings are remarkably adaptable. After a variable period of adjustment, we bounce back to our previous level of happiness, no matter what happens to us. There are, however, some scientifically proven exceptions, notably suffering the unexpected loss of a job or the loss of a spouse. Both events tend to permanently knock people down a notch.

Our adaptability works in two directions. Because we are so adaptable, points out Sonja Lyubomirsky, a professor of psychology at the University of California, Riverside, we quickly get used to many of the accomplishments we strive for in life, such as landing the big job or getting married. Soon after we reach a milestone, we start to feel that something is missing. We begin coveting another worldly possession or eyeing a social advancement. But such an approach keeps us tethered to the "hedonic treadmill," where happiness is always just out of reach, one toy or one notch away. It's possible to get off the treadmill entirely, Lyubomirsky says, by focusing on activities that are dynamic, surprising, and attention-absorbing, and thus less likely to bore us than, say, acquiring shiny stuff.

Happiness is not your reward for escaping pain. It demands that you confront negative feelings head-on, without letting them overwhelm you. Russ Harris, a medical doctor-cum-counselor and author of *The Happiness Trap*, calls popular conceptions of happiness dangerous because they set people up for a "struggle against reality." They don't acknowledge that real life is full of disappointments, loss, and inconveniences. If you're going to live a rich and meaningful life," Harris says, "you're going to feel a full range of emotions." The point isn't to limit that palette of feelings. After all, negative states cue us into what we value and what we need to change. Grief for a loved one proves how much we cherish our relationships. Frustration with several jobs in a row is a sign we're in the wrong career. Happiness would be meaningless if not for sadness. Without the contrast of darkness, there is no light.

Action toward goals other than happiness can make us happy. Though there is a place for vegging out and reading trashy novels, easy pleasures will never light us up the way mastering a new skill or building something from scratch will. And it's not crossing the finish line that is most rewarding; it's anticipating achieving your goal. University of Wisconsin neuroscientist Richard Davidson has found that working hard toward a goal, and making progress to the point of expecting a goal to be realized, doesn't just activate positive feelings. It also suppresses negative emotions such as fear and depression.

Yes, money does buy happiness, but only up to the point where it enables you to live comfortably. Beyond that, more cash doesn't boost your well-being. But generosity brings true joy, so striking it rich could in fact underwrite your happiness - if you were to give your wealth away.

Positive psychologist Chris Peterson, a professor at the University of Michigan, says the best piece of advice to come out of his field is to make strong personal relationships your priority. Good relationships are buffers against the damaging effects of all of life's inevitable letdowns and setbacks.

You can also increase positive feelings by incorporating a few proven practices into your routine. Lyubomirsky suggests you express your gratitude toward someone in a letter or in a weekly journal, visualize the best possible future for yourself once a week, and perform acts of kindness for others on a regular basis to lift your mood in the moment and over time. "Becoming happier takes work, but it may be the most rewarding and fun work you'll ever do," she says.

Harvard psychologist Daniel Gilbert discovered a deep truth about happiness: Things are almost never as bad - or as good - as we expect them to be. Your promotion will be quite nice, but it won't be a 24-hour parade. Your breakup will be very hard, but also instructive, and maybe even energizing. We are terrible at predicting our future feelings accurately, especially if our predictions are based on our past experiences. The past exists in our memory after all, and memory is not a reliable recording device. We recall beginnings and endings far more intensely than those long "middles," whether they're eventful or not. So the horrible beginning of your vacation will lead you astray in deciding the best place to go next year. Gilbert's take-away advice is to forgo your own mental projections. The best predictor of whether you'll enjoy something is whether someone else enjoyed it. So simply ask your friend who went to Mexico if you, too, should go there on vacation.

Not everyone can put on a happy face. Barbara Held, a professor of psychology at Bowdoin College, for one, rails against "the tyranny of the positive attitude." "Looking on the bright side isn't possible for some people and is even counterproductive," she insists. "When you put pressure on people to cope in a way that doesn't fit them, it not only doesn't work, it makes them feel like a failure on top of already feeling bad."

The one-size-fits-all approach to managing emotional life is misguided, agrees Julie Norem, author of *The Positive Power of Negative Thinking.* In her research, the Wellesley professor of psychology has shown that the defensive pessimism that anxious people feel can be harnessed to help them get things done, which in turn makes them happier. A naturally pessimistic architect, for example, can set low expectations for an upcoming presentation and review all of the bad outcomes that she's imagining, so that she can prepare carefully and increase her chances of success.

Finally, if you aren't living according to your values, you won't be happy, no matter how much you are achieving. Some people, however, aren't even sure what their values are. If you're one of them, Harris has a great question for you: "Imagine I could wave a magic wand to ensure that you would have the approval and admiration of everyone on the planet, forever. What, in that case, would you choose to do with your life?" Once you've answered honestly, you can start taking steps toward your ideal vision of yourself. You can tape positive affirmations to your mirror, or you can cut up your advice books and turn them into a papier-mâché project. It doesn't matter, as long as you're living consciously.

The state of happiness is not really a state at all. It's an ongoing personal experiment.

DISCUSSION

1. What is the (implied) thesis of the essay?
2. What logical evidence is provided in support of the thesis, and how convincing is it?
3. What other types of evidence - empirical and factual - are provided, and how effectively are they presented?
4. What common assumptions regarding happiness are disputed in the essay? Do you agree, and why?
5. What, if anything, did you learn about "happiness" from the essay? How might this knowledge influence how you live?

Writing a critique of an essay allows you to put into writing the kinds of evaluative analysis of the text readings you may have been doing during class discussions. You may have been discussing the impact of each essay, the strength of the support provided for the thesis, differing viewpoints relating to the topic, what you have learned from the essay, and what significance, if any, it may have.

In a more organized fashion, the same type of evaluative analysis forms the core of your critique of an essay. Readers are interested in what the essay was about, what you thought of it, and what you based those opinions on: the three primary functions of a critique.

Writing the Critique

As mentioned previously, writing an effective critique begins with a careful reading of the essay or article you are writing about. There are several things you want to take from the reading, which may require a rereading or two: a clear understanding of the topic, its thesis, the reasons in support of the thesis, and the evidence on which each reason is based. You want to subject the essay to the same scrutiny that you give your own essays and require, as you do of yourself, that the writer makes his case.

Beyond that, you want to try and understand the purpose behind the essay, to what extent that purpose was achieved from your perspective as a reader, and whether the essay was significant enough to matter to readers. Of course, as with any critique writer, you bring to your reading of an essay your own experiences and opinions, which may make you more or less sympathetic to the writer's viewpoint. As you read an essay, it is important to evaluate it as objectively as possible, allow it to stand on its merits or fall on its deficiencies, and leave those pre-conceived notions at the doorstep.

Activity 3.16

Write a critique of an essay from the text or with your instructor's approval, an outside essay or article. You may want to review the sections at the end of Unit One on "Critical Reading" and "Writing a Critique" and reread the critiques on pages 46 and 56 before writing your critique.

Unit Four
Comparative Evidence

O ne of the most effective ways that writers support their viewpoints and influence readers is through the use of comparisons. A relevant comparison can be used to support an alleged fact, to show the fairness or validity of a writer's position, or to help readers understand an issue better. Writers also use comparisons that relate to readers' personal experiences to engage their interest and influence their response.

In many cases, a writer draws on similar comparisons to provide evidence that supports his thesis. For example, in a previous sample essay, a writer opposed to an activity fee increase at her college revealed through comparisons with other colleges that her college's activity fee was already high. In another essay, a writer who opposed funding cuts for pre-school education compared the success in elementary school of children who had attended pre-school to children who hadn't, showing that children with pre-school education performed better. The type of comparison made in each essay - activity fee-to-activity fee, children's performance-to-children's performance - is similar, an "apples to apples" comparison that is easy for readers to follow and understand.

In other situations, a writer may use a dissimilar comparison, or *analogy*: a comparison of unlike things in a way that helps a writer explain or clarify a particular point. For example, in the sample draft where the writer opposed the activity fee increase, she compared the increase to the famed "taxation without representation" imposed upon the American colonies by England that ultimately lead to the Revolutionary War. While a college fee increase and England's taxation of her colonies have little in common, the one similarity - the lack of input by the students and by the colonists - reveals the writer's intent:

to show the unfairness of the increase and move readers to action.

Using an analogy, a writer can also compare and connect two things in a figurative rather than literal manner. For example, one writer compared prejudice to a cancer that spreads from generation to generation, making the point that prejudice has poisonous, traceable roots. A writer who helped to rebuild a dirt embankment after the Tuala River's annual spring flooding compared the effort to that of Sisyphus, a king in Greek mythology who continually rolled a huge stone up a hill only to have it roll down again, emphasizing the futile quest of rebuilding the embankment every year. The purpose of such comparisons is to lend a perspective to a topic that may strike a chord with readers and engage their interest.

Similar Comparisons

Using similar comparisons is one of the most effective ways that writers make their case. A simple comparison can be quite effective in showing the fairness, correctness, or good sense of a writer's position on an issue. For example, if a writer can show that the changes he is proposing to improve the registration process at the college have already proven effective at other colleges, he may have provided the best evidence to convince the college administration. If another writer can show that a new and promising cancer drug under FDA consideration is already legal and effective in other countries, she may convince readers to support its legalization in the U.S.

Comparative evidence can be used more effectively for some topics than others, and just because a writer uses a comparison doesn't mean that it will make an impression on readers. To use similar comparisons most effectively in your writing, consider the following suggestions.

1. **For any topic you are writing on, consider what comparisons you might use to support your position on the topic.** For example, for any issue related to your college, you might find out what other colleges are doing. For city, county, state, or national issues, you might investigate what similar cities, counties, states, or countries are doing. For a particular issue, ask yourself questions like, "Are there places where what I am proposing is already occurring? "Do situations similar to the one I am writing about exist?" "What results have occurred in places where my viewpoint (e.g. decriminalizing marijuana, increasing the legal driving age, legalizing high school locker searches) has been implemented?"

2. **Try to find the most similar group or situation to compare with to have the greatest impact on readers.** For example, in comparing the drop out rate of students in California's community colleges, a writer found great differences among schools. However, in looking at the location of the colleges, schools in middle-class, suburban areas had substantially lower drop-out rates than schools in poorer urban areas. However, the drop-out rate in some urban schools was relatively low. The writer decided, then, to compare "apples to apples" - urban area schools with higher drop-out rates to urban area schools with lower drop-out rates - to see what the high drop-out schools could learn from their lower drop-out counterparts.

3. **In using comparative evidence, sometimes a criteria needs establishing for the comparison: a standard or set of standards by which to judge the things being compared.** For example, if a writer contends that children with pre-school education perform better in elementary school than children who do not attend pre-school, what is the criteria for judging performance: standardized test scores? quarterly grades? advancement from grade-to-grade? If a writer states that the college's student health services are inferior to similar colleges, what is the criteria for evaluating health services: student-to-physician ratio? quality of health facilities? survey of student satisfaction? types of treatments available? In many cases when a comparison involves a judgment - one thing is better, worse, more effective, more viable, or of better value than another -, a writer needs to establish a criteria by which readers can evaluate that judgment.

4. **In the end, use comparisons that will have the greatest impact on readers**. Use comparisons that readers can understand and relate to, that seem the most reasonable, and that most strongly support your position. For example, a writer who supports the unionization of teaching assistants (TAs) at a college wants to convince the TAs that they will be better off with union representation. For comparison, she uses comparable colleges where TAs are unionized and are better paid. To help TAs understand the comparison best, she converts all salary information to hourly rates, which TAs clearly understand. She has made an "apples to apples" comparison of comparable colleges, used terms in making the comparison that TAs would understand and relate to, and

used a most significant criterion for comparison: salaries.

Activity 4.1

To support each of the following thesis statements, decide on a comparison or two that you might consider and the source(s) you might use to make your comparison.

EXAMPLE
Topic: Effect of loud music on teen hearing

Thesis: Listening to loud music over a period of time can cause hearing loss among many teenagers.

Comparison: Compare hearing of teens who listen to loud music to teens who don't.

Source: 1. Find studies that use comparisons to show the effect of loud music on teen hearing.
Source: 2. Research physicians' findings or talk to physicians regarding the relative hearing problems of teens who listen to loud music and those who don't.

1. Topic: Effects of television violence on boys
   Thesis: Viewing violence on television can lead to more aggressive, violent behavior among young boys.
   Comparison:
   Source(s):

2. Topic: Obesity in children
   Thesis Fast-food restaurants are a major contributor to obesity in children today.
   Comparison:
   Source(s):

3. Topic: Using animals for medical research
   Thesis: The use of animals for medical research is justified by the tremendous medical advances for humans that such research has produced.
   Comparison:
   Source(s):

4. Topic: Treatment of drug addicts
   Thesis: Drug addicts should be treated for their disease rather than incarcerated as criminals.
   Comparison:
   Source(s):

5. Topic: Performance of community college transfer students at four-year colleges
   Thesis: Community college transfer students have a high success rate at four-year colleges.
   Comparison:
   Source(s):

6. Topic: Cost of college textbooks
   Thesis: The cost of textbooks at the Walden College bookstore is excessively high.
   Comparison:
   Source(s):

Activity 4.2

For each of the following comparisons, decide on a criteria by which to compare subjects.

EXAMPLE

Topic: Living in college dormitories

Thesis: Living in a college dormitory is the least expensive way to attend school.

Comparison: Compare direct and indirect dormitory expenses to apartment or house rental expenses.

Criteria: cost of room, cost of food, cost of transportation (gas), cost of entertainment

1. Topic: Choosing a college major
   Thesis: Choosing a major early in one's college career can be a big mistake.
   Comparison: Compare after-college success of students who select a major early to students who wait until later.
   Criteria for "after-college success:"

2. Topic: Federal welfare-to-work program
   Thesis: The Federal welfare-to-work program is im-

proving the lives of millions of former welfare recipients and their children.
Comparison: Compare the lives of people while they were still on welfare to their current lives while being employed.
Criteria for "improved life:"

3. Topic: America's "war on drugs"
    Thesis: America's national "war on drugs" is a failure.
    Comparison: Compare drug situation today to when America's "war on drugs" began in 1988.
    Criteria for "failure" of program:

4. Topic: Marriage in America
    Thesis: In general, couples who marry later in life have the most successful marriages.
    Comparison: Compare the "success" of marriage for people married at different ages: teens, twenties, thirties.
    Criteria for "successful marriages:"

Activity 4.3

In the essay "A Violent Neighborhood," the writer uses comparisons to help make different points. Identify each comparison, its purpose, the criteria, if any, for the comparison, and the effectiveness of each comparison.

A Violent Neighborhood (reading audience: college board, city council)

Last month a murder occurred in the parking lot of an apartment complex one block west of the college. In a drug deal gone wrong, a female passenger in a car delivering drugs was shot to death by a college student making the purchase. In a similar incident three months ago at an adjacent apartment complex, a male college student was injured in a drug-related shooting.

Apartment complexes in the neighborhood west of the college have become a danger zone with the amount of drug trafficking occurring and the violence that it brings. Drug-related arrests in the area, according to the local police department, are higher than at any time in recent history, and college students are frequently involved. What was once a safe area for college students to live in has become a high-risk neighborhood. Such a dangerous situation should not exist around any college, and something must be done to change the environment.

Over the years, the neighborhood west of the college has grown older and seedier. Most of the apartment complexes are old and in various states of disrepair, and the lower rent that they draw has attracted a variety of occupants, according to apartment landlords: college students, non-college young adults, and recent immigrant families trying to make ends meet. College students remain in the area because of the relatively low rent and the walking distance to campus. Other students, however, are attracted to the area because of the availability of drugs.

Drug dealers have moved into the area and often reside next door to college students or families, according to student residents. The neighborhood also draws outside traffic as its reputation as a drug haven has grown, and on weekend nights, there are as many non-residents in the area as residents, as witnessed by the steady flow of traffic on a Saturday night. Gun shots ring out at night, according to apartment residents, and many of them stay away from the parking lots and don't walk the streets at night.

The more affluent neighborhoods on the east side of campus have few of the problems that the west side housing has. The higher rent attracts a more homogeneous population of student residents, and the drug activity and violence occurring on the west side aren't present, according to the local police. That is not to say that there aren't college students living on the east side who use drugs, but if they do, according to west-side student residents, they go "slumming" to the west side to make their purchases.

It is clear that the neighborhood west of the college needs cleaning up so that it is a safe place for anyone to live. The police department's drug and alcohol division estimates that just five-to-ten percent of residents are actually involved in using or trafficking drugs, but along with the outside drug traffic, that is more than enough to create a dangerous situation. Lower-income housing should not produce a violent environment and is not acceptable anywhere around a college campus.

Du Mont is not the first college to have a problem with its surrounding environment. The neighborhoods around colleges change over the years, sometimes improving and other times becoming more run-down. One thing appears clear, however: neighborhood conditions don't improve without a concerted city effort. These efforts have been made in college neighborhoods in other communities with encouraging results.

In every instance, the first step, according to city officials from other college towns, is that the cities and colleges acknowledge that there was a problem that needed fixing. The second step is for the cities to do what they could: compel apartment owners to renovate and comply with building and safety codes, work with owners to remove known drug traffickers from area apartments, increase the police presence in the neighborhood, and run weekend check-points on vehicles to discourage outside traffic. In addition, the colleges must do their part by expelling student drug offenders, providing matching funding with the cities to help clean up the areas, and making safe student housing a priority.

Some people argue that just because a particular neighborhood borders a college, it shouldn't get special attention. However, the city regularly gives special attention to other parts of the city where violence is commonplace. The only difference is that the college neighborhood has yet to be targeted by the city as a problem area. Others say that college students who live on the west side help create the problem and get what they deserve. However, based on the police's drug and alcohol division estimate, ninety to ninety-five percent of the students living in the area aren't involved in drugs or trafficking. They have just as much right to a safe living environment as any students.

At this point, neither Du Mont nor the city has made the commitment that other colleges and cities have made to make dangerous college neighborhoods safer. The blue print for success is available, but the commitment involves time, funding, and resources. If the college and city do nothing, it is only a matter of time before someone else is killed in a west-side shooting or before the college's west-side housing problem spreads to surround the campus.

Writers often draw upon their creativity to help make their case to readers. They ask themselves, "What can I do to help readers see or understand something more clearly?" The answer often lies in using an analogy: comparing dissimilar things in a way that makes a point. For example, in the famous Biblical analogy, "It is more difficult for a rich man to get into heaven than for a camel to fit through the eye of a needle," comparing the very dissimilar situations provides a clear point. Since it is impossible for a camel to fit through a needle's eye, a rich man stands little chance of getting into heaven.

The use of analogies in writing and conversation is more common than most people may realize. To make a point, people frequently draw on some analogy. For example, anti-tax politicians frequently make the analogy between a family's budget and a state's budget although the two have little in common. One version of the analogy goes like this, "If the state has a revenue shortfall, it wants to raise taxes rather than reduce its budget. However, if you and I have a salary shortfall, we reduce our budget to live within our means. Why shouldn't the state have to do the same?"

To use analogies most effectively in your writing, consider the following suggestions.

1. **Writers often use analogies to help readers understand something better**. To help readers understand his relativity theory, Einstein often used analogies comparing the movement of a train to the speed of light. Economists often use analogies to explain theories. Economists who were not fond of the "trickle-down" economic theory of the Reagan era compared it to rain water seeping into the ground: the farther down in the ground (or down the economic ladder) the water trickles, the less water (or money) there is.

2. **Figurative analogies, which use words metaphorically rather than literally, often have creative appeal to readers and remain in their minds.** The previously mentioned Biblical analogy of "a camel fitting through the eye of a needle" is so unusual and striking to today's readers that it is easily remembered. A writer who compared the difficulty of predicting trends in a volatile stock market to "catching moonbeams in a mason jar" showed the absurdity of such predictions in a way readers may remember.

    The power of a figurative analogy lies in its originality. Analogies that have become clichéd through overuse - "like a lead balloon," "like kissing your sister," "like a drunken sailor," "like talking to a brick wall," "like shooting fish in a barrel," "like finding a needle in a haystack" - possess little of the power of a striking, original comparison.

3. **Writers sometimes use extended analogies to make their points.** An extended analogy may run a few sentences and include an explanation of why or how one thing is like another. The following are examples of extended analogies.

A cultivated mind is like a cultivated garden. If planted thoughtfully, tended with care, and watered regularly, a garden will grow and flourish. If planted haphazardly, tended poorly, and watered irregularly, it will be undernourished, stunted in growth, and overrun by weeds.

State legislators are like lemmings. Once they choose an ideological path towards destruction, they don't turn back. They move inexorably closer to the ocean cliff, climbing over one another to get there first. Mindlessly, they jump into the water and swim until they drown. Learning nothing from experience, they do the same thing year after year with the same predictable results.

Writers use extended analogies to provide a sharper focus for a particular point or to help readers grasp its significance.

4. **Like any comparisons, analogies are most effective when they are appropriate to the situation and clearly understood.** For example, a writer comparing the Israeli-Palestinian conflict to a "spinning isosceles triangle" may be the only one who knows what he is getting at, and comparing the difficulty of deciding on a college major to "climbing Mt. Everest in flip flops" would seem incongruous to most readers. Creating effective analogies is not easy, and most writers use them rather sparingly. However, good analogies have the power both to entertain and influence readers, and when you are explaining your topic, supporting your thesis, responding to differing viewpoints, or showing the possible effects of an action, consider whether a well-placed analogy may help you make your case.

Activity 4.4

Come up with analogies to complete as many of the following comparisons as you can. Create analogies that are both appropriate to the situation and original in wording. Try using both literal and figurative analogies.

Trying to argue with the president of the student council
(an analogy showing the difficulty and frustration)

Trying to argue with the president of the student council
is like arguing with a mannequin.

The recent debate between mayoral candidates (analogy
showing how boring it was)

The recent debate between mayoral candidates was as
exciting as watching grapes grow.

1. Student interest over the upcoming student body elections (analogy showing students' lack of interest)
2. Stopping the flow of drugs into the United States from
   South America (analogy showing extreme difficulty)
3. Progress on the downtown renovation project (analogy
   showing slowness of progress)
4. Getting residents to comply with the new parking
   restrictions on Van Nuys Boulevard (analogy showing
   how willingly residents complied)
5. Getting neighborhood residents to come forward and
   testify against gang members (analogy showing extreme difficulty)
6. Finding a parking space on campus at 1:00 p.m. (analogy showing extreme ease)

Activity 4.5

Try your hand at writing an extended analogy running a few sentences.
Make the comparison in the first sentence and then elaborate on it in
subsequent sentences.

EXAMPLE

A teacher coming out of a poor teacher education program
is like a poorly constructed house. Initially it may look
good, but soon cracks start to appear in the walls and the
plumbing leaks. These problems are often the symptoms
of a weak foundation that ultimately affects everything
built upon it. In the end the house either needs extensive
repair to be brought up to code or is condemned and
eventually torn down.

Activity 4.6

Read the following short essay, find three or four places within the essay where an analogy might fit well, and write an analogy for each place which might strengthen the essay. You can add new sentences or add onto or change existing sentences to create the analogies.

Apartment Complex Swimming Pool

On occasion I like going to our apartment swimming pool to cool off. However, I find it hard to relax there because of the behavior of some of the kids. They completely ignore the written rules. In addition, some of them are very rude when their behavior is called to their attention. Rather than enjoying a relaxing couple hours at the pool, I often leave the area tense and irritated. The pool is not monitored during the day by any apartment staff, and that is the main issue.

Little kids love to run, and that is a problem at the pool. The large sign on the fence with the pool rules clearly states, "no running," but that doesn't seem to stop anyone. Kids run all over the place, and their parents don't seem to care. I've seen kids fall hard on the cement, but that's the only time they get their parents' attention. I'm not there to enforce the rules, but I end up telling kids to stop running, and they stop, at least for a few minutes. Some day a kid is going to have a serious accident because running kids and wet, slick cement are a bad combination.

It is the young teenage kids, however, that really get to me. Some of them are well behaved and cause no problems. There are a few, however, that make me angry. They ignore most of the rules like "no running," "no diving," and "no food or drinks." They do running dives and flips into the water and run all over the place playing tag. They act like they own the pool and expect the younger kids to stay out of their way. Some of them also use filthy language. The problem is that they come without parents and are totally unsupervised. They just do what they want.

I finally confronted their "leader" one day, who was throwing deck chairs into the deep end and diving over them. I told him to stop doing it and put the chairs back and he said, "You're not my boss," and continued what he was doing. That really got me mad. I went to the deep end and pulled the chairs out of the water. He threw them back in as his buddies watched. I jumped out, grabbed him by the arm, and dragged him to his bike by the gate. "Get out of here right now," I said, "or I'll call security." Screaming, cursing, and humiliated, he drove off on his bike shouting, "I'll get you, you bastard." By that time I was shaking with anger, and my afternoon was ruined.

At an apartment residents' meeting last week, I explained the terrible situation at the pool, and fortunately, several other residents backed me up and voiced similar complaints. I put my suggestions in writing: a life-guard on duty from 2:00-6:00 p.m. daily, a notice to all parents that they are responsible for policing their kids, and a "suspension" policy for kids who continually violate rules or behave rudely. I along with the other residents got the attention of the landlord and he said he'd pass everything along to the owners. He took particular notice when we mentioned the potential liability if a serious accident occurred at an unsupervised pool.

By the end of the meeting I had the feeling that we were going to get some results. After all, this is not a really difficult situation to handle. The problem is that no one had brought it to the owners' attention. Now they are very aware of it, and we'll see what happens. Interestingly, since the meeting, I've already seen a change in how some parents monitor their children's behavior, and the teenage boy who gave me trouble hasn't come back. The situation is already improving.

Prewriting

For your upcoming essay, you now have various types of development to draw upon, including empirical, factual, logical, and comparative evidence, responding to opposing viewpoints, and providing background and explanatory information. Which methods you employ and how extensively you use them will depend on your topic, thesis, purpose, and reading audience. Such decisions will be considered during this prewriting phase.

Since the focus for this unit is on comparative evidence, you will incorporate some comparisons in your essay to further your writing purpose. One consideration, then, in evaluating potential writing topics is deciding which topics can be developed effectively through comparative evidence. As you have seen in the writing samples from previous units, using comparisons is often an invaluable part of essay development, and you will no doubt find several topics for which you can use comparisons effectively.

Topic Selection

To select a topic for your upcoming essay, consider the following suggestions.

1. Select a topic that interests you from any field - education, politics, technology, business, social issues, college-related issues, children's issues, health issues, ethics issues - and at any level - local, state, national, or international.
2. Select a topic that people have different viewpoints on, that is serious enough to engage readers' interest, and that is specific enough to be developed in an essay-length writing.
3. Select a topic that is different from the topics you have selected for previous essay assignments.
4. Select a topic that can be developed in part from comparative evidence.

Activity 4.7

Considering the four suggestions for topic selection, select a potential topic for your upcoming essay. Take your time deciding on a topic, and keep two or three potential topics in mind to see which can best be supported by comparative evidence.

EXAMPLE

Potential topic: Downloading music on the Internet

As you know, your thesis for the upcoming essay presents your viewpoint on the topic that you develop and support. To decide on a thesis, consider the following suggestions.

1. **Generate a thesis that reflects your opinion on the topic: what you believe to be the fairest, most correct, or most defensible position on the issue.** You may already have a definite opinion, or you may need to learn more about your topic before drawing any conclusion.

2. **Generate a thesis that you believe is supportable through various types of evidence: factual, empirical, logical and comparative.** If the evidence ultimately does not validate your thesis, you may want to change your thesis or your topic.

3. **Since the focus for this unit is on comparative evidence, generate a thesis that can be supported by comparisons.** For example, let's say a writer is writing about a free speech controversy at your college. The college forum committee is bringing in a nationally known speaker on the topic of intelligent design as an opposing theory to evolution. Some students believe he shouldn't be given a platform, citing intelligent design as a "pseudo" theory rejected by the international scientific community. Others believe that in the name of free speech, he should be allowed to speak.

   After serious consideration, the writer generates the thesis, "Freedom of speech does not require a college to provide a forum for any speaker who would spread misinformation, quack theories, or racist ideas." For possible comparative evidence, the writer might compare the speakers' forum policy at different colleges, and the types of topics typically presented at your college's forum to the topic in question. In addition, she might consider using an analogy to show the wrongness of giving a platform to some speakers and topics (e.g. Allowing a speech on UFO landings and aliens living among us is like . . .).

Activity 4.8

Generate a potential thesis statement for your upcoming essay. You may want to do some reading or conduct interviews on your topic before making a decision.

EXAMPLE

Topic: Downloading music from the Internet
Thesis: Downloading music from the Internet is illegal, unethical, and hurts the music industry.

Support

How well a writer supports her thesis usually determines its impact on readers. If a writer shows a clear understanding of the issue, presents some good reasons to support her position, provides compelling evidence to validate each reason, and acknowledges and responds convincingly to differing viewpoints, she has given herself the best chance to have an impact on her audience. However, if a writer's knowledge of the topic is sketchy, her supportive reasons time-worn or weak, her evidence inconclusive, her sources questionable, or her response to opposing viewpoints unconvincing, she may lose her audience despite the soundness of her thesis.

To provide the best support for your thesis, consider the following suggestions.

1. **Based on what you know or what you discover through your research, generate some good reasons to support your thesis.** Come up with as many reasons as possible, and later you can evaluate their relative strength and the evidence to support them.

2. **Consider the type(s) of evidence you might provide to support each reason.** Can you use personal experience or observations for support? Is there factual evidence available? Are there logical arguments to make? What sources might you use to find some of your evidence?

3. **Given your topic and thesis, what comparative evidence might you use to influence readers?** Consider both similar comparisons and analogies and how you might use them to help make your case.

4. **Consider opposing viewpoints to your thesis and the main arguments that underscore them.** How might you respond to each argument in a way that could disarm its supporters?

Activity 4.9

For your upcoming essay, generate some reasons in support of your thesis, the types of evidence (including comparisons) you might use to validate each reason, possible sources for your evidence, and some opposing arguments and possible responses to them.

In addition, do the necessary research to get a good grasp of your subject and find supportive evidence.

EXAMPLE

Topic: Downloading music from the Internet
Thesis: Downloading music from the Internet is illegal, unethical, and hurts the music industry.

Potential reasons:
1. Downloading music from the Internet is stealing.
2. It hurts the recording artists whose music is being stolen.
3. The widespread practice doesn't make it right.
4. It is an affront to true music lovers.
5. It is another ethical breakdown in society.

Types of evidence (for reasons 1-5):
1. Cite illegality and legal sources that verify it.
2. Show impact on sale of CD's over past years.
3. Use comparisons to show that historically, different widespread practices were very wrong.
4. Provide testimony of credible, admired people who support thesis.
5. Compare downloading music to other unethical modern behaviors to show breakdown of morality.

Other possible comparisons:
1. Compare stealing music on-line with stealing music from a record store.
2. Compare the stealing of recording artists' music to stealing in other areas.
3. Make comparison by posing question, "What would you do if no one was looking and you wouldn't get caught?" Give different possible examples, stealing off the Internet being one.
4. Think of possible analogies.

Opposing arguments and possible responses:

1. Everyone's doing it. (Response: That doesn't make it right.)
2. Legality is a gray area. (Response: That is not true. Law is very clear.)
3. It keeps recording companies from ripping off consumers. (Response: That is a groundless argument that could be used to steal from any retail company.)
4. With the Internet, the game and rules have changed. (Response: Ethical behavior is ethical behavior, and the relative anonymity of the Internet doesn't change the rules, it just tests people's ethics.)

Audience and Purpose

The topic and thesis for your upcoming essay help determine the best reading audience and your purpose in writing to them. In deciding on a reading audience and purpose, consider these questions.

Audience

1. Whose viewpoint would I like to change on the topic? Who could make an impact on the future course of this topic?
2. What do I need to know about this particular audience to make the greatest impact? Given the topic, what factors should be considered: their age? gender? ethnicity? viewpoint on the issue? knowledge and understanding of the issue?
3. What connections might I make with this audience for them to consider my thesis seriously? What might we agree on regarding the topic? What common values might we hold? What might I understand about their opposing viewpoint?

Purpose

1. What is my main purpose in writing to this audience? What would I most like to accomplish? Realistically, what can I expect to accomplish given the topic?
2. Given the topic and audience, how can I best accomplish my purpose? What writing tone would be most effective, what arguments may be most influential, and how can I appeal to them in ways that will move them?
3. What is the most effective way to make readers aware of my purpose? Should I let them know from the beginning, wait until the end after I have made my case, or make it clear throughout the essay without raising it directly?

Activity 4.10

For your upcoming essay, decide on the best reading audience, what you need to know and keep in mind about them, and how you might best connect with them. Next, decide on your purpose for writing to this audience and how you might best accomplish that purpose: the best arguments, the strongest appeals, the best way to present your purpose.

EXAMPLE

    Topic: Downloading music off the Internet

    Thesis: Downloading music off the Internet is illegal, unethical, and hurts the recording artists.
(Note: writer changed thesis statement from "hurts the music industry" to "hurts the recording artists" because he felt readers would be more concerned about the artists than the industry.)

    Audience: People who download music off the Internet, particularly teenagers and young adults. They like music, are computer savvy, and are mostly good people whose better side can be appealed to. Best connection with audience would be mutual love of music and understanding of the temptation to download music online. It is important for readers to understand the law regarding downloading music since many people don't know it.

    Purpose: To get readers who download music illegally to stop. Probably best to emphasize the illegality and consequences and appeal to the readers' better self. Tone should be firm and serious - this is not an issue to be taken lightly - but also respectful and not scolding since many of them may not know that what they are doing is illegal. Purpose should be clear through the thesis and how it is supported, but it should also be emphasized in the conclusion for the strongest effect.

Drafting

Your prewriting preparation is valuable in helping you plan the first draft of your essay. However, in writing the draft, you face a number of new considerations: how best to open and conclude your essay, how best to organize your ideas, what prewriting material to include or leave out, and how to convey your ideas in ways that best accomplish your purpose.

Having written several essays for the course, you are familiar with all of these drafting considerations. However, with each new essay, as the topic, thesis, audience, and purpose change, you freshly tailor each aspect of your writing to fit most effectively. Each section on "Drafting," then, includes some similar writing suggestions which you apply uniquely to the essay at hand.

Drafting Guidelines

In writing the first draft of your essay, consider the following suggestions.

1. **Opening.** The purpose of the opening to is introduce your topic, engage your readers' interest, and present your thesis statement. Give some thought to how you might open your essay most interestingly: a powerful, relevant fact, an interesting anecdote, a brief synopsis of the issue revealing its importance, a relevant scenario, or an illustration showing how people are affected by the issue. There are many effective ways to open an essay, and you might try out two or three different options before settling on the best one.

2. **Middle**. First, consider how you might organize your middle paragraphs. If you need to provide some explanatory or background information to help readers understand your issue, present that first. Then decide on the best order for presenting your reasons supporting your thesis, one that highlights your most powerful points. Finally, decide on the best place to include your response to opposing viewpoints. Usually that response comes after you have made the case for your thesis, but sometimes a writer will address one or more opposing arguments early in her middle paragraphs to let readers know she is aware of them. Provide your evidence in the middle paragraphs - factual, empirical, logical, and comparative - to validate the supportive reasons for your thesis. Put the majority of evidence into your own words (*paraphrasing*), and enclose any directly quoted material within quotation marks.

3. **Ending.** Since the ending should follow smoothly and logically from the middle paragraphs, writers often don't consider how to end an essay until they reach that point. If you have an idea how you want to end the essay - a particular comparison, a powerful supportive point, a future scenario regarding the issue - that's great. If you don't, you may want to wait until you have completed the rest of your draft before deciding how to end it.

   When you get to that point, consider what you want to do: summarize the main points, reinforce your thesis in some manner, connect or reconnect with your readers, provide something new for them to consider, make your purpose clear, emphasize the importance of the issue, or present the probable consequences if people act or don't act on the issue. In addition, writers sometimes refer in some manner to their opening to tie the essay together and bring it full circle.

4. **Comparison.** Keep in mind the emphasis for this unit: using comparative evidence. Make sure to include some relevant comparisons in your essay along with other types of evidence, and consider including an analogy or two to help make a particular point.

5. **Paragraphing**. As a general rule, develop one main idea in each paragraph and change paragraphs when you complete that idea and move to something new. In the middle paragraphs, most of those main ideas will be the reasons you present to support your thesis, and each paragraph will be developed through the evidence provided to validate each reason.

6. **Source acknowledgment**. Whenever you provide information from a source, acknowledge that source so readers know where the information came from. If a writer states, "If the Talin Valley gets over an inch of rain in a twenty-four hour period this spring, the Kaweah River will flood its banks and wash out thousands of acres of crops," many readers would ask, "According to whom?" The statement becomes more credible with the introduction, "According to the lead hydrologist for the Talin Flood Control Board . . . ." When you provide source acknowledgments, readers know that you aren't pulling ideas out of the air, and they can distinguish the source information from your own thoughts and responses.

7. **Wording.** As with any first draft, get your ideas on paper without concern for "perfect" wording. Often when writers try to write a draft and revise their sentences simultaneously,

they take two or three times as long to complete the draft. In addition, they often end up rewording sentences a second time after completing the draft. In general, the most effective and efficient way to revise sentences is after a draft is completed, not while it is being written.

8. **Audience and purpose**. As you write, keep your audience in mind and your purpose: what you hope to accomplish.

Activity 4.11

Read the following sample draft and note the following: how the writer opens her essay, including her thesis statement; her explanation of the issue at the beginning of the middle section; the reasons she provides in the middle paragraphs to support her thesis and the evidence she presents to validate each reason, including making comparisons; the source acknowledgment for each piece of evidence; the response to opposing arguments at the end of the middle paragraphs; the connection she makes with readers during the essay; the way in which she expresses her purpose; and how she concludes the essay.

Then write the first draft of your essay, keeping the eight drafting suggestions in mind.

Sample first draft

Downloading Music from the Internet (audience: music download-ers)

Would you walk into an unattended record store, browse through the selection of CD's, grab ten or fifteen of your favorites, and then walk brazenly out the door without paying? Probably not, because you know that what you are doing is wrong and clearly illegal, and that you could get into big trouble.

However, stealing from a record store is the equivalent of what hundreds of thousands of people do every day when they illegally download music from the Internet without paying for it. Downloading a CD illegally from the Internet or stealing it from a record store has the same result: depriving the recording artists and the recording companies of the revenue they should be receiving from their creations. Illegally downloading music off the Internet is wrong, it is punishable by law, and it hurts the recording artists whose music the downloaders supposedly love.

Listening to music on computers took off when the MP3 file format was developed in the early 1990's. This format enabled computer users to compress music into digital audio files. Today you can create MP3 files quickly from a CD, store them and play them back on a personal computer, transfer them to a portable MP3 player, or burn them back onto a blank CD. Downloaders, according to the computer technology encyclopedia Webopedia, can go to one of many peer-to-peer file share programs on line, select the tracks they want, and download and burn them to a CD-ROM. The problem is that what they are doing is often illegal.

The U.S. Digital Millennium Copyright Act deems the copying of copyrighted music as illegal, according to Webopedia. The U.S. code protects copyright owners from the unauthorized reproduction or distribution of sound recordings. Since the vast majority of music on the Internet is copyrighted, the free downloading of this music is against the law. Being prosecuted for the on-line infringement of a music copyright results in more than a slap on wrist. The guilty person can receive up to three years in jail and a $250,000 fine, according to the RIAA (Recording Industry Association of America), and repeat offenders may serve up to six years. Such punishment is too big a risk to take just to steal a few songs off the Internet.

Illegal music downloading is not a victimless crime. People who illegally burn CD's of their favorite music don't turn around and buy those CD's at a music store. That results in the loss of revenue for many people including recording artists, recording companies, music technicians, music stores, and recording studios. According to Webopedia, the music industry has suffered around a 20% drop in revenues in the last ten years as a direct result of illegal music downloading off the Internet. You would think that music-loving downloaders who want to support their favorite artists would not turn around and take money out of their pockets, but that is apparently the last thing they think of when burning their CD's.

One of the problems is that many people who download music either don't know they are breaking the law or want to believe that the law is "gray" in the area of online copyright infringement. They may gather this impression from some of the online sights devoted to showing people how to download music, some of which expound the idea that "no one really knows" what is or isn't illegal, so until there is clarification, there is no risk to downloading. The fact, however, is that downloading copyrighted music for free is clearly illegal, and the risk is real.

Part of the confusion may also stem from the fact that, according to a July 2008 article at the World Law Direct website, there are on-line sights where you can legally download music, such as U Tunes and Amazon, and pay for it. These sites have sales contracts with the recording industry, and people pay for the music at less expensive prices than in music stores. Downloading music from these sites is perfectly legal since people purchase the music. For those who want to download music from the Internet, these sites offer a viable and legal alternative, one which doesn't take revenue away from the recording artists and doesn't put people at risk of being prosecuted for online copyright infringement.

Some people justify the illegal downloading of music by claiming that it gets the music into the hands of more people and therefore helps the music industry. However, as noted, revenue from music sales has dropped about 20% since 1999, so that justification doesn't work. Others claim that music should be accessible to anyone, and that free music from the Internet allows people to download music who couldn't afford to buy CD's. That argument, however, makes no more sense than arguing that automobiles, bottled water, or air conditioning should be freely accessible to anyone. Free food would certainly be wonderful, if we didn't mind destroying the agriculture and grocery industries. Basically, justifications for illegal downloading boil down to rationalizations that make little sense. And the worst of all is the rationalization, "Hey, it isn't illegal if you don't get caught," an appeal to the worst instincts in any of us.

Certainly free downloading of great music off the Internet is a temptation. Who wouldn't like to have hundreds or thousands of their favorite songs on free CD's? It's so simple that anyone can learn how to do it, and who's going to catch you downloading from your home computer? The problem, of course, is that it is illegal, unethical, and wrong. You may or may not get caught, but why take the risk? Most people love music, and there are legal ways to use the Internet to download and purchase music at very reasonable prices.

If you are a true music lover, remember that every song that you download illegally hurts the recording artist as well as other employees of the music industry. Not only are you hurting your favorite artists and the music industry in general, you are, of course, committing a criminal act. Most illegal downloaders, once they understand the clear-cut legal issue, the effect on recording artists, and the pay-to-download options, stop the practice. Most people understand right from wrong, and once they know that free downloading of music is wrong, they do the right thing.

Once you have completed the first draft, you are in the best position to evaluate the overall quality of the essay, its potential impact on readers, and how each part of the essay contributes to its success. You may find that some parts of the draft are stronger than others, indicating specific areas for improvement. You may also find "holes" in the essay - missing pieces that leave gaps in its logical progression or unanswered questions for readers - that can only be filled by your investigating the topic further and adding information as you revise.

For example, a writer who wrote an essay on college admittance from the viewpoint that an applicant's SAT scores carry too much weight realized on reading her draft that she had included nothing on the possible correlation between SAT scores and eventual college success. She felt this was something that writers might find lacking in her essay, and she needed to research the topic further before revising her draft. Such oversights are not uncommon in first drafts since it is impossible to think of everything you might include until you review the draft.

In addition, writers often have "revelations" as they reread a draft. New, relevant ideas emerge that they hadn't previously considered. For whatever reason, reading what is already on the paper can trigger related ideas that would otherwise remain untapped. Some of the most effective ideas in an essay may not even be present in a first draft, and rereading the draft can help generate new thoughts.

For example, a writer wrote an essay on the effects of room color on a person's mood and activity level. As she reread a part of the draft that related the calm, soothing effects of a light-blue colored room, it dawned on her that the one room in her house where she preferred to read and study was the light-blue colored den. She now had some empirical evidence to add to her essay that helped substantiate the studies on how room color affected mood. The more that writers reread drafts with their minds open to discovering new ideas, the more likely they are find them.

Writers revise their drafts in different ways. Some concentrate first on sentence-level wording improvements. Other may look first at organizational issues. Still others make revisions as they come upon things to improve: rewording a sentence here, adding a new idea there, moving a sentence elsewhere. However, whatever their individual approach may be, most writers revise in the same general areas: wording, content, and organization.

The following revision suggestions cover those three areas as they apply to your most recent draft. How you apply these suggestions is up to you. You may prefer evaluating each aspect separately, looking at different aspects simultaneously, or making revisions as you read through a draft and discover things that need improving. The goal, of course, is to make the best possible revisions for improving your paper, and achieving that goal is more important than the specific approach that you use.

Revision Checklist

The following revision checklist is rather lengthy as it covers a range of revision possibilities. However, a number of the suggestions are related in ways that will allow you to work on them simultaneously if you wish.

1. **Opening**: Read your opening and evaluate its impact on readers. What might you add or change to make it more interesting, introduce your topic more clearly, reveal its importance, or make your thesis sentence sharper or clearer?

2. **Background information**: At the beginning of your middle paragraphs, did you present some explanatory or background information on your topic to help readers understand the issue most clearly? How might you improve this section of your draft?

3. **Supportive reasons and evidence**: Read each paragraph that presents a reason supporting your thesis. Is each reason clearly stated and substantiated by some type of compelling evidence: empirical, factual, logical, and/or comparative? Have you put information from different sources into your own words (*paraphrasing*) and enclosed any directly quoted material within quotation marks? Could any reason be stated more clearly or any evidence improved upon or added to? Are there other reasons and evidence you might add to strengthen your support?

4. **Comparative evidence**: Since the emphasis for this unit is on making comparisons, evaluate the comparative evidence that you included and its effectiveness in validating your supportive reasons or reinforcing your thesis in some manner. Are your comparisons an effective part of the draft? Have you used any analogies to help make your points? What might you add or change to improve the comparisons?

5. **Source acknowledgment**: Do you provide a clear source acknowledgment for each piece of evidence that you included (e.g. According to a 2008 Times article, The online encyclopedia Wikipedia stated that, Several leading seismologists

agreed in *Geographic Journal*, According to a study conducted by clinical psychologists at Harvard University...)?

6. **Organization:** Are your supportive reasons presented in the best order for emphasizing your most important points? Are your responses to opposing viewpoints placed in the most effective location? Do any paragraphs or sentences seem out of place and might fit better in a different location?

7. **Opposing viewpoints**: Have you acknowledged and responded to the strongest or most common arguments that readers who hold opposing viewpoints to your thesis might have? How might you improve your responses to help readers see the flaws or misconceptions in their arguments?

8. **Paragraphing**: Check your paragraphing to make sure that you have changed paragraphs as you move to something new in your essay: a different part, a different supportive reason, a different opposing argument. Are there any paragraphs that don't have a clear focus or main idea and need revising? Are there any overly long paragraphs that could be divided into two effective paragraphs or strings of short paragraphs that could be combined or further developed?

9. **Wording:** Read each sentence to see how its wording could be improved. Delete unnecessary or repetitive words, rephrase awkward sentences, replace questionable word choices, and clarify vague sentences. Make sure that each sentence reads the way you want and that each word helps to convey the sentence's meaning.

10. **Audience**: Read your draft with your audience in mind. Does it read like you are writing to a definite audience? Are there any places in the draft where you connect with readers in ways that will help accomplish your purpose? Is your writing tone such that readers will be receptive to your message? What might you revise to make an even greater impact on readers?

11. **Purpose:** Have you made your purpose clear to readers by either stating it or making it obvious in other ways? What might you add or change in your essay to help accomplish your purpose?

12. **Ending:** Your ending is the last thing your audience will read. What kind of an impact will it have on them? How strongly does it reinforce your thesis and further your purpose? What will readers take from your ending that will help you accomplish your purpose?

Activity 4.12

Read the following first draft and apply the "revision checklist" suggestions. What types of revisions might you suggest the writer make to improve the draft?

First draft

Peer Counseling for Freshmen Students (audience: college administration)

Peer counseling for freshmen students sounds like a great idea. Pairing older students who have supposedly been through the trials that freshmen face and can advise them wisely with freshmen students makes a lot of sense. However, it doesn't always work out as well in reality.

The peer counselor I was paired with didn't seem particularly keen on his job. He seemed like he was going through the motions with me and would rather be somewhere else. He knew a lot less about majors and class scheduling and required courses than I would have thought, and I didn't learn a whole lot from him. We had coffee a couple of times, and he was a nice enough guy to talk to, but I'm not sure what I got out of it.

Some other freshmen I have talked to have similar stories. Some peer counselors aren't that knowledgeable about the academic side of things. They may say they'll find this or that out for a student, but usually that student can find it on her own just as well. In addition, much of their "counseling" is less than profound, and they often serve up the obvious, like, "You'll probably be homesick the first semester," or "You'll have a lot more free time on your hands and have to learn how to use it," or, "You can expect your grades to drop a little from high school," or "Get involved in social activities or join a club so you'll feel more connected." None of this is news to most freshmen who have been told similar stuff by the high school counselors and their parents for some time in the past.

There's more. Some older male counselors apparently get into the program to hit on younger girls, and I've heard more than one freshman say that her counselor wanted to date her. I guess the word is out that the peer counseling program is a good place to pick up on freshmen girls, and there are some guys that are in it apparently for just that reason.

One of the problems is that peer counseling at our college can serve "in lieu" of regular counseling. In fact, peer counselors can even sign off on a student's class schedule, and some of them, including mine, would sign off without looking at it or knowing whether some of the classes may have prerequisites or whether the classes were all transferable or whether they fulfilled graduation requirements. That a freshman can get his class schedule signed off without a real counselor looking at it or approving it doesn't sound right, and it doesn't seem to be in the best interests in freshmen.

Of course, there are good peer counselors who befriend the freshmen, give them good advice, provide good academic assistance, and really have their best interests at heart. However, from what I've seen and heard, there are just as many bad and mediocre counselors who are little help and who could actually end up hurting students. That is why the peer counseling program should never be "in lieu of" regular counseling by trained college professionals. All freshmen should be required to see real counselors and get their class schedules checked off by them. Relying on peer counselors for such services doesn't work in many cases, where it is like the blind leading the blind.

In researching other peer counseling programs in area colleges, I found the practice is spotty; some schools offer peer counseling and others don't, according to the counseling departments. However, only one college other than our own allows peer counselors to sign off on a student's class schedule. In fact, one college counselor from Bryant College said, "That's a very unusual and questionable practice. We try everything possible to get our freshmen in to see us, and this practice seems to have the opposite effect."

Should the peer counseling program at our college be discontinued? Not necessarily. However, at least three things should happen if it does continue. First, peer counseling should never be "in lieu" of real counseling by trained professionals, the only people who would be allowed to sign off on class schedules. It should be supplemental, and in that role, would make more sense. Second, many peer counselors need to learn more about what they are supposed to do and know before being accepted into the program. From what I have heard from peer counselors, all they have to do is sign up and have a respectable GPA to be in the program. Where is the training they should receive to be of any real value? Third, there should be an evaluation process that every freshman who has a peer counselor should participate in. Bad counselors should not be allowed to continue in the program, but right now unless a student takes the trouble to complain, no one hears about it.

The school definitely has a problem with its peer counseling program, but it is one that can be solved if some clear steps are taken. As it is, the program doesn't seem to help a lot of students, and it definitely hurts some of them. That is the last thing that the college or its freshmen students need.

Activity 4.13

Considering the revision checklist suggestions, revise your draft, making any changes that you feel will improve the essay and help accomplish your purpose. Before doing your sentence wording revision, you may want to do the sentence revision practice in Activity 4.14.

Activity 4.14

This sentence revision activity provides more practice in improving first-draft sentences. Revise the sentences by eliminating unnecessary or repetitive words, rewording or rephrasing awkward sentences, moving words or phrases around to more effective locations, clarifying vague sentences, replacing questionable word choices, or making two sentences out of one long, cumbersome sentence. There may be several ways to revise a particular sentence effectively.

EXAMPLE

> **First draft:** The water has eroded the sand along the section of beach between the pier and trestle to the extent that the layer of small rocks below the sand is exposed in many places, making it difficult to walk barefooted out into the water or along the beach.
>
> **Revised:** Water has eroded the sand between the pier and the trestle, exposing the underlying layer of small rocks in many places, and making walking along the beach or into the water difficult.

1. Stealing from a music store is the equivalent of what hundreds of thousands of people, mostly teens and young adults, do every day when they illegally download music from the Internet without paying for it.
2. You would think that music-loving downloaders who want to support their favorite artists would not turn around and take money out of their pockets, but that is apparently the last thing they think of when burning their CD's.
3. Downloaders may gather the impression that the illegality of downloading copyrighted music is questionable from some of the on-line sites devoted to showing people how to download music, some of which expound

the idea that "no one really knows" what is or isn't il-legal, so until there is clarification, there is no risk to downloading.

4. For people who want to download music from the Internet, some sites offer a viable and legal alternative, one which doesn't take revenue away from the recording artists and which doesn't put people at risk of being prosecuted for on-line copyright infringement.

5. Pairing older students who have supposedly been through the trials that freshmen face and can advise them wisely with freshmen students makes a lot of sense.

6. Some peer counselors aren't that knowledgeable about the academic side of things.

7. None of this is news to most freshmen who have been told similar stuff by the high school counselors and their parents for some time in the past.

Editing

The final step in preparing your essay for "publication" is to proof-read it for errors and make any needed corrections. At this point you are no doubt aware of your error tendencies, so make sure to look in particular for those types of errors that you are most prone to make.

Editing Checklist

The following checklist will ensure that you cover every aspect of grammar usage, punctuation, and spelling as you proofread your paper for errors.

1. **Spelling.** Use the spell check on your word processor and also proofread your paper for spelling errors. Most spell checks do not flush out words that are spelled correctly but used incorrectly (e.g. Their motives aren't as altruistic as one might imagine.), so pay particular attention to homophones, words that sound the same but are spelled differently, and similar sounding words.

2. **Punctuation**. Check to make sure you used the following correctly:
    End marks (periods, question marks, and exclamation marks) to designate the end of each sentence. As you read your sentences, look for any run-on sentences, comma splices, or sentence fragments, and punctuate them correctly to eliminate the problems.
    Commas to separate words or phrases in a series; after introductory dependent clauses and preposition, participial, and gerund phrases; after conjunctions in a compound sentence; after "interrupters" such as "by the way," "incidentally," or "of course" at the beginning or within a sentences; before and after appositives or unrestricted relative clauses; to set off ending participial phrases, or at a point in a sentence where a pause is essential for the sentence to be read and understood correctly.

    Semi-colons to connect two closely related sentences or to separate phrases within a series that also contain commas within the phrases.

    Colons to set off a summary, series, or example following a main clause.

Dashes to set off a summary, series, or example within a sentence: The most difficult part of helping a child with school work - letting her learn from her own mistakes - is also one of the most important.

Apostrophes to identify possessive words and contractions.

Quotation marks to set off direct quotations.

3. **Grammar**.   Check to make sure that your verbs agree with their subjects, pronouns agree with their antecedents, the correct pronoun subject and object forms are used, the correct comparative and superlative adjective forms are used, the correct adverb forms are used, and the correct irregular past tense verb forms are used.

4. **Parallelism**.   Make sure that in sentences that contain a series of two or more words, phrases, or clauses, frequently joined by "and" or "or," all parts of the series are parallel in construction.

5. **Active/Passive Voice**.   Make sure that most of your sentences are in the active voice, and use the passive voice only for special emphasis.

6. **Dangling/Misplaced Modifiers**.   Check your sentences for any dangling or misplaced modifiers and make the necessary revisions. (See the following section on "Dangling and Misplaced Modifiers."

Dangling and Misplaced Modifiers

Even the most experienced writers will occasionally "dangle" or misplace a modifier. For example, the following sentence contains both a dangling and misplaced modifier.

Drawing the blinds, the bright morning light struck Juan in his bedroom like a laser, intensifying the pain in his head.
The participial phrase "Drawing the blinds" is a dangling modifier because it doesn't modify the subject "light." Obviously, the morning light can't draw the blinds. The prepositional phrase "in his bedroom" modifies "blinds" but is misplaced in the middle of the sentence. Here is a corrected version of the sentence that eliminates the problems:

As Juan drew the blinds in his bedroom, the bright morning light struck him like a laser, intensifying the pain in his head.

To eliminate the dangling modifier, the participial phrase "Drawing the blinds" was changed to the clause, "As Juan drew the blinds in his bedroom." The misplaced modifier "in his bedroom" was moved from the middle of the sentence to directly after the word it modifies: "blinds in the bedroom." The revised version of the sentence is clearer and smoother.

To detect and eliminate dangling or misplaced modifiers in your drafts, consider these suggestions.

1. **A dangling modifier is most frequently an introductory participial phrase that does not modify the subject of the sentence:**

    Dazed by the accusations hurled at her, the room began spinning and Gretchen struggled to keep her balance. ("Dazed by the accusations hurled at her" doesn't modify the subject "room." A room isn't dazed by accusations.)

    Driving through the Maine countryside, the maple trees were awash in brilliant reds, oranges, and yellows. ("Driving through the Main countryside" doesn't modify the subject "trees." Trees can't drive.)

2. **To eliminate a dangling modifier, do one of two things**:
    a. Change the subject of the sentence so that the introductory phrase correctly modifies it:
    Dazed by the accusations hurled at her, Gretchen struggled to keep her balance as the room began spinning.
    b. Change the dangling modifier to a clause with an appropriate subject:
    While I was driving through the Maine countryside, the maple trees were awash in brilliant reds, oranges, and yellows.

3. **A misplaced modifier is most frequently a phrase or clause placed some distance from the word it modifies, resulting in an awkward or unclear sentence:**
    The judge ordered Felipe to pay the maximum fine who was usually lenient on first-time traffic offenders. (The clause "who was usually lenient on first-time traffic offenders" does not follow directly after the word it modifies, creating an awkward sentence.
    There were broken bottles that had been hurled from vehicles

on the shoulder of the road. (The phrase "on the shoulder of the road" isn't near the word it modifies: "bottles.")

4. **To eliminate a misplaced modifier, move the modify phrase or clause directly after or near to the word it modifies:**

The judge who was usually lenient on first-time traffic offenders ordered Felipe to pay the maximum fine.

There were broken bottles on the shoulder of the road that had been hurled from vehicles. ("Bottles" has both a modifying phrase - "on the shoulder of the road" - and a modifying clause - "that had been hurled" - following it. In this sentence, putting the phrase directly after "bottles" produces the smoothest, clearest sentence.)

Activity 4.15

The following paragraph contains some sentences with dangling and misplaced modifiers. Revise the sentences to eliminate the problems. You may add words, move words around, or change the wording of a sentence.

EXAMPLE

Nothing indicated that Claudette was suffering from an acute case of nerves by her manner. Sitting calmly in the dentist's waiting room, you would think she was waiting in a restaurant to be seated.

Revised:
Nothing in Claudette's manner indicated that she was suffering from an acute case of nerves. As she sat calmly in the dentist's waiting room, you would think she was waiting to be seated in a restaurant.

Listening to the President's speech on tort reform, the division between Democrats and Republicans was obvious. The Democrats applauded frequently while the Republicans sat with folded arms throughout the speech. Overcome with anger and frustration, a shout of "Liar!" emitted from a Republican legislator at one point, which was met by shocked silence from the crowd. The Democratic legislators gave the President ten standing ovations while the Republicans remained seated. Undeterred by the lack of Republican support, the tone of the speech was enthusiastic and optimistic. No one doubted the President's sincerity or good intentions in the room. The split was over the shape that tort reform should take between Democrats and Republicans. Noting the obvious split in the chambers, pessimism reigned in next-day articles by reporters over a tort reform agreement being reached.

Activity 4.16

Proofread your latest draft for errors and make any necessary corrections.

If Same-sex 'Marriage' Is Legalized, Why Not Polygamy?
by Michael Foust

Late last year, months after the landmark Lawrence vs Texas decision striking down anti-sodomy laws, two Utah polygamists filed suit in state court, asking that their relationships with multiple wives be validated by the government. Laws against polygamy, they said, are unconstitutional.

"Everyone should be free unless there's a compelling state interest that you shouldn't be," John Bucher, one of the lawyers, told The Salt Lake Tribune. "The state is not able to show that there's such an evil to polygamy that it should be prohibited."

As the nation continues to debate same-sex "marriage," some have begun examining the logical extension of its legalization. If the legal benefits of marriage are awarded to homosexual men, then why aren't they also given to, say, three polygamists?

"There isn't a single argument in favor of same-sex marriage that isn't also an argument in favor of polygamy - people have a right to marry who they love, these relationships already exist ... we have no right to deny the children of their protections," columnist Maggie Gallagher, an outspoken supporter of a Federal marriage amendment, told Baptist Press.

Jennifer Marshall, director of domestic policy studies at The Heritage Foundation, said she sees no "logical stopping point" if same-sex "marriage" is legalized. "This is the dissolution of the parameters around marriage," she said. "You'd be hard-pressed to say, 'Why not any other kind of arrangement?'"

Conservatives and traditionalists say the debate over same-sex "marriage" is the result of marriage being separated from its religious roots and from procreation. If marriage is not tied to childbearing, traditionalists warn it literally could mean anything.

In its landmark ruling on same-sex "marriage" last year, the Massachusetts high court ruled that marriage's purpose is not procreation, but instead the commitment of two people to one another for life. That argument troubles Gallagher, who asserts that government benefits are awarded to married couples because they, in turn, benefit society by raising the next generation of adults.

"If marriage is only about private love, why is the government involved?" she asked, rhetorically. "Why does the government care? Why is the [government] involved if you have this view of marriage that's just kind of a private, emotional lover's vow? But for some reason, you record it in law and it changes your tax status."

The issue of polygamy has been one that has frequently stumped supporters of same-sex "marriage." During a January debate, University of Louisville law professor Sam Marcosson, a supporter of homosexual "marriage," called the polygamy argument a "red herring." Candice Gingrich, a homosexual activist, made the same assertion during an appearance on Sean Hannity's radio program.

Last November on ABC's "This Week," conservative columnist George Will asked two homosexual men - Rep. Barney Frank and columnist Andrew Sullivan - to give him a "principle" as to why polygamy should be banned in light of the Lawrence and Massachusetts decisions. "Some distinctions are hard to draw," Frank answered. "But the difference between two people and three people is almost always clear. It is responsible for a society to say, 'Look, you can do what you want personally. If three people want to have sex together, that's not against the law. But when it comes to being married and institutionalizing these legal relationships with regards to the ownership of property and children, then we believe a three-way operation is likely to cause difficulty, friction with the children.'" Sullivan responded: "I don't want the right to marry anyone. I just want the right to marry someone."

Sociologist Glenn Stanton of Focus on the Family said one reason same-sex "marriage" has made advances is because marriage itself is viewed as a means of receiving legal benefits. "If we have to honor the relationship that two guys have, then we have to honor the relationship that a guy and his three wives have," Stanton said. "We have to honor the relationship that two heterosexual single moms have. If we are going to offer health benefits and government benefits to other configurations, why keep anybody from joining together and saying, 'Our relationship is significant, too,' regardless of what that relationship is?" Gallagher said there is "no logical reason" for not awarding benefits to polygamists if they are given to same-sex couples.

The irony of the current debate is that polygamy is rooted far deeper in human history - and is accepted in far more cultures today - than is same-sex "marriage." Polygamy once dominated the Mormon church, and Utah was not given statehood until it outlawed the practice. The church officially disavows it now, although estimates say that up to 100,000 people in the West still practice it. Worldwide, polygamy is legal in some countries and is common among Muslims. Islam's founder, Muhammad, had multiple wives. The United Nations allows employees to divide their benefits among multiple wives, as long as they come from a country where polygamy is practiced, The Washington Post reported.

Seeing the logical extension from same-sex "marriage," some in America have begun to argue for the legalization of polygamy, too.

Anthropologist Robert Myers wrote in a USA Today editorial March 14 that the United States has a "narrow view" of marriage. "We will allow marriage to any number of partners, as long as it is to only one at a time," he wrote. Gallagher said she believes that polygamy is less of a departure from traditional marriage than is same-sex "marriage." After all, she said, it involves procreation. Of course, Gallagher and other traditionalists aren't arguing for polygamy's legalization. They're showing the logical inconsistency of same-sex "marriage."

"The argument in the 19th century that Congress made is that polygamy is associated with despotic forms of government, because basically the most powerful men start hogging all the women," Gallagher said. "There is something to be said for that. I think it's also associated with less investment by fathers in their children. Some children get subordinated in polygamous marriage systems. The attention of the father and the family tends to focus on the heir." Other arguments against polygamy include an increase in child and spousal abuse, welfare fraud and forced marriages. Many Christians base their opposition to same-sex marriage, as well as polygamous marriage, on Scripture. In Matthew 19, Christ points to Old Testament law as limiting marriage to one man, one woman. Any other "marriage" configuration goes against the word of God.

Marshall, of The Heritage Foundation, said the onus must be placed on same-sex "marriage" supporters as to why marriage should not include polygamy and other forms of relationships. The polygamy question is not a "red herring," she said. "It seems to me," she said, "that those who are trying to argue for the redefinition of marriage should have to answer the question, 'What is the logical stopping point after this?' It seems to me that that question should be turned around, and the ones who are answering it should be the ones who are proposing the redefinition of marriage." So far, no satisfactory answer has come forth.

DISCUSSION

1. What is the topic of the essay, and what is its (implied) thesis?
2. What comparisons are drawn between same-sex marriage and polygamy, and why? Do you think the comparisons weaken the case in support of same-sex marriage?
3. What other arguments are presented against same-sex marriage and how effective are they?
4. Same-sex marriage proponents argue that comparing same-sex marriage with polygamy is a "red herring." Do you agree, and why?

5. What is your viewpoint on the legalization of same-sex marriage? On the legalization of polygamy? Do you believe that the Bible should inform people's viewpoint on same-sex marriage and polygamy, and why?

Is America Really On the Decline?
By Thomas Omestad

The financial crisis of 2008 has not just toppled once-proud corporate giants and eviscerated American assets, livelihoods, and credit. It has touched off an anxious debate over whether the debacle heralds a long-predicted decline in U.S. global power, nothing short of the beginning of the end of the American century.

Overseas and in America, the meltdown is being widely interpreted as a bellwether event, the moment when the American colossus is forced by its own imprudence to throttle back on its globe-straddling ambitions and begin climbing down from the summit of its primacy. A dramatic sign is the emergency Washington summit of the G-20 on November 15. The leaders of 20 key economies will start remaking the power structure of global finance to give rising nations a bigger role.

The rumblings about America's decline are understandable. The financial crisis represents this year's third shock, coming after spiking energy and food prices. Even with a bold intervention by Washington to shore up financial markets, the scope and velocity of the made-in-America financial tumble have thrust forward doubts about the future - and the attractiveness - of the freewheeling U.S. capitalist model, about America's true strength overseas, and about the durability of a post-Cold War order with the United States as the unchallenged, full-service superpower. "The U.S. will lose its status as the superpower of the world financial system." Peer Steinbrück, the finance minister of Germany, declared in September. "This world will become multipolar."

That prediction came from the top ranks of a close U.S. ally and trading partner. From would-be rivals and those nursing resentments of Washington, the reaction has been more caustic. "Economic egoism is also a consequence of the unipolar vision of the world and of the desire to be its mega-regulator," Russian President Dmitry Medvedev said last month. He blamed the United States for having "let slip" a chance for a more democratic world order after the rush of global solidarity with America following 9/11. Why? Because of Washington's "desire to consolidate its global rule," he said. Even as world leaders gathered at the United Nations in September, the chatter behind the public speechifying veered onto one topic: U.S. decline. "The corridors are full of it," said a senior U.N. diplomat with no track record of U.S. bashing. He shook his head over "America's blindness to recognize how the world has changed."

The Bush administration, by contrast, sought to reassure Americans that their status as the premier economic and military power - U.S. "centrality," as Secretary of State Condoleezza Rice puts it - will endure. Indeed, some measures of American pre-eminence remain impressive and relatively unchanged. With less than 5 percent of the world's population, the United States still produces about one quarter of the global gross domestic produce, more than three times the share held by Britain at the height of its empire in the mid-1800s. Some 60 percent of the world's reserve currencies are held in U.S. dollars. One-third of the world's 500 largest companies are American, and one-third of its patent filings are, too. America's military budget represents just under half of the world's total defense spending. Seventeen of the world's top twenty universities are in the United States, and American popular culture penetrates into nearly every corner of the world.

Yet Americans are feeling sour about their country's international standing. The need to preserve American primacy remains, for the time being at least, a given to most Americans. A Chicago Council on Global Affairs opinion poll released in September found that 53 percent of Americans worry that the United States has already lost leverage for achieving its aims overseas. Improving U.S. stature received more backing as being of the highest priority than any other goal, with 83 percent calling it "very important."

Bush administration officials dismissed the talk of decline as a predictable and episodic ritual. This time, however, might not turn out as well for America, some analysts worry, because the trends eroding America's pre-eminence run deeper. "It's not simply that we've run into a rough patch, shaking our self-confidence," warns Andrew Bacevich, an international affairs specialist at Boston University and author of this year's *The Limits of Power: The End of American Exceptionalism.* "It's different this time." That there is some sort of big change is widely accepted, and even mainstream Defense Secretary Robert Gates now speaks of a "multipolar world." In its 2007 annual survey, the International Institute for Strategic Studies referred to "the profound loss of authority suffered by the United States since its invasion of Iraq."

Yet more troubling was the vista painted by Thomas Fingar, the U.S. intelligence community's top analyst. Foreshadowing a conclusion of a coming report called "Global Trends 2025," he said in September that "American dominance will be much diminished over this period of time" and "will erode at an accelerating pace with the partial exception of the military." In future competition, he added, the military will be "the least significant" factor. Fingar labeled U.S. pre-eminence since World War II a "truly anomalous situation." Indeed, shifts in economic and military power - played out slowly, over decades and centuries - are the norm, as Yale historian Paul Kennedy pointed out in his 1988 work, *The Rise and Fall of the Great Powers*. Some analysts conclude that if the reality of America's power position has changed, so must American attitudes. "We should disenthrall ourselves from the idea that the well-being and security of the United States can only be attained by seeking to maintain primacy," says Bacevich.

Something else is different about the current debate over U.S. decline. Without any contraction of its daunting military firepower or the size of its economy, other nations are bound to assume more influential positions. The world geo-political map is being redrawn: Several powers are rising, some rapidly. China takes top billing on the list. Back when economic reforms began in 1978, China contributed but 1 percent of the world's GDP and its trade. Last year, it reached 5 percent of world GDP and 8 percent of trade. China's growth has hummed along at nearly 10 percent annually - for three decades. That is three times the global average.

China's "peaceful rise," as officials call the strategy, aims to restore China to the status it had enjoyed for many centuries: the world's largest economy. A recent Goldman Sachs report has bumped up the time by which China's economy is expected to surpass America's in size to 2027. China's growth is fueling a rapid expansion of military capabilities and, in effect, promoting a model competing with that of the United States - authoritarian capitalism.

At the same time, India, the world's most populous democratic state, has also found a surer path to prosperity that is broadening its influence and enabling a military buildup. Along with the economic recovery of Japan and the growth of what used to be called the "tigers" of South Korea and Southeast Asia, predictions of a "Pacific century" or an Asian one look more plausible. Asia is returning to its historical norms, Kishore Mahbubani, dean of the Lee Kuan Yew School of Public Policy at the National University of Singapore, argues in his book *The New Asian Hemisphere.*" The era of Western domination has run its course," he writes.

There are shifts elsewhere, too. The once slumbering giant of South America, Brazil, is overcoming its past weaknesses. Russia is undergoing a resurgence of uncertain duration, courtesy of massive sales of oil and natural gas. Its invasion of neighboring Georgia and support for separatist regions there may mark a new period of strategic challenges to the West. Meanwhile, the European Union, in fits and starts, continues to evolve into a more coherent force in global affairs that, as a 27-nation collective, already presents the world's largest economy.

The erosion of U.S. global standing - at least in the eyes of the world

- has been hastened by a foreign policy routinely portrayed overseas as one of arrogance and hubris. The charge of U.S. unilateralism, stoked above all by a costly and unresolved war of choice in Iraq, has fortified a troubling caricature of America as a militaristic and hypocritical behemoth that frittered away the outpouring of global goodwill after 9/11. The damage to America's reputation has weakened its "soft power" - the attractiveness abroad of its society and politics.

The go-it-alone instincts of the Bush administration - though tempered in its second term - came into play on issues from climate change to international justice to arms control. Old allies felt a cool wind from Washington. Grand ambitions for a democratic Middle East went unfulfilled. The Americans championed the war on terrorism with a "with us or against us" zeal. Fairly or not, friends and foes alike saw a lecturing, moralistic American style of leadership. It sat badly. "We exited the Cold War with amazing prestige and an automatic followership," says Freeman. "Nobody will charge a hill with us anymore."

And yet, for all the deflating news, the time-tested ability of American society to assess and overcome problems should interject caution about proclaiming the American century over and done with. The restorative capacity of America, reasons Thérèse Delpech, a leading French strategic thinker, "is constantly underestimated abroad and even sometimes at home." Those who contend American decline is being exaggerated - or not happening - say that the unipolar moment was never destined to last and that the degree of deference actually accorded to Washington in happier days was never as much as is portrayed. Take, for instance, the disfavor visited on the United States because of its racial segregation and bigotry and a polarizing war in Vietnam.

Further, the current credit crash follows in a long tradition of occasional panics and meltdowns in both the British Empire and the United States. "Those crises haven't sunk us in 300 years," reasons Mead. "We seem to find a way to manage them." Skeptics of U.S. decline believe that other weaknesses are exaggerated and that the U.S. economy remains central. Says George Schwab, president of the New York-based National Committee on American Foreign Policy, "When Wall Street coughs, the rest of the world catches a cold." No other currency, including the euro and the Chinese renminbi, is yet ready to replace the dollar.

Nor, in general, should the rise of others stir angst, say the anti-declinists. It reflects, by contrast, the near globalization of the U.S.-initiated postwar system, whose very openness should accommodate the peaceful rise of newer powers. "It was American strategy to see them get stronger," says Robert Kagan, a senior fellow at the Carnegie Endowment and author of The Return of History and the End of Dreams.

The interdependence woven into the existing system creates mutual vulnerabilities that might deter efforts to weaken the United States directly. John Bruton, the European Union ambassador in Washington, says, "If the West goes into decline, so do they." U.S. policy aims to make China a "responsible stakeholder." If China were to sell off its trove of U.S. public debt, it would undercut the value of its own assets. More likely, Beijing sees buying treasury bills as both a good investment and a way to balance a relationship in which it has to sell to the American market to make its long climb out of poverty. "The Asians are not happy about America being so weakened," says Mahbubani. The anti-declinists also count America's demographics as a key source of vigor. Through its acceptance of immigration and its higher birthrates, America's population is projected not only to grow but to avoid taking on the aging profiles of China, Russia, and Western Europe.

Few doubt that America's global position will experience "relative shifts," to use the diplomatic language of State's Cohen. But, he insists, "there is no other country's hand I'd rather play." Says a senior U.N. diplomat, "Bet against America at your peril." Even so, in the 21st century, it might be prudent to spread a few wagers on others as well.

DISCUSSION

1. In question form, what is the topic of the essay? What is its thesis?
2. What comparisons are drawn in the essay to support a decline in America relative to other countries, and how convincing are they?
3. What comparisons are drawn to support the "anti-declinists'" position, and how convincing are they?
4. Based on the essay as well as your own opinions, do you think that America is on the decline, and why?

U.S. Workers in a Global Job Market
By Ron Hira

Among the many changes that are part of the emergence of a global economy is a radically different relationship between U.S. high-tech companies and their employees. As late as the 1990s, a degree in science, technology, engineering, or mathematics (STEM) was a virtual guarantee of employment. Today, many good STEM jobs are moving to other countries, reducing prospects for current STEM workers and dimming the appeal of STEM studies for young people. U.S. policymakers need to learn more about these developments so that they can make the critical choices about how to nurture a key ingredient in the nation's future economic health: the STEM workforce.

U.S. corporate leaders are not hiding the fact that globalization has fundamentally changed how they manage their human resources. Craig Barrett, then the chief executive officer (CEO) of Intel Corporation, said that his company can succeed without ever hiring another American. In an article in Foreign Affairs magazine, IBM's CEO Sam Palmisano gave the eulogy for the multinational corporation (MNC), introducing us to the "globally integrated enterprise" (GIE): "Many parties to the globalization debate mistakenly project into the future a picture of corporations that is unchanged from that of today or yesterday.... but businesses are changing in fundamental ways - structurally, operationally, culturally - in response to the imperatives of globalization and new technology."

GIEs do not have to locate their high-value jobs in their home country; they can locate research, development, design, or services wherever they like without sacrificing efficiency. Ron Rittenmeyer, then the CEO of EDS, said he "is agnostic specifically about where" EDS locates its workers, choosing the place that reaps the best economic efficiency. EDS, which had virtually no employees in low-cost countries in 2002, had 43% of its workforce in low-cost countries by 2008. IBM, once known for its lifetime employment, now forces its U.S. workers to train foreign replacements as a condition of severance. In an odd twist, IBM is offering U.S. workers the opportunity to apply for jobs in its facilities in low-cost countries such as India and Brazil at local wage rates.

As Ralph Gomory, a former senior vice president for science and technology at IBM, has noted, the interests of corporations and countries are diverging. Corporate leaders, whose performance is not measured by how many U.S. workers they employ or the long-term health of the U.S. economy, will pursue their private interests with vigor even if their actions harm their U.S. employees or are bad prescriptions for the economy. Simply put, what's good for IBM may not be good for the United States and vice versa. Although this may seem obvious, the policy and political processes have not fully adjusted to this reality. Policymakers still turn to the CEOs of GIEs for advice on what is best for the U.S. economy.

U.S. universities have been a magnet for talented young people interested in acquiring the world's best STEM education. Many of these productive young people have remained in the United States, become citizens, and made enormous contributions to the productivity of the U.S. economy as well as its social, cultural, and political life. But these universities are beginning to think of themselves as global institutions that can deliver their services anywhere in the world.

Cornell, which already calls itself a transnational institution, operates a medical school in Qatar and sent its president to India in 2007 to explore opportunities to open a branch campus. Representatives of other top engineering schools, such as Rice, Purdue, Georgia Tech, and Virginia Tech, have made similar trips. Carnegie Mellon offers its technology degrees in India in partnership with a small private Indian college. Students take most of their courses in India, because it is less expensive, and then spend six months in Pittsburgh to complete the Carnegie Mellon degree.

If students do not have to come to the United States to receive a first-rate education, they are far less likely to seek work in the United States. More high-quality job opportunities are appearing in low-cost countries, many of them with U.S. companies. This will accelerate the migration of STEM jobs out of the United States. Even the perfectly sensible move by many U.S. engineering programs to provide their students with more international experience through study-abroad courses and other activities could contribute to the migration of STEM jobs by preparing these students to manage R&D activities across the globe.

The emerging opportunities for GIEs to take advantage of high-skilled talent in low-cost countries have markedly increased both career uncertainty and risk for the U.S. STEM workforce. Many U.S. STEM workers worry about offshoring's impact on their career prospects and are altering career selection. For instance, according to the Computing Research Association, enrollment in bachelors programs in computer science dropped 50% from 2002 to 2007. The rising risk of IT job loss, caused in part by offshoring, was a major factor in students' shying away from computer science degrees.

Offshoring concerns have been mostly concentrated on IT occupations, but many other STEM occupations may be at risk. Princeton University economist Alan Blinder analyzed all 838 Bureau of Labor Statistics standard occupation categories to estimate their vulnerability to offshoring. He estimates that nearly all (35 of 39) STEM occupations are "offshorable," and he described many as "highly vulnerable." By vulnerable, he is not claiming that all, or even a large share, of jobs in those occupations will actually be lost overseas. Instead, he believes that those occupations will face significant new wage competition from low-cost countries. Further, he finds that there is no correlation between vulnerability and education level, so simply increasing U.S. education levels, as many have advocated, will not slow offshoring.

Workers need to know which jobs will be geographically sticky and which are vulnerable to being offshored so that they can make better choices for investing in their skills.

But there is a great deal of uncertainty about how globalization will affect the level and mix of domestic STEM labor demand. The response of some workers appears to be to play it safe and opt for occupations, often non-STEM, that are likely to stay. Further, most employers, because of political sensitivities, are very reluctant to reveal what jobs they are offshoring, sometimes going to great lengths to mask the geographic rebalancing of their workforces. The uncertainty introduced by offshoring aggravates the already volatile job market that is characteristic of the dynamic high-tech sector.

Private companies will have the final say about the offshoring of jobs, but the federal government can and should play a role in tracking what is happening in the global economy and taking steps that help the country adapt to change. Given the speed at which offshoring is increasing in scale, scope, and job sophistication, a number of immediate steps should be taken.

Collect additional, better, and timelier data. We cannot expect government or business leaders to make sound decisions in the absence of sound data. The National Science Foundation (NSF) should work with the appropriate agencies, such as the Bureaus of Economic Analysis (BEA) and Labor Statistics and the Census, to begin collecting more detailed and timely data on the globalization of innovation and R&D.

Establish an independent institute to study the implications of globalization. Blinder has said that the economic transformation caused by offshoring could rival the changes caused by the industrial revolution. In addition to collecting data, government needs to support an independent institute to analyze the social and economic implications of these changes and to consider policy options to address the undesirable effects. A $40 million annual effort to fund intramural and extramural efforts would be a good start.

Facilitate worker representation in the policy process. Imagine if a major trade association, such as the Semiconductor Industry Association, was excluded from having any representative on a federal advisory committee making recommendations on trade and export control policy in the semiconductor industry. It would be unfathomable. But we have precisely this arrangement when it comes to making policies that directly affect the STEM workforce. Professional societies and labor unions should be invited to represent the views of STEM workers on federal advisory panels and in congressional hearings.

Create better career paths for STEM workers. STEM offshoring has created a pessimistic attitude about future career prospects for incumbent workers as well as students. To make STEM career paths more reliable and resilient, the government and industry should work together to create programs for continuing education, establish a sturdier safety net for displaced workers, improve information about labor markets and careers, expand the pool of potential STEM workers by making better use of workers without a college degree, and provide assistance for successful reentry into the STEM labor market after voluntary and involuntary absences.

Improve the competitiveness of the next generation of STEM workers. As workers in other countries develop more advanced skills, U.S. STEM workers must develop new skills and opportunities to distinguish themselves. They should identify and pursue career paths that are geographically sticky, and they should acquire more entrepreneurship skills that will enable them to create their own opportunities. The National Academies could help by forming a study panel to identify necessary curriculum reforms and best practices in teaching innovation, creativity, and entrepreneurship to STEM students. NSF should encourage and help fund study-abroad programs for STEM students to improve their ability to work in global teams.

Public procurement should favor U.S. workers. The public sector - federal, state, and local government - is 19% of the economy and is an important mechanism that should be used by policymakers. There is a long, strong, and positive link between government procurement and technological innovation. The federal government not only funded most of the early research in computers and the Internet but was also a major customer for those new technologies. U.S. taxpayers have a right to know that government expenditures at any level are being used appropriately to boost innovation and help U.S. workers. The first step is to do an accounting of the extent of public procurement that is being offshored. Then the government should modify regulations to keep STEM-intensive work at home.We are at the beginning of a major structural shift in global distribution of STEM-intensive work. Given the critical nature of STEM to economic growth and national security, the United States must begin to adapt to these changes. The responses that have been proposed and adopted so far are based on the belief that nothing has changed. Simply increasing the pool of STEM workers and the number of k-12 science and math teachers is not enough. The nation needs to develop a better understanding of the new dynamics of the STEM system and to adopt policies that will advance the interests of the nation and its STEM workers.

DISCUSSION

1. What is the thesis of the essay?
2. What comparisons are made between the present and the past regarding STEM employment in the U.S.? How does each comparison support the thesis in some manner?

3. "U.S. Workers in a Global Job Market" is a problem/solution essay. How successful do you feel the solutions presented will be in helping to solve the problem, and why? Can you think of other possible solutions?

4. How do you think the "offshoring" of traditional American jobs will affect our country in the next twenty years? How does "offshoring" affect your personal educational and employment plans, if at all?

Writing about Writing

At the end of each "Readings" section you are given the opportunity to write a critique of an essay based on the main criterion by which you evaluate your own essays: how well does the writer make his case?

By having written several essays and scrutinized a number of readings, you have no doubt developed some expertise in essay analysis and evaluation. You are aware of different types of evidence that writers use and how effectively they employ them to support their thesis. You are also aware of apparent "holes" in an essay - unsubstantiated claims, a lack of opposing viewpoints - that can weaken its impact. You are knowledgeable about a number of elements of effective essay writing, which help you evaluate how well a particular essay measures up. In short, you are well prepared to write an informed, insightful critique.

Writing the Critique

In simplest terms, an essay critique tells what the essay is about, what you thought of the essay, and why. What the essay is about may include the topic, its thesis, its main supportive points and substantiating evidence. What you thought of the essay is usually expressed in your thesis: how effective you felt the essay was. How you reach this conclusion may include how well the essay makes its case, its impact on you, and its significance. As you write your upcoming critique, keep in mind the three basic questions that most readers want answered: What is the essay about? What do you think of it? Why do you think that way?

Activity 4.17

Write a critique of an essay in the text or an outside essay or article with your instructor's approval.

Unit Five
Causal Evidence

In essay writing, writers often deal with thorny problems that have no simple solution: colleges trying to cope with increasing costs and declining enrollment; states trying to develop a budget with decreasing tax revenues; counties dealing with overcrowded jails and nowhere to house new prisoners; social workers trying to reduce the physical abuse of children with so much abuse unreported and undetected; students searching for a greater voice in college decision-making without a legal right to participation.

Solutions to difficult problems often begin with identifying the root causes of the problems and determining how best to address them. If a writer can convince readers that the causes presented for a particular problem are valid, they will be more inclined to accept them or help work towards a solution.

If a writer can find *causal evidence* to validate the causes for a particular problem, she can be confident that whatever solution she proposes will address the right causes. She also has the strongest evidence for convincing readers to accept the causes and consider the solution(s) on which they are based.

For example, let's say that someone is writing an essay on the difficulty of college graduates finding jobs. She has discovered that a commonly held belief - that once a person has a college degree, a job awaits him - is fiction. There are several causes that she feels may contribute to the problem: the loss of jobs in the U.S. due to companies outsourcing them to other countries; the disparity between the numbers of students graduating with a particular major and the number of jobs in that field; the unwillingness of many students to accept entry-level positions; the downsizing of many companies during hard times. However, she isn't sure which causes are valid.

After doing some research, she discovers that there is evidence to confirm that there are more students graduating in certain fields than there are jobs to fill, and that many companies have downsized in recent years, reducing the number of available jobs in many fields. There was little evidence, however, to support that outsourcing has had a substantial impact on the types of jobs that college graduates seek, or that students rejecting entry-level jobs was a cause of the problem.

Based on the causal evidence that shows the disparity between the numbers of graduates in particular fields and the number of jobs available, and the jobs that have been lost through company downsizing, the writer can fashion a possible solution that addresses those causes. Part of that solution may be for colleges to do a better job of letting students know the fields where the most employment opportunities await and those that are flooded with applicants.

Finding solid causal evidence is critical for getting at the real causes of a particular problem, which is important for finding a viable solution. Whether the topic is global warming, the declining U.S. automobile industry, the high cost of medical insurance, or the alarming increase in sexual transmitted diseases (STDs) among young adults, addressing the actual causes of these problems provides the best chance for finding a solution that works. If a purported cause of a particular problem is in fact valid, there should be evidence available to confirm its validity. It is the writer's job to find that evidence, present it to readers, and fashion a solution that helps eliminate the cause.

Cause, Correlation, and Coincidence

Before elaborating on the role of causal evidence in writing effective problem-oriented essays, it is useful to distinguish among *cause*, *correlation*, and *coincidence*: three types of relationships that writers may encounter in investigating why a particular problem exists. The following information will help you distinguish among the three and focus on relevant causes and correlations.

Cause

When one thing produces an effect on another, it is the *cause* of that effect. For example, if we heat water on a stove and it begins to boil, we know that heating the water was the *cause* of its boiling. There is a direct cause and effect relationship between the heating and the boiling of water.

Of course, the causes of problems are seldom as obvious or clear-cut as boiling water, and problems often have multiple causes, some having a greater impact than others. For example, the tremendous decline in home sales that precipitated the 2007 recession had multiple causes, according to housing experts: the large increase in home prices that created a dwindling pool of people who could afford to buy a home; the unprecedented number of people who bought homes between 2003 and 2007, leaving fewer available potential buyers; and the increase in interest rates, which helped drive people out of the market. Each of those causes no doubt contributed to the housing collapse, but whether one cause was more responsible than another is a topic for further research.

When you write about one specific cause of a problem, you are saying that if that cause did not exist, neither would the problem. When you write about multiple causes of a problem, you are saying that if those causes didn't exist, neither would the problem. However, if only some of the causes were eliminated, the problem could still exist due to the remaining causes. For example, lowered interests rates could have attracted more potential home buyers to the declining market, but if the housing prices remained high, the lowered rates by themselves probably wouldn't have solved the problem.

Sometimes the most that we can infer about a particular action or condition is that it is a *probable cause* of a particular effect. For example, a woman works out at a fitness center and while doing the bench press, feels a twinge of pain in her right shoulder. The next morning, she wakes up with a sore, stiff right shoulder that hurts when she tries to lift her arm. While she can't say with perfect certainty that the weight lifting caused the shoulder problem - it could have been caused by how she slept that night - she knows it is highly probable that the weight lifting was responsible, certain enough to refrain from lifting weights until her shoulder heals.

Police frequently operate on probable cause in trying to solve crimes and identify suspects. For example, conditions may indicate that the probable cause of a house fire was arson, that the probable cause of a death was homicide, or that the probable cause of a home break-in was robbery. Further, they may determine that the probable cause, or motive, for the arson was insurance fraud, that the probable cause for the homicide was gang retaliation, or that the probable cause for the robbery was to obtain money for drugs. Based on probable cause, police can narrow down a pool of potential suspects and in many cases, identify a primary suspect. While probable cause does not have the certainty of indisputable cause - e.g. catching an arsonist, murderer, or robber in the act -, it is often the best that we have to work with, and the higher the probability, the more assuredly we can base a solution on it.

Correlation

A *correlation* is a relationship in which one thing has some effect on another. For example, studies reveal a correlation between children eating a healthy breakfast and performing well in grade school. While eating a healthy breakfast may not be a *direct cause* of good school performance, it may be a *contributing factor* for some children. Due in part to this correlation, many school districts have created free breakfast programs for children from poorer backgrounds. Of course, it can not be said that all children who eat a healthy breakfast will perform well or that all children who don't eat a healthy breakfast will perform poorly. The best we can say is that eating a healthy breakfast appears to have a positive effect on school performance for some children, that there is a *correlation* between the two.

What role do correlations play in writing about problems and solutions? If there are no direct causes that are evident for a particular problem, the next best thing is to discover correlations that link a problem to specific *contributing factors*. For example, the gap in educational performance between children from middle-class and poorer socio-economic backgrounds is a problem that schools have struggled with for years. However, it has been impossible to identify specific causes of the gap: conditions that have proven responsible for the problem in every situation

At the same time, there are a number studies that have shown a link between school performance and certain contributing factors: nutrition, pre-school preparation, parental involvement, teacher expectations, class size, and overall school quality. While none of these correlations rises to the level of cause, since they don't produce the same effect, or student outcome, in every situation, they do provide specific concerns for educators to address. Since poor nutrition, lack of pre-school preparation, weak parental involvement, low teacher expectations, large class sizes, and poor quality schools all contribute to poor school performance, eliminating those factors should help close the educational gap. The lack of clear-cut causes is perhaps one reason that the gap still exists today, but addressing the relevant correlations is probably the best available solution.

Coincidence

A *coincidence* - the chance concurrence of specific events or situations - has no causal or correlational value, and therefore no role in problem-solution essays. For example, let's say the stock market rises three hundred points on the same day that New York City employees end a six-month garbage workers' strike. That the two events occurred simultaneously is a *coincidence,* and no one knowledgeable of the stock market would suggest that the end of a local strike would have any impact on the market's direction. Another example would be the sky clearing and the sun appearing for the first time in days as the Pope stepped out on his Vatican balcony to address the waiting throng, a fortuitous occurrence but coincidental nonetheless.

Some people, however, try to make more out of a particular coincidence than exists, especially when it fits a particular bias. For example, some people believe that it was not a coincidence that Hurricane Katrina hit New Orleans most directly and caused great devastation. In the eyes of some, New Orleans was being "punished" by God for being an immoral city, a modern-day Sodom and Gomorrah. Most would agree, however, that imputing some divine cause to the disaster is utter nonsense. Writers should be aware that coincidences, while sometimes intriguing, have no causal value.

Activity 5.1

Identify the relationship in each of the following sentences: cause, probable cause, correlation, or coincidence. Assume for this activity that all of the information presented is factual. If there is not enough information to determine whether a causal or correlational relationship exists, write "insufficient information."

EXAMPLES

The powerful earthquake left a large crack in the living room wall of the apartment.
Relationship: cause

The mailman happened to pull up to my mailbox as I was putting out a letter to be mailed.
Relationship: coincidence

1. The electricity in the dormitory went out during a heavy rain and lightning storm.
   Relationship:

2. The center fielder lost sight of the fly ball in the sun, and it dropped to the ground in front of him.
   Relationship:

3. Adults who were abused as children are more likely to abuse children than adults who were not abused.
   Relationship:

4. Traffic on Highway 50 is the heaviest between 8:00 and 10:00 a.m. and 4:00 and 6:00 p.m. when commuters are on the road.
    Relationship:

5. In many U.S. cities, violent crime peaks during the hottest summer months and is lowest during the winter.
    Relationship:

6. Several baseball fans suffered from heat prostration during an afternoon game in Detroit where temperatures soared to 108 degrees.
    Relationship:

7. Children who attend church regularly with their parents are more likely to be church-goers as adults than children who do not attend church regularly.
    Relationship:

8. A study at Hart University concluded that students scored significantly higher on tests when they studied in groups rather than by themselves.
    Relationship:

9. On the day that over one-hundred detainees from Middle Eastern countries were released from Guantanamo Bay prison, large celebratory rallies occurred in Afghanistan, Iran, Syria, and Saudi Arabia.
    Relationship:

10. While the U.S. prison population increased by 5% in the past year, college enrollment dropped by 5%.
    Relationship:

To incorporate causal and correlational evidence effectively in your writing, consider the following suggestions.

1. **Before considering causal evidence, identify potential causes for a particular problem.** You may have in mind some possible causes for a problem, but you also may need to research the problem to find causes.

   For example, if you were writing about the high rate of teenage pregnancy in the U.S., you may think that its causes include the increasing number of teenagers who are sexually active and the lack of sex education among many teenagers. However, on researching the topic, you may learn that many teenage girls want to get pregnant and have babies, and that among some teenagers, being pregnant carries a status rather than a stigma. You never know what potential causes you may discover as you learn more about a topic, nor which causes will be validated by evidence.

2. **Whenever you present a cause (or a significant correlation) for a particular problem, provide the evidence that confirms its validity.** For example, if you write that a major cause of students dropping out of college is that they can't afford tuition, what evidence might you provide? A survey of college dropouts who confirm that they left school for financial reasons may provide good evidence. In addition, testimony from financial aid officers concluding that financial problems are a main cause of students leaving school could further convince readers.

3. **Providing sound causal evidence can eliminate the speculation that often leads to false causes.** For example, farmers in the Alhambra Valley who were struggling financially blamed the below-average availability of irrigation water for their woes and asked for an increased share of water released from the Alhambra Dam to solve the problem. However, a careful investigation of the problem revealed that the farmers' current financial problems were the same as in years when the irrigation water was plentiful. In other words, although the water situation probably didn't help the problem, it didn't cause it, so more water wouldn't solve the problem. Strong evidence, however, was found that supported other causes: the overproduction of crops which led to lower market prices, and competition from imported crops which cut into sales of

locally produced crops. In searching for evidence to support a particular cause, writers may turn up false causes, which activates their search for valid causes.

4. **Like causes, correlations should also be supported by evidence.** In the earlier example of educational studies revealing a correlation between good nutrition and successful school performance, what evidence did the studies provide? One study compared the performance of the same children in the school year prior to the implementation of the free breakfast program to the year the program was implemented. It found that the majority of children who regularly ate breakfast at school performed better than they had the previous year. While other factors may have also contributed to the children's improvement, the school district found the evidence encouraging enough to continue the program.

Activity 5.2

For each of the following causes (or correlations) presented, determine the type of evidence you might use to try and verify the cause.

EXAMPLE

One reason that students eat off campus more than in the cafeteria is that off-campus food is cheaper.

Evidence:
1. Do a survey of students who eat off campus to determine whether the relative cost is a significant reason.
2. Compare the price of food at nearby fast-food restaurants to the price of food in the cafeteria.
3. Research online for any articles or studies on college students' eating habits.

1. Unionizing undocumented agricultural workers is difficult because of the transient nature of their employment. **Evidence:**

2. The high administrative charges for administering medical insurance claims is one cause for the escalating cost of health insurance today. **Evidence:**

3. The large majority of high school drop-outs have a long history of poor academic performance.
Evidence:

4. The extremely low voter turn-out in the mid-year Buffalo election was caused by the severe snow storm on election day.
Evidence:

5. Financial problems cause a severe strain on marriages and contribute to the divorce rate.
Evidence:

6. Most young girls who have working mothers expect to have jobs themselves some day.
Evidence:

7. There is a shortage of doctors in many rural areas in the U.S. because most medical school graduates want to live and work in more desirable places.
Evidence:

8. One of the reasons that obesity among children has risen dramatically in the past fifteen years is that they get less exercise than in the past and consequently don't burn off as many calories.
Evidence:

9. The average age at which people marry is much higher than thirty years ago because it is more acceptable today for couples to live together without being married.
Evidence:

10. Binge drinking occurs frequently among college students because at many schools, it has become a "normal," accepted part of partying.
Evidence:

Finding Causal Evidence

Finding causal evidence to verify a possible cause of a problem can require some serious digging. You don't know exactly what your investigation will turn up or where it will lead you, making the investigation both interesting and at times perplexing. You may not find the kind of evidence you would like, and sometimes you have to reject an alleged cause that doesn't stand up to scrutiny.

For example, let's say that enrollment at a particular college has declined, and since the college receives state funding based on the size of enrollment, it is going to lose significant funding. It is important for the college to increase enrollment in future semesters, but until it knows the causes for the decline, it can't develop a plan.

Possible causes for the enrollment decline abound: an increase in the college's tuition; an improved employment situation in the area; a decline in the number of graduates from area high schools; a change in the overall population in the area; and the opening of a new college center by a rival college district nearby. In order for the college to address the most probable causes of the decline, it needs to find clear evidence of their existence.

To that end, the college might do some of the following:

1. **Surveying**. Specific surveys could be done to find out the following: the number of newly hired employees in the area who chose work over attending college; the number of students who opted to attend the rival district's college center rather the college; the number of potential students who didn't enroll due to the college's tuition increase.

2. **Comparing.** Relevant comparisons can be made by obtaining the following information: the number of graduating seniors in the area compared to the number in each of the past five years; the percentage of college students over thirty compared to the percentage under thirty to determine where the greatest decline occurred; the size of the overall population in the area compared to previous years to determine whether the population is declining; the college's enrollment decline compared to other community colleges to determine whether the problem is widespread and the causes similar.

3. **Interviewing**. Interviewing knowledgeable individuals may prove useful in corroborating other evidence: interviewing financial aid officers to help determine the impact of the tuition increase on students; interviewing high school counselors to determine the impact of the rival district's new center on their students' choice of colleges; interviewing different employers to help determine whether their newest employees had opted out of college; interviewing administrators from other colleges to find out the types of evidence-supported trends they have discovered that affected enrollment.

4. **Reading**. A significant amount of evidence may be found by

reading about similar situations in other times and/or places. While such research may not produce direct causal evidence, it can help determine the probability of a particular cause. For example, through reading different sources, the college may discover the following: similar situations in the college's history and how it responded to them; similar situations in other colleges' histories and how they responded to them; a cyclical pattern of declines and increases in the college's enrollment that has appeared immune to change; a nation-wide trend of declining enrollments in peak employment years and increased enrollments in lower employment years.

After thoroughly researching the possible causes for the enrollment decline, the college determined that there was substantial evidence supporting three causes: a decline in the number of area high school graduates, meaning fewer available college applicants; the sizable tuition increase, which had an impact on college enrollment throughout the state; and an improved employment situation in the area, which drew high school graduates and older adults away from the college. The new college center of the rival district appeared to have little effect on enrollment, and the overall population of the area had not declined appreciably. The college, then, fashioned a solution to the enrollment decline that addressed the three clearest causes of the problem based on the evidence.

Activity 5.3

For each possible cause (or correlation) given for the problem presented, determine what type of evidence might verify the cause and where it might be found.

EXAMPLE

Problem: The increase in prescription drug use by children

Possible causes:
1. America's prescription drug culture, where every problem has a drug to make it disappear.
2. The increasing amount of drugs prescribed by physicians for children diagnosed with various conditions.
3. The aggressive marketing of prescription drugs for children by pharmaceutical companies.

Causal evidence:

1. Try to find evidence of increased prescription drug use throughout the population, which would include children. Look on the Internet and in the library for articles and books on prescription drug use, and talk to local long-time pharmacists.

2. Try to find evidence of an increase in the number of children diagnosed with conditions such as ADHD, hyperactivity, and affective disorders, and the frequency with which drugs are prescribed.. Look on the Internet and in the library for articles and books on children's medical and mental disorders and prescription drug remedies, and talk to local physicians.

3. Provide as evidence specific television and magazine marketing campaigns by pharmaceutical companies aimed at children. Try to find evidence of a correlation between television marketing of specific drugs and an increase in public usage. Look on the Internet and in the library for articles on the effects of drug marketing on public consumption.

1. **Problem:** While Hanford University's football team is always one of the best in the conference, its men's basketball team is always near the bottom.
   Possible causes:
   1. Hanford gets better football coaches than basketball coaches.
   2. Hanford has a reputation as a football school, not a basketball school, so it gets better football recruits.
   3. Hanford's budget for the football program is four-times larger than for the basketball program.
   Causal evidence:

2. **Problem:** Criminal activity on the Landsford College campus has increased.
   Possible causes:
   1. Crime in the area surrounding the college has increased and carried over onto the campus.
   2. More non-students are coming on campus and committing much of the crime.
   3. Alcohol and drug use among students has increased, which has led to increased criminal activity.
   Causal evidence:

3. **Problem:** Binge drinking among students is a major problem at many colleges.

   Possible causes:

   1. Binge drinking is acceptable party behavior, a part of the drinking culture at many colleges.

   2. Many students binge drink because of peer pressure.

   3. Many students "drink to get drunk" to escape the stress and anxiety of going to college.

   4. Binge drinking is the worst at colleges with neighborhood stores that regularly market alcohol and have sales.

Activity 5.4

For practice, research one of the four possible causes of binge drinking among college students from the previous activity. Try to find evidence of its validity, and either provide the supporting evidence or explain why the cause does not appear to be valid.

Prewriting

For this unit's essay assignment, you write on a particular problem that interests or concerns you. Among your prewriting considerations is to identify the problem clearly, generate possible causes of the problem, find evidence to validate the actual causes (or correlations), determine the effects of the problem, and consider possible solutions that address the causes. A significant part of your prewriting time may be spent researching the problem and evaluating its causes based on the evidence you discover.

While the emphasis on causal evidence is new, your essay will have much in common with your previous essays: a thesis indicating your viewpoint on the topic; opening, middle, and ending sections; supportive reasons for your thesis; evidence to validate the reasons; addressing opposing viewpoints, which may mean responding to faulty causes or questionable solutions; and writing with a clear purpose for a specific reading audience.

The prewriting goal for most essay writers is similar: to do the preparation necessary to help them write an effective paper. How much preparation you do for a particular essay depends on many things: the complexity of the topic, how much you know or need to learn about it, how much material you want to generate before beginning to write, and the extent to which you want to organize your ideas. Prewriting preparation is an individual matter, and the text provides suggestions to use in ways that work best for you.

For some writers, the suggestions may provide a clear path that leads to writing the first draft with confidence. Other writers prefer a generalized plan with little detail and are comfortable exploring where their ideas will lead them. How you prepare for an essay depends on your writing personality and what approach seems most effective for you. Therefore, the upcoming prewriting suggestions may at the least help you begin thinking and planning for your essay, and at the most, provide a specific plan for marshaling potential essay material in a relatively organized fashion.

Topic Selection

Your topic for the upcoming paper is a problem that is serious and difficult enough that no easy solution is apparent. Part of your writing task is to come up with potential solutions that address the causes of the problem. It is of little value to write about problems that have already been solved or are of little consequence.

To help you decide on a topic for your upcoming essay, consider the following suggestions.

1. **Select a problem that concerns or affects you, and that**

may also affect others. It may be in any field - politics, education, sports, technology, health, law enforcement, finance, college-related, child-related, or a social problem - and at any level: local, state, national, or international.

2. **Select a problem that is serious enough to engage readers' interest**. Any problem that affects readers and is not easily solvable may pique their interest.

3. **You may select a difficult long-standing problem or a relatively new problem.** Long-standing problems present the challenge of fashioning a different solution from the ones that have failed, and newer problems often require significant probing to determine their actual causes.

4. **You may want to do some research before deciding on a topic: reading or talking to experts about problems in different fields.** You will be spending considerable time working on the problem you choose, so take your time to find a topic that you really want to investigate.

Activity 5.5

After considering the four suggestions presented, select a problem as the topic for your upcoming essay.

EXAMPLE
      Potential topic: High school drop-out rate

Causal Evidence

Once you have selected a problem, you are ready to start digging into it, trying to identify and understand the problem clearly and determine its causes. With each potential cause that you generate or discover, try to find evidence to validate it. If there is no such evidence, or if the evidence indicates that it is not valid, you would probably not use it, or if it was a commonly held cause, present it in a way that readers would discount it.

    To determine the causes of your problem and provide evidence to validate them, consider the following suggestions.

1. **Before looking into causes, determine exactly what the problem is.** For example, the writer who selected the "high school drop-out rate" as her topic wanted to know how schools defined their drop-out rate. She found that most schools defined a high school drop-out as someone who left

school sometime between their freshman year and the end of their senior year, and didn't return. She used that definition of a "drop-out" for her essay.

2. **From your own ideas and research, generate some possible causes for the problem**. Your "causes" may turn out to be probable causes or correlations (contributing factors), but you don't need to make a distinction at this point.

3. **Evaluate each cause by trying to find evidence to validate it.** Your evidence might be factual, empirical, logical or comparative, depending on the cause. Question any possible cause that you can't substantiate with evidence.

4. **In some cases, you may be evaluating correlations rather than causes**. For example, as previously noted, in addressing the problem of the success gap in grade school between children of different backgrounds, studies have indicated a correlation between parental involvement and a child's success. While parental involvement is not a direct cause of the success - it is still the children who have to perform -, it may contribute to that success, enough so that many elementary schools today stress parental involvement.

   If a correlation appears to contribute to a problem significantly, try to find evidence validating the correlation just as you would a cause.

5. **In compiling evidence to validate a cause, consider any type of compelling evidence.** This evidence may include studies by credible institutions, large surveys, relevant statistics, significant comparisons, confirmation by experts, and personal experiences and observations. Make use of any evidence that lends credibility to the cause or correlation.

6. **Don't accept that a cause or correlation is valid just because it is presented as such.** Many times articles on problems simply present causes without substantiating them or distinguishing cause from correlation.

   For example, an article on steroid use among high school students cited the following as causes for students taking steriods: wanting to get" bigger and faster" to perform better in sports; mimicking the behavior of older athletes who take steroids; conforming to the culture of a particular sports program where steroid use is common; coaches "turning their backs" and ignoring the problem; students wanting to "bulk up" to look better and gain status. The article provided no evidence to validate any cause, and it mixed causes - e.g. wanting to get "bigger and faster" - with correlations - e.g.

coaches ignoring the problem. Some of the causes and correlations may have been valid, but if the writer provides no evidence, readers should question them, which weakens the essay's impact.

Activity 5.6

Following the suggestions presented, identify possible causes (and in some cases correlations) for your problem. Then investigate each cause, trying to find evidence to validate it, and reject or question any cause for which no evidence is found.

   As you read, you may find other causes or correlations you want to include.

EXAMPLE

Topic: high school drop-out rate

Possible causes for students dropping out:
1. lack of success in school
2. lack of support from parent or parents
3. getting expelled
4. getting into criminal activity, e.g. selling drugs
5. following older siblings or friends who dropped out
6. having to work
7. not having friends in school or being an outcast
8. not seeing a connection between school and success
9. an "anti-school" culture where success in school is ridiculed

Evidence:
1. Several articles confirmed the lack of success as a factor based on surveys of student drop-outs.
2. Several articles confirmed lack of parental support as a factor based on surveys of educators, i.e. teachers, counselors, administrators.
3. No compelling evidence to support getting expelled as a significant factor.
4. Several articles confirmed that students who were heavily into drugs or alcohol or into criminal or gang activity were more likely to drop out.
5. Several articles confirmed that students who had siblings or friends who had dropped out or were not in school contributed to their dropping out.

6. Several articles confirmed that having to work caused many students to drop out, based on surveys of drop-outs.

7. No evidence to support that not having friends is a significant factor.

8. No compelling evidence to support that not seeing connection between school and success is a factor.

9. No compelling evidence to support that an anti-school culture is a significant factor.

Additional causes discovered:

1. Several articles agreed that dropping out derives from a culmination of years of failure that begins in elementary school.

2. Several articles agreed that factors contributing to a student dropping out are often multiple and tied together.

3. Several surveys of drop-outs noted that they were bored with school and had no interest in continuing.

Effects

An important part of providing the "total picture" in a problem/solution essay is to identify the effects of the problem and who or what is affected. To understand the seriousness of a problem, readers want to know its impact. If a writer can show that the effects of a problem can be devastating, his readers' interest will pick up.

Effects, like causes, should be substantiated whenever possible. For example, for the sample topic on high school drop-outs, let's say one of the alleged effects on drop-outs is that they are more likely to be incarcerated than students who graduate. This may or may not be true, and it is the writer's task to find the evidence to confirm the effect.

Sometimes writers use alleged effects as a "scare tactic" to influence readers' behavior. For example, some opponents of stem cell research argue that if embryonic stem cells can be used for medical purposes, the ultimate effect will be that human embryos will be harvested for medical purposes. While there is no evidence to support the speculative allegation, some readers may be influenced by the fearful scenario. As writers and readers, we need to separate actual effects from speculation, which often appeals to readers' fears at the expense of their reason.

To present the effects of a problem most effectively, consider these suggestions.

1. From your own ideas and research, identify as many alleged

effects as you can.

2. Try to find evidence to substantiate each effect, and move forward with those that appear valid.

3. Evaluate the relative seriousness or impact of each effect to determine what to include in your essay.

Identify who or what is affected by the problem so that any solution focuses on those who are most affected. For example, if the problem is the performance gap in math and science between boys and girls in high school, and it is determined that the gap appears from sixth grade on, the solution to the problem could focus on girls in the sixth and seventh grade, where the problem seems to originate.

Activity 5.7

Following the suggestions provided, identify possible effects of the problem and find evidence of their validity. You may also find additional effects through your research. In addition, identify who or what is most affected by the problem.

EXAMPLE

    Problem: high school drop-out rate

    Possible effects:
1. Drop-outs are more likely to be unemployed than high school graduates.
2. Drop-outs are more likely to work in lower-paying jobs than graduates.
3. Drop-outs are more likely to be involved in crime and to be incarcerated.
4. Drop-outs are more likely to be on welfare than graduates.
5. Drop-outs are more likely to have children who eventually drop out of school.
6. Drop-outs are more likely to abuse drugs and alcohol.
7. Drop-outs are more likely to live in poverty.

    Evidence:
1. Several articles based on studies agreed that the financial effects of dropping out of school were significant: higher unemployment, lower-paying jobs, being on welfare, and living in poverty.
2. Several articles confirmed through research evidence

that drop-outs were more likely to be incarcerated and abuse drugs and alcohol.

3. Two articles based on studies concluded that the children of drop-outs were more likely to drop out themselves.

Additional effects:

1. There is a financial effect on the economy as drop-outs contribute less and cost more as a result of incarcerations and welfare.

Who is affected:

Studies show that a larger percentage of African-American, Latino, and Native American students from lower socio-economic backgrounds drop out of school than white and Asian American students.

Solutions

Difficult, persistent problems are not easy to solve. Sometimes the solutions are not focused on the root causes of the problem. For example, America's "war on drugs," which has not stemmed the tide of drug use in the U.S., has concentrated unsuccessfully on the "supply" side of the problem while failing to address adequately the "demand" side: people's appetite for illicit drugs.

Sometimes the problems are so complex or the causes so entrenched that progress is very slow. For example, poverty in America, the richest nation in the world, is still pervasive in our inner cities and rural belts despite years of governmental and private sector attempts to reduce the problem. Other times the solutions are quite evident but the public or political will to solve them isn't strong enough. For example, if all Americans replaced their gas-guzzling vehicles with hybrids, electric cars, and bicycles, air pollution, atmosphere-warming emissions, and America's dependence on oil would be significantly reduced. However, at this point, most Americans are not willing to make the change.

To consider a possible solution or solutions to your problem, keep the following in mind:

1. **Realistically, what would it mean to "solve" the problem?** Would it mean to eliminate it completely, reduced it significantly, or make some demonstrable headway?

2. **Given the major causes (or correlations) of the problem, how might each best be addressed?** What approach would have the best chance of reducing or eliminating each cause?

What causes are most significant and need the greatest attention?

3. **What, if anything, is currently being done to address the problem, and what is working?** You are probably not the first person to consider your topic a problem, and including current solutions that show promise may be a part of your proposal.

4. **What solutions may realistically work, given possible financial, political, or logistical limitations?** For example, a solution to global warming could be to ban the burning of all fossil fuels for industrial or vehicular use, but we know that isn't a viable solution. The most idealistic solution may not be the most workable one.

5. **How can progress towards eliminating or reducing the problem be determined?** For various problems, how might progress be shown: by a world-wide reduction in greenhouse gases? By a reduced percentage of students dropping out of high school? By a reduced percentage of teenage pregnancies? By an increase in economic productivity in the city's downtown area? By a significant reduction in the cost of college tuition? Some yardstick is needed to measure progress and determine whether a solution is working.

6. **Solutions may come in a variety of packages: new, creative approaches that haven't been tried; dusted-off approaches that may work in a new environment; or new solutions added to on-going approaches that appear promising.**

   For example, the government's latest attempt to reform the country's health care system includes an old solution - offering government-sponsored health care for all Americans - with a new twist - offering the government program alongside the existing private health insurance options to provide competition and reduce the cost of insurance. Solving a persistent problem doesn't always mean finding a completely new approach. Your solution might include something old, something new, and something on-going, configured in the best way to solve the problem.

Activity 5.8

Based on your own ideas and research, generate a possible solution(s) to your problem which addresses its most significant causes or correlations. Feel free to include in your solution approaches that have proven successful, perhaps in other colleges, cities, or countries, or on a small scale.

EXAMPLE

Problem: high school drop-out rate

Possible solutions:
1. Intervention program that identifies and helps elementary students who aren't succeeding since they are at risk to be high school drop-outs.
2. Mentoring program by community members who take an interest in students' progress and encourage them to stay in school.
3. Intervention program that identifies and helps students in their freshman year who are at risk of dropping out.
4. Greater parental involvement at high school level.
5. Creating a "connection" between high school students and school by encouraging participation in school activities and developing more activities of interest to students.

Thesis

As in your previous essays, your thesis for the upcoming essay presents your viewpoint on the topic. It may touch upon the seriousness of the problem, the importance of solving it, the need to consider new solutions, the belief that the problem can be solved, the need for readers to recognize the problem, or some combination of ideas.

To generate your thesis for the upcoming essay, consider these suggestions.

1. **Generate a thesis that best reflects your viewpoint on the problem that you can develop and support in your essay.** For example, if the effects of the problem are a critical part of the essay, those effects may be a strong focus for the writer's thesis: *If students continue to drop out of high school at the current rate, the problems of poverty, overcrowded*

prisons, and long welfare roles will only get worse. If getting readers to buy into the solution is critical for reducing the problem, a writer's thesis may reflect that: *The student drop-out problem is definitely solvable, but only if the community gets behind the solution and demands that the school district steps up to the plate.*

2. **Generate a thesis that helps create a perspective for readers to view the problem from.** For example, if it is important that they understand the great challenge the problem presents and the great rewards if it is solved, the thesis could help provide that perspective: *No educational problem has proven more challenging than the high school drop-out rate, and nothing offers greater rewards than keeping millions of potential drop-outs in school.*

3. **Generate a thesis that is consistent with the evidence you present.** If your thesis doesn't mesh with the evidence, or if your evidence points more clearly to a different thesis, that disparity can confuse readers and weaken the impact of your essay.

Activity 5.9

Based on what you have learned about the problem, generate a thesis statement that reflects your viewpoint and that you can develop and support in your essay.

EXAMPLE

> **Topic:** High school drop-out rate
>
> **Thesis:** The high school drop-out rate is a major educational problem, but any school district that is determined to keep students in school can be successful.

Audience and Purpose

As a writer, there are many benefits to writing a problem/solution essay: learning to distinguish between cause and correlation, researching and providing evidence to validate causes and effects, understanding the connection between causes and solutions, creating solutions different from what has been tried, and using relevant causal, factual, logical, empirical, and comparative evidence to help make your case.

The practical value in writing a problem-oriented essay, however, is to contribute towards solving a serious problem. That is generally the primary reason for writing a problem/solution essay although there may be other purposes, such as shedding light on a problem that has gone largely unnoticed, or emphasizing the need to pursue a new and different direction to solve a particular problem.

A major consideration in trying to solve a problem is to influence an audience that can help carry out the solution. The best solution is of little value if it doesn't resonate with the people who can make it happen. Sometimes the greatest challenge in writing a problem/solution essay is to convince readers to take action.

To determine the audience and purpose for your upcoming essay, consider the following questions:

1.   **What is my primary purpose in writing the essay?** Do you want to help solve a particular problem? Raise the consciousness of readers about an existing problem? Change the fruitless direction that a current solution is taking?

2.   **What is the best audience to reach to accomplish my purpose?** What group of people is in the best position to implement a solution to the problem? Who might be affected by the problem that could help convince that group of people to take action? For example, if a school district has been reluctant to implement a comprehensive plan for reducing the high school drop-out rate, the parents of high school students might be the best audience to put pressure on the district to do something.

3.   **What do I need to know and keep in mind about my audience?** How knowledgeable are they about the problem? What differing viewpoints might they hold? How are they affected by the problem?

4.   **What is the best way to accomplish my purpose with this particular audience?** How can they be convinced that the problem needs addressing and that your proposed solution will work?

Activity 5.9

Following the suggestions presented, decide on a purpose and audience for your upcoming essay, what you need to know and keep in mind about your audience, how you might best accomplish your purpose, and the best way to reach your audience.

EXAMPLE

   Topic: High school drop-out rate

   Purpose: To provide a solution that will help reduce the current drop-out rate

Audience: Local K-12 district trustees and administrators, and parents of potential drop-outs. I need to assume district officials and I are on the same side on this issue - wanting to reduce the drop-out rate - and to communicate with them as fellow problem-solvers. It would do little good to belittle their current efforts at keeping students in school.

Success: To accomplish my purpose, district officials need to be convinced that the problem is serious in their district, that the consequences for drop-outs are devastating, and that there are things to do that aren't being done to help solve the problem.

Means: Deliver copies of essay to district officials at a board meeting, prefaced by a brief oral presentation to explain purpose. I don't yet know how I could communicate directly with parents of at-risk students.

Drafting

Through your prewriting efforts, you have the basic components of your essay in mind: the problem, its causes, its effects, and possible solutions. During the drafting and revision process, your task is to present this information, as well as your personal insights, in the best manner to accomplish your purpose.

A writer cannot always assume that her reading audience feels the same way that she does about the problem. Readers may know little about the problem, consider it less of a problem than the writer, have little concern for its effects or who is affected, question the efficacy of the writer's solution, or feel that what is currently being done to solve the problem is enough.

An important part of your writing task, then, is to convince readers that what you have to say is worth reading and considering seriously. Merely presenting information, no matter how impressive you feel it is, may not convince readers or engage their interest. To have the greatest impact on readers, how you present the information, with your readers' response in mind, is as important as the information that you present.

Drafting Guidelines

In writing the first draft of your essay, consider the following suggestions.

Opening. Engage your readers' interest and draw their attention to the problem in a compelling way. Your choice of possible openings is substantial: an anecdotal incident or situation relating the problem, factual information revealing the enormity or gravity of the problem, a disturbing future scenario if the problem is not solved, a personalized example of how the problem affects one individual, a particularly devastating effect of the problem, a surprising or shocking statistic that reveals the seriousness of the problem, or some combination of approaches. You can present your thesis in the opening or save it for the conclusion, as a lead-in to the solution. Read the optional openings presented with the sample draft to see different approaches.

Middle. Most typically with a problem-oriented essay, the middle paragraphs present the causes (or correlations) and effects of the problem, who or what is affected, and the evidence to validate each cause or effect. In addition, you might begin the middle paragraphs with some explanatory and background information on the problem and conclude by acknowledging and responding to opposing viewpoints.

1. **Opposing viewpoints.** In a problem-oriented essay, oppos-

ing viewpoints may include disagreement over the seriousness of a problem, its causes or effects, or the best solution. For example, on the topic of the high school drop-out rate, some readers may not agree that the problem is that serious, that the effects are that devastating, or that what is already being done to keep students in school is not enough. The writer may decide to respond directly to only one argument - that what is already being done is sufficient - and let her evidence speak for itself on the seriousness of the problem and its effects.

In writing your draft, consider the most critical points of opposition and how best to respond to them. Ask yourself, "What opposing viewpoint could be most detrimental to my solution being implemented?" and respond to that viewpoint.

2. **Source acknowledgment**. As in your previous essays, it is important to acknowledge the source of any information that you have found through your research. Providing sources makes your evidence most credible and distinguishes source information from you own thoughts and responses.

For some causes or effects of your problem, you may find widespread agreement within the literature that you read or experts that you talk to. Rather than provide source acknowledgments for every source that presents the same cause or effect, you may reference the sources as a group: A number of educational studies agreed that parental involvement is critical to the educational success of grade school children.

Another way to present broadly corroborated findings is to reference the sources as a group but also acknowledge one particularly credible source: A number of educational studies, including a 2008 study by the Harvard School of Education, concluded that parental involvement is critical to the educational success of grade school children.

3. **Organization**. Organize your middle paragraphs to present your ideas most effectively. While the causes of a problem are often presented before the effects, some writers lead with the effects to get the readers' attention, then follow with the causes. Whether you present the causes or effects first, and whether you provide some background information before presenting either, depends on what seems the best approach for your topic.

Sometimes as you get into writing your draft, an organic flow develops that provides a sense of what most naturally comes next. For example, in the upcoming sample draft on the high school drop-out rate, the writer realized that providing the devastating effects of dropping out followed most naturally from the background information she presented on the seriousness of the problem. The organizational "flow" that developed from her writing countermanded her preconceived organizational plan.

4. **Ending**. Your ending to a problem-oriented essay usually provides the solution or solutions that you are proposing. It should be clear to readers how your solution will address the problem's causes. In addition, your ending should clarify your purpose: why are you writing to this particular audience about this problem? What does it have to do with them, and what can they do about it? A problem-oriented essay should focus clearly on the solution. Write an ending that will give that solution the best chance of seeing the light of day.

5. **Paragraphing**. The paragraphing of a problem-oriented essay is rather straightforward. The opening paragraph or two introduce the topic and present the thesis statement. Each middle paragraph presents and develops a different cause or effect, including evidence to validate it. The ending paragraph(s) presents the proposed solution to the problem and emphasizes the writer's purpose. Change paragraphs as you move to something new in your essay: a different cause, a different effect, a response to an opposing viewpoint, or from beginning to middle or middle to ending.

6. **Audience and purpose**. As you write, keep in mind your readers and purpose, writing in ways that will have the greatest impact on readers and give you the best chance of accomplishing your purpose.

     Write in a tone that you feel is most effective for presenting the problem, establish any connections with readers that will help you accomplish your purpose, and consider the impact of everything that you write on your audience.

Activity 5.10

Read the following sample first draft, including the three optional openings that show some alternative ways to begin an essay. Read the first draft of the essay, noting the organization of the essay; the evidence provided to validate the effects and causes; the source acknowledgments for all researched information; the acknowledgment and response to differing perspectives; the solutions (strategies) presented to attack the problem; and the ending paragraphs, which summarize key elements and convey the writer's purpose to readers.

Then write the first draft of your essay, keeping in mind the drafting suggestions presented.

Sample First Draft

Dropping Out of High School (audience: local K-12 school officials)

Optional Opening #1
Three years ago Jonathan Edwards was a freshman at Lincoln High School. Today, he is an inmate at the Haskins Juvenile Facility, where he will spend the next two years for armed robbery before being transferred to a men's state prison. Three years ago Maria Gutierrez was a classmate of Jonathan's and a promising student. Today, Maria works at a garment factory to help support her one-year-old daughter who stays with Maria's mother while she works. Neither Jonathan nor Maria will walk the halls of Lincoln High again.

Jonathan and Maria are among the millions of high school dropouts across the country who never graduate and face the bleak futures of undereducated young adults in America. Their life circumstances may not mirror either Jonathan or Maria's, but the outcome for most students who leave school early is similar: a future of limited and stark options. The high drop-out rate among high school students is one of the most severe problems facing our schools today, and the results are devastating and far-reaching not only for the drop-outs but for our society as a whole. It is a problem that every school district must confront and do everything possible to eradicate.

Optional Opening #2
Of the five hundred incoming freshman walking the halls of Reed High School, over one-third of them will vanish sometime within the next three years, never to walk the halls again. This silent epidemic strikes like an educational plague that takes students from their schools before their time, leaving them to face the outside world before they are prepared. The results are devastating and lasting, and the plague continues year after year.

Nothing is more damaging to a young person's future than dropping out of school, and millions of high school students drop out every year across America. The problem seldom makes newspaper headlines, most school districts keep their student drop-out rates relatively quiet, and many parents of drop-outs either are not in a position to make waves or are a part of the problem themselves. The high drop-out rate is not, however, a problem without solutions. Any school district that dedicates itself to reducing the number of students who drop out can have success, and while it isn't easy, we owe it to every student students to make a monumental effort.

Optional Opening #3

What if there were a way to get many Americans off of welfare, significantly reduce the prison population, improve the economy, reduce the unemployment rate, reduce the crime rate, reduce the teenage pregnancy rate, and improve the lives of millions of young adults by doing just one thing? This probably sounds like the false promise of some political candidate desperate for votes or an infomercial that promises more than it can deliver. However, there is a way to accomplish these goals that relies neither on smoke and mirrors nor works only on paper. What needs to be done is to drastically reduce the drop-out rate of America's high school students, a challenging but achievable goal.

Over a million high school students drop out of school every year. The results are not only devastating and long-lasting for the young people who drop out, but the negative impact ripples through our society. The high school drop-out rate is one of the biggest problems facing our schools today across the country. The difference between a young person dropping out or graduating from high school can be the difference between a bleak or a successful future. Every school district needs to be on a crusade to keep students in school. Their future, and a better future for our country, depend on it.

Sample First Draft

Senior graduation night at Hawthorne High School is an exciting event. Over a thousand people gather to celebrate the achievements of the three-hundred and fifty graduates who have successfully navigated the waters of their twelve-year school careers. Everyone is proud: the young people graduating, their parents and friends, and school officials, who praise this current class of graduates as one of the finest ever.

However, how would the mood change if among the three-hundred and fifty seated graduates were one-hundred and fifty empty chairs, each silently representing a member of the class who had dropped out somewhere along the way? Certainly there would be a sense of loss and sadness, not unlike the mourning of soldiers who never make it back from war. The one-hundred and fifty empty chairs would be powerful testimony to an educational problem occurring in most school districts in the country: the high drop-out rate among America's high school students. Until those one-hundred and fifty empty chairs are filled with graduates, no school district should feel proud or celebratory. There is still much work to be done in keeping students in school and millions of lives to be saved.

Estimates of the percentage of students dropping out of high school range from as high as thirty per cent, according to separate reports by the public policy firm Civic Enterprises and the Manhattan Institute, to twenty percent, according to the National Department of Education and state education reports from California and Massachusetts. There is agreement among reports that the dropout rate for African-American, Latino, and Native American students is higher than among other students. Even if the actual dropout rate is nearer the twenty percent range, more than a million students are dropping out of school every year across the nation, a disturbingly high number.

But is dropping out of high school all that bad? Don't we read about self-made millionaires who quit school to pursue their dreams? Such is not the case for the vast majority of dropouts. Report after report agrees with the profound and long-lasting effects chronicled in the Civic Enterprise's publication, "The Silent Epidemic." Students who drop out of high school are more likely to live in poverty, be unemployed, be in prison, receive Federal or state assistance, have health problems, or be in minimum-wage, dead-end jobs. In short, their futures appear bleak and dismal compared to high school graduates, who conversely are more likely to be employed and in higher paying jobs, and much less likely to be in prison or on welfare. It is not an exaggeration to say that for every young person who can be helped to stay in school, a life has been saved.

The repercussions of dropping out of school go well beyond the individual. People who are unemployed don't contribute to the economic well-being of the community or the country. Dropouts who end up in prison or on welfare cost taxpayers millions of dollar annually. Dropouts who are involved in crime make our neighborhoods and communities more dangerous. And as dropouts are more likely to live in poverty, their children suffer the same plight. The effects of millions of dropouts annually touch many lives, making it a societal as well as an individual problem.

Given the devastating effects of dropping out of school, why does the dropout rate remain so persistently high? Obviously, most students who drop out don't see the connection between their decision and its effect on their future. Young people tend to live in the moment and not consider the ramifications of their actions years down the road. The reasons that students drop out seem to be relatively well known, but knowing the causes and solving the problem are two very different things.

According to a 2008 U.S. Department of Education report , there are several significant reasons that students drop out of high school before graduating, all of which appear throughout the literature on the dropout issue. The lack of parental support is a common factor for students dropping out. If parents aren't concerned about their children's education, why should their children be? Outside influences are another factor: friends or relatives who aren't in school, or gangs who lure teens from school to the streets. A number of teens drop out because of learning disabilities such as ADHD or dyslexia, which prevent them from succeeding and often aren't addressed in overcrowded classrooms. Teens also drop out to find jobs to help out their family in poor financial condition, and they seldom return.

A lack of interest in school is a big reason for students dropping out, confirmed by several surveys on students who drop out. They are bored with their classes and don't see the value of being in school. Drug and alcohol abuse is another major reason for students to drop out. Not surprisingly, students who are on drugs or who abuse alcohol are seldom going to succeed in school. Depression and physical illnesses both contribute to the dropout rate, as does physical, sexual, and verbal abuse. Teens who are abused often run away from home and consequently drop out of school.

Teen pregnancy is still a cause of many students dropping out of school although the numbers have dropped significantly, according to the U.S. Department of Education, since many schools have made it possible for pregnant teens to remain in school, and some districts have even created alternative schools for pregnant teens. Finally, there is an anti-educational culture among some teens that views school as a waste of time and school achievement as something to belittle, a culture that accepts drug dealing and prostitution as acceptable lifestyles.

Curiously, the U.S. Department of Education report ignores two factors that are prominent among the literature on why high school students drop out: lack of educational success and regularly missing school. Clearly, students who don't do well in school year after year are likely candidates to drop out, and the more that a student misses school, the less likely his chances for success. An additional factor confirmed by various surveys of high school dropouts is students not feeling connected in any way to the school. They don't join teams or clubs or participate in school activities, have nothing to look forward to at school, and take no pride or feel any loyalty towards the school. Another common finding is that for most teens, dropping out is not a spur-of-the-moment decision. Rather, it comes from a culmination of negative experiences that often go back as far as elementary school - lack of success, lack of parental support, lack of connectedness - that finally take their toll.

The number of factors that influence a student's decision to leave school is rather daunting. Given the myriad of factors, where does one start in crafting a viable solution that addresses those factors? The complexity of the problem is certainly one of the reasons that it has remained so resistant to change, but the problem is not unsolvable, and there are schools across the country that are attacking the problem with some success. Can these successes be duplicated across the country in every school district?

Certainly a first step in reducing the dropout rate is acknowledging the problem and marshaling a network of people to begin working on it. In Jackson, Mississippi in 2008, for example, a group of educators, students, community, and church leaders from across the state met to find ways to improve dramatically on Mississippi's dropout crisis. The goal of the created On the Bus program was to inspire community members to action and to build a plan to be initiated in all school districts across the state. The ultimate goal: to reduce the state dropout rate by fifty percent in the next five years. The state of Mississippi acknowledged the seriousness of the problem, involved community members as well as educators in confronting the problem, crafted a plan to implement in every school district, and set an ambitious and exciting goal to achieve. There is no reason that every state, or every individual school district, can't take similar steps.

An extensive report by the National Dropout Prevention Center, "Dropout Risk Factors and Exemplary Programs," highlights the types of programs across the country that have proven effective in reducing the high school dropout rate. The most successful programs were multifaceted, targeting a range of factors that contribute to students dropping out. The following strategies were found to be effective in combating the high dropout rate.

Academic support and intervention. Targeting "at risk" students at various educational stages and providing remediation, academic skills enhancement, and using instructional methods designed to increase student engagement in the learning process.

After school programs. Providing rewarding, challenging, and age-appropriate after-school activities in a safe, positive, structured environment.

Behavioral intervention. Individualized interventions designed to decrease a specific behavior by shaping and reinforcing a desirable alternative behavior, designed to improve an individual's overall quality of life and enhance the chances for school success.

Career development/job placement. Providing social, personal, and vocational skills and employment opportunities to help youth achieve economic success, avoid involvement in criminal activity, and increase educational functioning.

Case management. Coordinating services for youth/families, linking child and/or parents to resources and services such as job counseling, mental health counseling, financial management, and medical care.

Conflict resolution/anger management. Encouraging non-violent dispute resolution through a variety of processes including negotiation, mediation, community conferencing, and peer mediation.

Court advocacy/probation/transition. Individuals serve as advocates for youth with social services, the juvenile system, or school system to make sure they receive appropriate services and have support during transition and reintegration after they have been released.

Family engagement. Educating parents on particular parenting skills, management skills, and communication skills, and providing training on ways to assist children academically; focus on improving maladaptive patterns of family interaction and communication; create activities that involve families in their children's education.

Gang prevention/intervention. Prevent youth from joining gangs and intercede with existing gang members during crisis conflict situations.

Mental health services. Substance abuse treatment programs and counseling related to substance abuse.

Mentoring. Relationships created over a long period of time where an older, caring, more experienced person provides help to the younger person as he or she goes through school.

Pregnancy prevention. Aims to reduce teenage pregnancy rate through education.

School/class environment. Reorganizing classes or grades to create smaller units where students get more individual attention and feel more connectedness.

Substance abuse prevention. Reduce the use or abuse of illegal drugs and alcohol by educating youth to the effects.

Teen parent support. Providing training and assistance to assist teen parents in staying in school and developing family life.

Truancy prevention. Promoting regular school attendance through an increase in parental involvement, participation of law enforcement, and the use of mentors.

The list of effective strategies proven in specific programs to reduce the dropout rate is extensive and addresses the range of factors that contribute to students dropping out. Each individual district, according to the California Dropout Research Project affiliated with the University of California system, needs to assess its own situation and create a program based on its students' needs. It is also obvious by the strategies presented that solving the dropout problem requires the involvement of much more than just the school district. That is why Philadelphia's Project U Turn, aimed at turning around the dropout rate problem, is a collaborative effort involving the public school system, city agencies, family court, community-based organizations, literacy providers, and researchers. The most successful dropout prevention programs have the support and involvement of the community.

There is little question that the high school dropout rate in American schools is a significant and persistent problem affecting over a million students every year. There is also evidence across the country that there are programs and strategies to reduce the dropout rate that are having a positive effect. Defenders of the status quo argue that it is the ills of society that create the dropout problem and that the schools can't change the world outside their doors. However, the success of numerous programs shows that no matter how difficult, dangerous, distracting, or depressing the environment that children grow up in, there are ways to keep them in school and make their futures brighter.

As the California Dropout Research Project attests, the success of any dropout reduction program begins with a school district acknowledging the problem, having the will and determination to solve it, and creating a collaborative, comprehensive plan that involves the community. There are a number of successful programs available for districts to emulate, and successful emulation, according to the National Dropout Prevention Center, means duplicating the program verbatim rather than revising or scaling it down for budgetary purposes.

Creating a successful dropout prevention program is a huge undertaking for any district, one that requires funding, community involvement, and the patience to continue with a program, perhaps for years, before significant results may be seen. However, the results of significantly reducing the dropout rate are stunning: improving the lives of millions of our youth, reducing the crime and incarceration rate, reducing the welfare rolls, reducing unemployment, improving family life, improving the economy, and creating more unified, involved, and caring communities.

In states where the government does not feel school districts have done enough, such as California and Virginia, legislation is being considered to force districts to implement changes to reduce the dropout rate. However, the most successful dropout prevention models are grassroots efforts, with the commitment coming from the school districts and communities to fix their own problems. Top-down governmental intervention programs would seem a last resort, but that prospect may be a wake-up call for districts who are lagging in implementing a comprehensive dropout prevention program.

Revision

Once your first draft is on paper, you can see most clearly what can be improved. You can view the draft more critically from the readers' perspective and evaluate how well you have accomplished your purpose. Revision often results in more fine-tuning than major overhauling, but those changes may be significant in how readers respond to your essay.

Revision Guidelines

To revise your current draft most effectively, consider the following suggestions.

1. **Opening**. Read your opening to see how well you have introduced the problem, engaged your readers' interest, and presented your thesis. What might you add or change to make your opening stronger and more effective?

2. **Explanatory/Background Information**. Immediately following the opening, do you provide any explanatory or background information that will help readers understand the problem, its seriousness or pervasiveness, or how it began? Ask yourself what readers should know to understand and take the problem seriously and whether you have provided such information.

3. **Organization**. Read the essay from your readers' perspective. Are the various aspects of the problem - its causes, effects, solutions - presented in the best order? Is it most effective to present the causes before the effects, or vice-versa? Are there any paragraphs or sentences that might fit better in a different location? What organizational changes might you make to improve the essay?

4. **Causes/effects**. Do you present the causes and effects of the problem in a clear and effective manner? Do readers understand which causes and effects are most important? What might you add or change to highlight the causes or effects of the problem more strikingly?

5. **Evidence/acknowledgments**. Do you provide enough evidence to convince readers that each cause, correlation or effect that you present is valid? Do you put most of the source evidence in your own words? Do you provide source acknowledgments to add credibility to your evidence and clearly distinguish the research information from your own thoughts and responses? Check to make sure that readers

know where your source evidence came from and when you are presenting your own ideas.

6. **Differing viewpoints**. Are differing viewpoints that readers might hold acknowledged and addressed in the essay? Opinions may differ on the seriousness of the problem, its causes or effects, or ways to solve it. Have you responded to viewpoints that could get in the way of readers considering your solution?

7. **Solutions**. Is your solution to the problem presented in a way that will have the greatest impact on readers? Is it clear which aspects of the solution may be most critical to solving the problem? Have you convinced readers that the solution is workable and attacks the causes of the problem?

8. **Paragraphing.** Check your paragraphing to make sure you change paragraphs as you move from opening to middle and middle to ending, and as you complete one idea and move to the next. Consider dividing an overly long paragraph into two and combining or developing pairs or strings of short, successive paragraphs.

9. **Wording.** Read each sentence to see how the wording might be improved. Eliminate unnecessary words or phrases, reward awkward or vague sentences, and replace questionable word choices.

10. **Ending.** Read your ending to assess its impact on readers. Have you presented your solution clearly, reinforced your thesis in some manner, or emphasized your purpose? What might you add or change to your ending to leave the strongest impression on readers?

11. **Audience and Purpose**. Read your draft a last time, evaluating everything you have written from your readers' perspective. Do you connect with readers in any way that would help accomplish your purpose? Is your purpose clear, and have you written in ways that help readers respond favorably to it? What might you add or change to make a greater impact on readers and help you accomplish your purpose?

Activity 5.12

Applying the revision suggestions presented, read and evaluate the sample draft on "The High School Dropout Rate" on page 246. Make specific suggestions that the writer might use to improve the draft.

Activity 5.13

Considering the revision suggestions, evaluate and revise your draft, making any changes that you feel will improve the essay.

Editing

Now that you have edited several essays, you no doubt have an "error detection" process that works well for you in proofreading your papers. Whether you scan your draft for one type of error at a time, for similar types of errors simultaneously, or for any type of error that you come across, the goal is the same: to produce a polished, error-free final essay for your reading audience.

Editing Checklist

The following checklist will ensure that you cover every aspect of grammar usage, punctuation, and spelling as you proofread your paper for errors.

1. **Spelling**. Use the spell check on your word processor and also proofread your paper for spelling errors.

2. **Punctuation**. Check to make sure you used the following correctly:
   End marks (periods, question marks, exclamation marks) to designate the end of each sentence. As you read your sentences, look for any *run-on sentences, comma splices, or sentence fragments,* and punctuate them correctly to eliminate the problems.

   Commas to separate words or phrases in a series; after introductory dependent clauses and preposition, participial, and gerund phrases; after conjunctions in a compound sentence; after "interrupters" such as "by the way," "incidentally," or "of course" at the beginning or within a sentences; before and after appositives or unrestricted relative clauses; to set off ending participial phrases, or at a point in a sentence where a pause is essential for the sentence to be read and understood correctly.

   Semi-colons to connect two closely related sentences or to separate phrases within a series that also contain commas within the phrases.

   Colons to set off a summary, series, or example following a main clause.

   Dashes to set off a summary, series, or example *within* a sentence: The most difficult part of helping a child with school work - letting her learn from her own mistakes - is also one of the most important.

Apostrophes to identify possessive words and contractions.

Quotation marks to set off direct quotations.

3. **Grammar.** Check to make sure that your verbs agree with their subjects, pronouns agree with their antecedents, the correct pronoun subject and object forms are used, the correct comparative and superlative adjective forms are used, the correct adverb forms are used, and the correct irregular past tense verb forms are used. (See the upcoming section on "Common Pronoun Problems.")

4. **Parallelism.** Make sure that in sentences that contain a series of two or more words, phrases, or clauses, frequently joined by "and" or "or," all parts of the series are *parallel* in construction.

5. **Active/Passive Voice.** Make sure that most of your sentences are in the active voice, and use the passive voice only for special emphasis.

6. **Dangling/Misplaced Modifiers.** Check your sentences for any dangling or misplaced modifiers and make the necessary revisions.

Common Pronoun Problems

In most instances, experienced writers have little problem with basic pronoun usage: subjects, objects, and pronoun-antecedent agreement. The three situations where problems most frequently occur involve faulty pronoun references, pronouns shifts, and pronoun-antecedent agreement involving indefinite pronouns.

Faulty Pronoun Reference

A faulty pronoun reference occurs when more than one word in a sentence could be the antecedent of the pronoun:

The tax bill in the Senate was similar to the tax measure in the House, so it had a good chance of passing both houses.

What antecedent does the pronoun "it" refer to: "bill" or "measure?"
It isn't clear, so the sentence needs revising. Here are two possibilities:

The tax bill in the Senate was similar to the tax measure in the House, so the tax bill had a good chance of passing both houses. (Pronoun "it" was replaced by "tax bill" to eliminate problem.)

The tax bills in the Senate and House are very similar, so they both have a good chance of passing both houses. ("Tax bill" and "tax measure" are replaced by "tax bills," creating a single antecedent for the plural pronoun "they," which replaces "it.")

To avoid faulty pronoun references in your writing, consider these suggestions:

1. Most faulty pronoun references occur when there are two nouns in a sentence that could be the antecedent for the pronoun:

    The major duties of the student body vice-presidents are outlined in the student handbook, and they have equal power. ("They" could refer to "duties" or "vice-presidents.")

    Sarah is an animal rights' activist while her sister Vanessa adamantly supports green energy projects, and she also is involved in college government. ("She" could refer to "Sarah" or "Vanessa.")

2. To eliminate a faulty pronoun reference, either eliminate one of the possible antecedents or eliminate the pronoun by replacing it with a noun or rewording the sentence:

    The major duties of the student body vice-presidents are outlined in the student handbook, and the *vice-presidents* have equal power. (The noun "vice-presidents" replaces the pronoun "they.")

    Sarah is an animal rights' activist and is involved in college government while her sister Vanessa adamantly supports green energy projects. (The pronoun "she" is eliminated by rewording the sentence so that a pronoun isn't needed.)

3. Sometimes although there are two or more possible anteced-

ents for a pronoun, one antecedent is so clearly correct that the sentence doesn't need revising:

The tigers in the Grantland Zoo had been housed beside the pandas, but since young children were often frightened by their roar, they were moved to a more remote area of the zoo. (The pronouns "their" and "they" obviously refer to the roaring tigers although the nouns "Pandas" and "children" could technically be antecedents.)

Unnecessary Shifts in Pronoun

Sometimes writers will unnecessarily shift to different pronouns within a sentence or paragraph, which can confuse readers:

You need to read the entire ballot proposition on property tax reform before *one* can understand its magnitude.

Shifting from "you" to the indefinite pronoun "one" is unnecessary and awkward. Replacing "one" with "you" is the simple solution:

You need to read the entire ballot proposition on property tax reform before *you* can understand its magnitude.

To avoid unnecessary shifts in pronouns, consider these suggestions:

1. Pronoun shifts usually occur when the pronouns refer to a generalized group of people or individuals. Pronouns such as *we, you, one, someone,* and *everyone* and the nouns *person* or *people* are often involved:

   A *person* should do *his or her* best to avoid unnecessary confrontations, but sometimes *you* need to stand up for *yourself*. *One* can't always walk away from a confrontation despite *your* desire to avoid it.

   The two sentences contain numerous pronoun shifts that are easily correctable:

   You should do *your* best to avoid unnecessary confrontations, but sometimes *you* need to stand up for *yourself*. *You* can't always walk away from a confrontation despite *your* desire to avoid it.

2. To eliminate pronoun shifts, choose the pronoun that seems best for the sentence or paragraph and stick with it. In the

following paragraph, full of italicized pronoun shifts, the writer decided the best pronoun was "we," which referred to all students including herself, and she also eliminated some pronouns.

Students who wait until the last minute to apply for *their* grants sometimes panic. *We* try to fill out a lengthy application in a few minutes, and *you* feel pressure with every click of the clock. Sometimes *we* are asked for financial information that isn't at *our* fingertips, and *you* can't just make up income figures. The financial aid office always tells students to schedule *their* appointments early to have time to complete the process, but *we* don't always listen. Sometime students learn the hard way, losing out on *their* grant opportunity for a semester.

Revised:
When students wait until the last minute to apply for grants, *we* sometimes panic. *We* try to fill out a lengthy application in a few minutes and feel pressure with every click of the clock. Sometimes *we* are asked for financial information that isn't at *our* fingertips, and *we* can't just make up income figures. The financial aid office always tells *us* to schedule appointments early to have time to complete the process, but *we* don't always listen. Sometime *we* learn the hard way, losing out on *our* grant opportunity for a semester.

3. Try to avoid awkward or stilted pronoun references. For example, if the previous paragraph began with "When a *student* waits until the last minute to apply for grants, *he or she* sometimes panics," the entire paragraph would be filled with awkward "he or she" and "his or her" references. To avoid having to repeat "he or she" or "his or her," change the singular antecedent to plural - "students" instead of "student" or "people" instead of "a person."

    In addition, using the indefinite pronoun "one" - "One should do one's best to avoid confrontations" - is considered somewhat stilted and formal compared to using "you" or "a person."

Pronoun-Antecedent Agreement

Most writers have little problem with basic pronoun-antecedent agreement: making sure a pronoun agrees in number and gender with its antecedent:

Floyd parked *his* new car at the back of the stadium lot where *it* wouldn't get scratched by an adjacently parked car.

In such cases, the correct pronoun forms clearly look and sound right. However, with *indefinite pronouns*, sometimes the incorrect form may not sound bad to some writers:

No one in the stadium left *their* seats until the end of the game.

Since we know that "no one" refers to a lot of people in the stadium, the pronoun "their" seems to make sense. However, since the antecedent "no one" is singular, the plural "their" does not agree with it in number. The correct pronoun reference is "his or her:" No one in the stadium left *his or her* seats until the end of the game."

To avoid pronoun-antecedent agreement problems with indefinite pronouns, consider the following suggestions.

1. The following indefinite pronouns are always singular, and as antecedents, require singular pronouns for agreement: *anybody, anyone, another, each, either, everybody, everyone, nobody, no one, neither, one, other, someone, somebody.* If the indefinite pronoun refers to both men and women, the correct pronoun reference is "he or she" or "his or her:" Nobody left *his or her* seat until long after the concert had ended. If the indefinite pronoun clearly refers only to men or to women, the correct pronoun reference is "she," "her," and "hers" for women and "he," "his," and "him" for men: No one on the women's tennis team wants *her* season to end early. Someone at the men's tennis club left *his* racket at the court.

2. The following indefinite pronouns are always plural, and as antecedents, require plural pronouns for agreement: many, both, few, several, others. Plural indefinite pronouns pose little problem as antecedents since the plural pronoun forms that agree with them look and sound right: Several of the shoppers camped out in *their* sleeping bags to be the first in the doors at the Macy's 6:00 a.m. sale.

3. The following indefinite pronouns are plural when they refer to *number* and singular when they refer to *quantity*: *all, any, some, none.* The modifying phrase following the indefinite pronoun will indicate whether the indefinite pronoun is singular or plural:

None of the monkeys left *their* cages when the gate was left open.
("None" is plural since it refers to a number of monkeys.)

None of the cake was eaten after *it* had fallen on the floor.
("None" is singular since it refers to an amount of cake.)

4. To avoid awkward pronoun-antecedent agreement situations with singular indefinite pronouns, make the antecedent plural:

    Everybody has a stake in the upcoming board of supervisor's election, so *he or she* should make *his or her* vote count. (The antecedent "everybody" leads to the awkward-sounding pronoun references "her or she" and "his or her.")
    Revised:

    All voters have a stake in the upcoming board of supervisor's election, so *they* should make *their* votes count. (Changing the singular "everybody" to the plural "all voters" requires the use of better-sounding "they" and "their" references.

Activity 5.13

Revise the following paragraph by eliminating any problems with pronoun shifts, faulty pronoun references, or pronoun-antecedent agreement.

EXAMPLE

The U.S. is slowly recovering from the recession that began in 2007, but it is far from over. Unemployment remains stubbornly high, and a person who has a job should probably hold on to it, even if you aren't thrilled with the work. Most of the jobs that were lost came from companies downsizing, and they aren't going to come back soon. For anyone who has lost a job, the recession is still very real, and they need all the support they can get from family and friends.

Revised:

The U.S. is slowly recovering from the recession that began in 2007, but *the recession* is far from over. Unemployment remains stubbornly high, and *people* who have a job should probably hold on to it, even if *they* aren't thrilled with the work. Most of the jobs that were lost came from companies downsizing, and *those jobs* aren't going to come back soon. For *all of the people* who have lost a job, the recession is still very real, and they need all the support they can get from family and friends.

(Sentences were revised to eliminate the following problems: sentence one - faulty pronoun reference; sentence two - pronoun shift and a "he or she" pronoun reference; sentence three - faulty pronoun reference; sentence four - pronoun-antecedent agreement problem and a "he or she" pronoun reference.)

Foreclosure Effects

Many couples are having problems paying their home mortgages, and they sometimes view foreclosure as their only option. However, foreclosures carry some serious consequences, and you need to be aware of them. If one goes through foreclosure, your credit rating is destroyed, meaning a person can't get any kind of loan for several years, including home or car loans. In addition, you lose whatever equity you have in the foreclosed house, and rebuilding one's savings for a future home down payment is extremely difficult for most couples. There are other options available to couples besides foreclosure, and they need to take a look at them. Renegotiating mortgage terms with the lender, going through a "short sale" on your home, or renting are options to consider. In today's economy, anyone could lose a job and face a mortgage payment dilemma, but they don't have to view foreclosure as the only alternative.

Activity 5.14

Proofread your latest draft for errors and make the necessary corrections.

For Latinos in the Midwest, A Time to be Heard
By Randal Archibold

The pro-immigration rally here two weeks ago was not the largest or most sophisticated, considering the tens of thousands of people who marched in places like Washington, Los Angeles and New York. It came together in just a few days, spread by word of mouth and a hastily written flier posted in stores. People picnicked or milled about as children played and vendors sold ice cream. They chanted "Sí, se puede" - yes, we can - but did not venture many more slogans than that.

But the turnout of 800 or so in this windswept prairie town reflects the activism around the immigration debate that has rippled to rural areas in the Midwest, where the Latino population has soared in recent years but opposition to illegal immigration remains deeply ingrained. "We've never been united like that, all of us Latinos," said Jose Torres, a meatpacking plant worker who attended the rally. "We are here and not leaving, and we need to let people know that."

The main elements of the national debate are here, just somewhat hidden beneath the surface: the mutually dependent relationship of employers and immigrant workers, the financial benefits and setbacks an influx of immigrants brings to a community, and the awkward question of who is legal and how much it should matter.

There have long been Latinos in southwestern Kansas, a place steeped in Americana. One of the towns, Dodge City, still promotes the legend of Wyatt Earp. Liberal celebrates an annual pancake festival and stakes a tourist-minded claim as the hometown of Dorothy from the "Wizard of Oz" - complete with a yellow brick road. Mexican laborers first arrived more than a century ago to help build railroads, and some of their descendants remain.

The marches here and in nearby towns, however, underscored the other, parallel world of newly arrived Mexican laborers living impoverished in trailer parks and working in the unglamorous meatpacking industry. With the growth of the meatpacking industry here in the early 1980's came droves of new immigrants. At $10 an hour, the messy, taxing and sometimes dangerous assembly-line work of slaughtering cows and processing them into steaks and hamburger was a bonanza compared with jobs in Mexico, El Salvador and elsewhere in Latin America.

By 2000, the Latino share of the population of this town of 20,000 had quadrupled to 43 percent from 10 percent in 1980, reflecting a pattern throughout southwest Kansas. "They came to fill important jobs in the community and work, and people in our world respect hard workers," said Donald D. Stull, an anthropologist at the University of Kansas who has studied the demographic changes across the region.

Liberal got its name, the story goes, from the generosity of its founder, S. S. Rogers, who would give out water to settlers passing through. That welcoming spirit pervaded many prairie towns and continues to some extent today. Still, many people here who are not Hispanic take offense at the waving of foreign flags - during the rally here a few carloads of young white men drove past pointedly brandishing American flags - and chafe at hearing so much Spanish spoken on the streets. In a Survey USA poll earlier this month for The Wichita Eagle and KWCH-TV, nearly three-quarters of 500 adults statewide answered "yes" when asked if the United States should find and deport all illegal immigrants.

Even so, there has been a respect here, sometimes grudging, that the majority of the immigrants have come to work and have helped keep Liberal and other towns hanging on, in contrast to dying farm towns. But complaints about the strain on services and crowded schools are growing, too. "We don't look at it as growth and progress always because we are getting the growth and progress, but from the lower incomes that are a drain on government services," said Sally Cauble, a longtime resident who is running for the state school board.

The imprint of Latinos in Liberal goes well beyond the schools. Bakeries, Mexican food stands, Spanish-language radio and other businesses catering to them have sprouted up over the years. On Pancake Boulevard, a main drag dotted with fast food restaurants and cheap motels, a restaurant, El Amigo Chavez, rubs shoulder with the KFC, and the counter girl at McDonald's takes orders in Spanish while a group of older white men hold court at a table. "They work hard and don't cause too much trouble, so I guess it's been good for these parts," said one of the men in the McDonald's, Fred Sanders, a former Liberal resident on a visit.

It is common belief, if difficult to prove, that many of the new arrivals are illegal, but this town generally has taken a "don't ask, don't tell" approach. For many years, it was better not to know - the work that needed to get done was getting done.

Nonetheless, the nationwide crackdown by the Department of Homeland Security on illegal immigrants and those who employ them has caused a stir here, as many believe the meatpacking plants, despite assurances from executives that identity documents are checked, employ some workers with fake work permits and Social Security cards.

The state's political leadership has been split on how to deal with the problems of illegal immigration. Last month, state legislators beat back a proposal to repeal college tuition breaks for the children of illegal immigrants, a proposal the governor, Kathleen Sebelius, a Democrat, had criticized. Senator Sam Brownback, a Republican, broke with fellow conservatives to favor a provision in a Senate bill that would allow a guest worker program that ultimately would steer illegal immigrants to citizenship. That put him in the company of major agriculture and industry leaders here.

The state's other senator, Pat Roberts, also a Republican, has emphasized a crackdown on the border to keep illegal immigrants out. The congressman from this region, Representative Jerry Moran, a Republican, voted for a House bill in December that, apart from strengthening border security, would make it a felony to be an illegal immigrant or aid one.

Against the uncertain political backdrop, some Latinos see opportunity. In recent months a generation of longtime workers and their relatives, some of whom have moved on to better-paying work, opened businesses and raised families here, have seized on the immigration debate in an effort to increase Latino political power. "I went to a meeting in Topeka and they said, 'What, there are Hispanics in southwest Kansas?' " said Concha Aragon, a custodial worker in Ulysses who is organizing a chapter of an advocacy group, Hispanos Unidos, in the area. "I said, 'Yes, and we're taking action.' "

The younger generation, especially the children of the immigrants, who make up nearly two-thirds of the public school enrollment now, are also beginning to assert themselves. Kasmine Hidalgo, 25, whose father came here years ago to work in a meatpacking plant, National Beef, recalled an awkward moment when a local radio reporter approached her during the demonstration here on April 10. "He asked me, well, 'Are you Mexican or American?' " Ms. Hidalgo said. "I said: 'I am Mexican-American. I was born here.' People do not realize a lot of us are from here. We do need more political leaders, and maybe this is a step."

As in a lot of the country, much of the focus these days is on May 1, when immigrant groups in many states are threatening a work stoppage. Organizers here are discussing the possibility of joining the boycott, but some church leaders argue against it and some workers fret over antagonizing their bosses at the plants. National Beef, which operates plants here and in Dodge City, issued a letter before the April 10 demonstration sympathizing with the cause of immigration law reform but discouraging employees from skipping work.

Fresh from her shift at the plant, Adela Torres sat at the kitchen table of her Liberal home in a neighborhood of small houses and mobile homes. "We have to keep this going, to claim our rights," Ms. Torres said. "We're just deciding how."

DISCUSSION

1. What is the thesis of the essay?
2. What are the cause/effect issues in the essay, and what causal evidence is provided?
3. What conflicting attitudes do non-Latinos in the area have regarding the Mexican immigrant population, and what causes the conflict?
4. What impact do you feel the increasing Latino activism will have on the situation, and why?
5. Mexican immigrants, legal and illegal, have been coming to America, working, and setting down roots for a century. Why do you think immigration has become such a hot-button issue in recent times?

Heroin Hits the Suburbs - Hard
By Jessica Calefati

When the vomiting, tremors, and chills she felt each morning became overwhelming, Jessica Polmann started selling her body to finance her heroin addiction and halt the debilitating physical symptoms of withdrawal. The petite, blond cheerleader, who made the honor roll before she started doing heroin at age 13, received $60 and some cigarettes each time she had sex with a man in his 50s who lived near her suburban New Jersey home. Jessica also traded sex for drugs with her dealers and male friends if they had extra bags of dope. She even introduced her friends and boyfriend to heroin to expand the pool of people she could call on to pick up more drugs. "I was," she says now, "really disgusting."

Polmann, now 18, is just one in a wave of teens and 20-somethings in suburbs across the Northeast who are becoming addicted to and dying from abuse of heroin and prescription opiates like OxyContin. Once prevalent mostly in big cities, heroin has been spreading out to smaller towns in New England and the mid-Atlantic as the drug is becoming more widely available in a highly pure, inexpensive form that can be snorted. Many of these young addicts get started on prescription drugs, move on to cheap heroin that can be snorted, and end up injecting it for a more potent high. Either way, the effects have been deadly.

In Massachusetts, for example, the number of opiate-related deaths, which include overdoses and fatal drug interactions among people ages 13 to 30, was five times as great in 2006 as it was in 1997. And according to drug intelligence, law enforcement, and treatment officials at both the federal and state level, the trend has not yet shown signs of reversing or slowing down.

Heroin has been available in the Northeast's inner cities for a long time, in part because much of it is funneled through well-worn trafficking routes like New York's busy airports. Five years ago, the National Drug Intelligence Center noted in its annual report that heroin was just beginning to move into the suburbs, but it concluded that the drug's popularity was stable or even declining. By 2008, the NDIC's National Drug Threat Assessment, which is based on interviews with local law enforcement and public-health officials across the country, struck a very different tone, warning that heroin abuse "is increasing among young adults in a number of suburban and rural areas." Low-level dealers had found the suburbs could be quite lucrative because they could more easily monopolize the local heroin market.

The 2009 report has not yet been released, but Allison Stombaugh, an intelligence analyst for the NDIC, says it will cover the growing threat of prescription opiates. She adds that prescription drug abusers often graduate to heroin within a few years, suggesting that heroin abuse could rise even more in the near future. "Prescription opiates are seen as acceptable because they are doctor prescribed. But abusing them to get high frequently leads users to try heroin," Stombaugh says.

Douglas Collier, a Drug Enforcement Administration agent in New Jersey, has seen the risks firsthand. He worries that parents in these suburban areas don't realize how frequently prescription opiate abuse is leading to heroin. An annual survey by the U.S. Department of Health and Human Services found that 2.1 million people ages 12 or older who tried an illicit drug for the first time in 2007 chose prescription pain relievers, 57,000 more than the number who tried marijuana. Collier frequently meets with groups of parents to discuss these risks. When he asks audience members whether they lock their liquor cabinets before leaving the house, Collier sees a sea of raised hands. But when he asks how many lock their medicine cabinets, he often sees just a single hand.

"A mother approached me after one of these presentations, weeping," Collier says. "She said, 'I couldn't figure out why my kids were visiting my mom, who had been diagnosed with stage three cancer and prescribed Fentanyl and OxyContin for her pain. But then a bell starting ringing in my head during your presentation, and I connected the dots. I realized my kids were visiting their grandma every day to steal her medication and get high,' " Collier says. The mother later told him that her teenage daughter had overdosed on the stolen prescription opiates but that she survived.

David L'Esperance, the police chief of Salisbury, a coastal Massachusetts town where heroin and prescription opiate abuse is extensive, endured an even more painful trauma. His son died of a methadone overdose a year and a half ago. For L'Esperance, who spent most of his career working on a drug task force, the loss was particularly painful. "Salisbury is a hardworking, middle-class community with an excellent school system and great people, but we also have a problem with painkillers and heroin, and we recognize it," L'Esperance says. "Kids are into this stuff, and hell, if it can happen to the police chief, it can happen to anyone."

Last year, Salisbury and the surrounding beach communities lost at least six people to opiate overdoses, according to L'Esperance. Across Massachusetts, 149 teenagers and 20-somethings died from opiate use in 2006. Unsurprisingly, the number of heroin addicts entering state-operated drug treatment programs also increased over the same period. Indeed, the gap between the number of addicts entering state facilities to treat heroin addiction and the larger number seeking treatment for alcohol abuse shrank dramatically, from 21 percentage points to only 5.

The frequency with which prescription opiate abusers switch to heroin, a drug that is arguably more likely to result in fatal overdoses, does not surprise Michael Botticelli, director of the Massachusetts Bureau of Substance Abuse Services. He says that when OxyContin users exhaust their finances or opportunities to steal from medicine cabinets, they become shrewd consumers. They can either purchase a single OxyContin pill for up to $80 or spend as little as $5 on a bag with one tenth of a gram of heroin. Both options offer a comparable high, and because heroin no longer carries the stigma of a drug that users must inject, the decision to graduate to heroin is an all-too-easy one, Botticelli says.

Though Massachusetts and other northeastern states have not yet seen a decline in the number of young people addicted to and dying from opiate addictions, Botticelli is hopeful that strategies he helped implement this year to address the problem will soon provide some relief. In January, the bureau launched a program to train addicts and their relatives on how to administer nasal Narcan, a drug commonly used by first responders to reverse the effects of an opiate overdose. To deter more people from developing opiate addictions, the bureau also distributed $2 million among the 15 Massachusetts communities with the highest incidences of opiate overdoses. The money will fund prevention strategies that each town must devise.

Law enforcement and treatment officials in New Jersey agree that education about their state's heroin and prescription opiate problem is the best way to prevent more young adults from losing their lives. Between 2004 and 2007, the number of opiate-related deaths per year in New Jersey rose from 129 to 173. In 2006, the annual number of deaths hit 215 when a rash of addicts died from using heroin cut with Fentanyl, a synthetic opiate more powerful than morphine. One of the young adults who lost her life that year was a friend of Polmann's. In total, Polmann lost seven of her school friends during her five years addicted to heroin.

Polmann now lives at Daytop, a drug rehabilitation and treatment facility in northern New Jersey, and she has been clean for nearly five months. She has made significant strides in repairing what were once broken relationships with her family and even has plans to go to college and join the Army, accomplishments that were seemingly beyond her reach earlier this year. "When I came to Daytop on June 23, I walked in here with my face yellow, tracks up and down my arms, saying f---this," she says. "Now that I'm in the program, I love it. I love being clean, and never in a million years did I ever think I would say that."

But she is never far from reminders of her life as an addict. An album she keeps in her bedroom at Daytop is filled with photos of her former friends. Some have died or gone to prison while others have attempted suicide or contracted diseases through their IV drug use. The first photo in the album shows Jessica in a vibrant green front yard wearing a silky, white dress and preparing to leave for her middle school dance. She had snorted heroin earlier that night and was high when the photo was taken.

DISCUSSION

1. What is the thesis of the essay?
2. What are the cause/effect issues in the essay, and what causal evidence is presented? How convincing is the causal evidence?
3. What issues related to teenage drug abuse does the essay not address, and what effect, if any, does this have on the essay?
4. What is the purpose of beginning and ending the essay with the personal story of Jessica Polmann? What impact does this have on you as a reader?
5. The essay focuses on particular types of drug abuse in the suburban Northeast. To your knowledge, how does this compare to the teen drug problem in your area?
6. What solutions to the problem of teen drug abuse does the essay present, and how effective do you think they are? What other solutions might you propose?

Is Adult Prison Best for Juveniles?

By Marilyn Elias

Get-tough laws that have put more teenagers in adult prisons since the early '90s conflict with a wave of new research suggesting how children can be set straight and society protected at the same time. At a two-day summit starting Thursday in Washington, leading researchers will meet with juvenile justice decision-makers - directors of state juvenile justice systems, judges, prosecutors and defense attorneys - to discuss how the new evidence should affect treatment of teen offenders. It is becoming increasingly clear that sending teens to adult prisons does more harm than good.

We know so much more about the adolescent brain and behavior than we used to, and we want to get these facts into the hands of people who can make a difference," psychologist Laurence Steinberg says. He heads a network of researchers and juvenile-justice workers financed by the MacArthur Foundation, which sponsored the meeting.

Since 1992, every state but Nebraska has made it easier to try juveniles as adults, and most states have legalized harsher sentences. Many states limit judges' discretion, sending all teens who commit serious offenses to adult courts, or allowing prosecutors to opt for adult prosecution.

That may sound reasonable, but it can be unfair, says Kimberly O'Donnell, chief judge of the Juvenile and Domestic Relations District Court in Richmond, Va. She points to 14-year-olds tried as adults for "assault by a mob" - in effect, the same as ganging up on and hurting a child at school. "And once you're tried as an adult, you're always an adult, which can have awful consequences," she says. For example, if these teens are arrested again, prosecutors can use the threat of lengthy prison sentences as leverage to gain a plea bargain agreement that might not be in a child's interest, O'Donnell says.

There's firm evidence that teens prosecuted as adults are much more likely to commit crimes when they get out than comparable young people tried as juveniles, says Shay Bilchik, president and CEO of the Child Welfare League of America. Juvenile facilities tend to offer better education, job training, and drug abuse and mental health treatment, Steinberg says. Plus, teens aren't learning from adults how to be career criminals, he adds.

That's not to say kids don't commit serious crimes before landing in adult jails. Some even score in the psychopathic range on written tests that predict which adults are likely to commit future crimes. These tests are sometimes used in deciding whether young people should get severe punishments or be tried as adults, says psychologist Elizabeth

Cauffman of the University of California-Irvine. She says, however, that it's a dubious practice. Her studies show that adolescents tend to move away from this psychopathic profile when they're tracked for a couple of years, while adult scores are usually stable. Some hallmarks of psychopathy - thrill-seeking, impulsivity, failure to accept responsibility - are all too familiar to parents of teenagers, Cauffman says. In effect, youths grow out of this behavior.

Many younger children aren't even competent to stand trial because they don't understand the trial process or can't make decisions about pleas, says Thomas Grisso, a psychologist at the University of Massachusetts Medical School in Worcester. He has developed guidelines to determine juvenile competence and is training U.S. juvenile court workers in using them.

New findings of other MacArthur network scientists challenge common assumptions about teenage criminals. For example, a study that has tracked 1,355 serious offenders for three years finds that less than 10% of those involved in a lot of criminal activities at the outset continued to be heavily involved over the years. "A lot of policy is driven by the view that if a kid does a felony assault, he must be a bad actor from here on forward," says study leader Edward Mulvey of the University of Pittsburgh Medical School. In Mulvey's study, better parenting and long-term treatment for drug or alcohol abuse correlated with less criminal behavior.

Still, 57% had at least one more arrest within two years. "Plus, we know arrests represent only the tip of the iceberg. Who really knows how much else they did that they weren't caught for?" asks Adrian Raine, a psychologist at the University of Southern California who studies criminal behavior. Long-term studies of highly aggressive children suggest that some are headed for a life of violent crime and should be locked up early because they're dangerous, he says. Brain damage or family qualities may cause their behavior, Raine says. "But it's naive to think many of these very violent kids are going to stop, and we don't need to be protected from them." Locking them up in adult facilities, however, seems to exacerbate the problem more than help.

Frank Bilchik, a former prosecutor of juvenile cases in Miami for 16 years and former head of the federal Office of Juvenile Justice and Delinquency Prevention, can understand why research has been slow to translate into action. "When you've got a kid in front of you who's done a vicious armed robbery with a beating, it's different than an intellectual argument about what works," Bilchik says. "Prosecutors think, 'Can I really make myself try him as a juvenile? Can I even get permission from my boss?' " Sometimes prosecutors know a juvenile system has scant mental health treatment or rehabilitation, and they'd rather lock up a dangerous teen with adults than risk a slap on the wrist, Bilchik says. And often there's little follow-up monitoring by youth workers when troubled young people are let out.

Still, he says adult prisons, despite their short-term appeal, aren't usually the long-term answer. "We have the research that tells us what to do. The tragedy is, we're not capitalizing on it." Hopefully, the substantial research will eventually overcome the "tough on crime" mentality that is responsible to sending teenagers to adult prisons despite the negative outcomes for both the teens and society.

DISCUSSION

1. What is the thesis of the essay?
2. What cause/effect relationships are used to support the thesis? What causal evidence is provided, and how convincing is it?
3. What counter argument to the thesis is presented, and how is it addressed?
4. Based on the essay, do you agree with its thesis, and why?
5. Why do you think the current trend towards trying juveniles as adults and the evidence presented showing its negative impact are in such conflict? How does the essay help to answer the question?

Writing about Writing

Since the writing and reading focus in Unit Five was on problem/solution essays, you now have the opportunity to do a written critique on a problem/solution essay of your choice. You will evaluate the essay similarly to how you evaluated your own problem/solution essay and the essays in the "Readings" section: determining the exact problem, the validity of the causes, the validity and seriousness of the effects, the soundness and viability of the solution, and the appropriateness of the thesis.

Critiques of problem/solution essays often answer questions such as, "How well did the essay present the problem and its seriousness?" "Are the effects serious enough to concern readers?" "Are the causes of the problem clear, and does the solution address those causes?" "What concern is the problem to me, the reader, and what if anything can I do?" Consider such questions as you prepare to write your essay.

Writing the Critique

Your critique of a problem/solution essay follows the same basic format as your previous critiques: telling what the essay was about, what you thought of the essay, and why. There are a couple of different ways to organize the essay: 1) by evaluating each aspect of the essay - presentation of the problem, its causes, its effects, the solution - after you present that aspect; or 2) by presenting all aspects of the problem and then evaluating them at the end of the essay. Use whatever organizational method seems most appropriate and effective for your particular critique.

Assignment 5.15

Write a critique of a problem-solution essay from the text or an outside essay or article with your instructor's approval.

Unit Six
Moral Evidence

Sometimes a writer takes a particular position on a topic not because it is necessarily the most logical or factually supported viewpoint but because it represents the *right* thing to do. *Moral evidence* - arguments that appeal to the readers' sense of right and wrong - can sometimes transcend other types of evidence when readers agree that doing the right thing is the most important consideration.

Perhaps the best argument, for example, in support of national health care reform is that a nation has a moral obligation to make sure that every man, woman, and child has adequate health care. Even though health care reform may raise some people's taxes, increase the national debt, and possibly create a more cumbersome health system, many Americans believe that those concerns are less important than ensuring health coverage for all Americans.

Moral evidence can be a powerful persuader because in general, people prefer being on the side of "right" when an issue has a moral component. When given a choice, most people feel good about supporting issues or taking action that helps others and that is consistent with widely held standards of right and wrong. Times of disaster - flood, hurricane, or earthquake - often bring out the most helpful, selfless side of people, revealing how strongly the human urge is to do the right thing. Writers often tap into that urge to make their most convincing arguments.

Writers frequently capitalize on their readers', and their own, sense of morality and justice in framing particular issues. Issues that lend themselves best to moral arguments often involve the treatment of humans or animals. Is it right, for example, to allow heterosexual marriage but not gay marriage? To torture laboratory animals to find cures for human diseases? To guarantee health care only to those who can afford it? To "imprison" wild animals in zoos? To legally kill people under any circumstances? To allow urban areas to deteriorate? To devastate the planet with pollution and global warming? To kill a human fetus?

The writing focus for this unit is on providing moral evidence to support your opinion on an issue where principals of right and wrong are involved. You can also supplement your moral arguments with any other evidence that you find useful: empirical, factual, logical, causal, or comparative.

In philosophy, a distinction is sometimes made between *moral* and *ethical* behavior, the former referring to personal behavior, the latter to conduct within a social or professional context. However, since both moral and ethical behavior involve principals of right and wrong, and since all behavior involves personal choice no matter the context, for our purposes, no distinction is made between the two.

Using Moral Evidence

To provide the most compelling moral evidence in your writing, consider the following suggestions.

1. **Determine the moral element(s) of an issue which may appeal to the readers' sense of right and wrong.** For example, with the issue of euthanasia, several moral concerns may be raised: whether it is right to kill a suffering, terminally ill person; whether it is right to allow a terminally ill person to suffer against his or her will; whether anyone other than a terminally ill person has the right to decide when and whether he should die; whether anyone, including physicians, should be allowed to "play God" in determining when another person lives or dies.

2. **Use moral evidence that supports your viewpoint and would be most convincing for readers.** For example, if a writer favored patient-requested euthanasia, perhaps her strongest moral argument would be that no suffering, terminally ill person should be forced to continue living against her will, or put another way, that a suffering, terminally ill person should have the right to decide when her life should end. Readers may relate to this argument since they may have considered what they would want done in such a situation or have had friends or relatives in a similar situation.

3. **Provide moral evidence based upon the most widely held principals of right and wrong.** Readers will have trouble accepting a moral argument if they don't believe in the principal upon which it is based. For example, one argument in support of health care reform purports that all men, women, and children are entitled to adequate health care. However, some

people don't accept the underlying principle that a nation has a moral obligation to ensure health care for all citizens. Some people believe that having health care is not a right but the responsibility of the individual, and therefore reject the "entitlement" argument. The more widely held the principle upon which a moral argument is based, the more likely it will resonate with readers.

4. **Writers often personalize a moral argument to make the greatest impact on readers.** For example, writers who favor capital punishment will sometimes pose questions to readers like, "What if it were your mother or daughter who was brutally raped, tortured, and murdered? Would you consider it just to allow the murderer to continue living?" Writers who oppose term limits for elected politicians sometimes ask readers, "What if you were forced out of your job after six or eight years, just when you were becoming very knowledgeable and good at it? Would that be right or fair?" If you can put readers in the position of those people affected by a particular issue, they may view it in a different light.

5. **Moral arguments often come in the form of syllogisms.** In using syllogisms to make a moral argument, the major premise(s) is the widely held principal of right and wrong upon which the argument is based, the minor premise(s) is the specific situation which is either adherent or contrary to the principle, and the conclusion is the moral argument upon which the principal is based. Here are two examples:

Major premise: Everyone should have the right to an education.
Minor premise: Attending college is an important part of one's education.
Conclusion: Everyone should have the right to attend college despite their financial status.

Major premise: Everyone should have an equal right to a fair trial.
Minor premise: Wealthy people can afford the best lawyers.
Minor premise: Poor people are often provided minimal legal services.
Conclusion: The justice system must change to guarantee every person the same quality of legal assistance.

Activity 6.1

Identify possible moral issues for the following topics and consider how you might use them to support your viewpoint on each topic.

EXAMPLE

Topic: global warming

Possible moral issues:

1. Does man have the right to subvert the natural climatological conditions of the planet?
2. Is it morally acceptable for one generation of mankind to leave the planet in worse condition for future generations?
3. Is the potential damage of global warming offset by the progress that man has made in creating the problem?

Using moral issues:

To support my viewpoint that global warming is a dangerous problem I would use the moral arguments that man doesn't have the right to destroy the ecological balance of the planet through global warming, and that it is morally wrong for one generation to leave the planet in worse shape for future generations.

1. **Topic:** Drilling for oil in environmentally sensitive areas to end U.S. dependence on foreign oil
2. **Topic:** Allowing a time for "silent prayer" in schools where children can pray to whomever they want
3. **Topic:** Giving athletes cortisone shots to "play injured" without pain
4. **Topic:** Implementing a single 15% flat tax rate on income to replace current complex tax system
5. **Topic:** Trying pre-teens who commit murder as adults
6. **Topic:** Legalizing Las Vegas-style gambling in all states

---

Activity 6.2

For reach of the following moral arguments, identify the underlying principal of right and wrong on which it is based.

EXAMPLE

Moral argument: It is not right that drug addicts are incarcerated like criminals.
Principle: Man has a moral obligation to help the afflicted.

1. **Moral argument:** It is not right for people to down-

load music off the Internet without paying for it.
Principle:

2. **Moral argument:** It is only fair that people selling their homes disclose to potential buyers any structural problems with the house.
Principle:

3. **Moral argument:** The torturing of terrorists by the military to reveal information that might thwart future terrorist attacks is not defensible.
Principle:

4. **Moral argument:** The legalization of prostitution is morally indefensible.
Principle:

5. **Moral argument:** It is wrong for a writer to use source information in an article without divulging the source.
Principal:

6. **Moral argument:** It is morally wrong for American companies to buy clothing from foreign manufacturers who use child labor.
Principal:

7. **Moral argument:** It is wrong for an employer to hire a person on the basis of affirmative action when there are more qualified applicants.
Principal:

Activity 6.3

Complete the following syllogisms to provide moral arguments in support of each thesis presented.

EXAMPLE

Major premise: Forced child labor is immoral.

Minor premise: Some American shoe companies rely on foreign manufacturers who exploit child labor.

Conclusion: Americans should not buy shoes from companies that use child labor to manufacture their shoes.

1. **Major premise:** In a country as wealthy as the U.S., no child should go hungry.
    Minor premise:
    Conclusion: America must devise a better system to ensure that all children are adequately fed.

2. **Major premise:** Entertainment that exposes children to violence and increases their aggression level is morally wrong.
    Minor premise: Many children's video games are filled with violence.
    Conclusion:

3. **Major premise:**
    Minor premise: Today's government is leaving future generations with the largest Federal deficit burden in history to pay off.
    Conclusion:

4. **Major premise:** Every American has the right to protect his family from harm.
    Minor premise: Having a gun in the home can provide protection against intruders.
    Conclusion:

5. **Major premise:**
    Minor premise:
    Conclusion: Students should be allowed to park free on their college campus.

Activity 6.4

Read the following essay and identify and evaluate the moral evidence presented in support of the thesis. In addition, identify and evaluate other forms of evidence presented, how opposing arguments are addressed, and the overall impact of the essay.

If a new policy being considered by the local unified school district board goes into effect, a high school student will soon be able to get free condoms from the school nurse, under strictest confidentiality, to use for safe sex with a classmate after school or on the weekend. Perhaps the district should also provide a nice, safe on-campus location for sexual trysts so students wouldn't have to use back seats of cars or worry about distracting interruptions.

Yes, a lot of high-school age students have sex, and if they are going to do it anyway, it would certainly be better that they use a condom to avoid pregnancies and STD's. No one would argue that. But is it a school district's responsibility to provide the condoms for the students? If so, shouldn't it also provide a good, pure grade of marijuana to high school dope smokers so they wouldn't get some tainted stuff off the street? If the school district provides condoms for high school students, it is essentially promoting a behavior that it should be helping to reduce. It is essentially saying, "We know you're going to have sex, we accept the behavior, and we want to help you be responsible about it." That is the wrong message to send to any teen.

The Guttmacher Institute, a nonprofit organization that focuses on sexual and reproductive health research and public education, reports that by their senior year in high school, over 60% of teenagers have engaged in sex. However, it has also been demonstrated that there are several sexual abstinence programs that reduce the amount of sexual activity in teenagers, according to Robert Rector, senior research fellow for The Heritage Foundation. In other words, school districts don't have to throw up their hands and accept that students' sexual behavior can't change. By dispensing condoms to students, however, they slant the change in the direction of more sexual activity rather than less.

While pregnancy and STD's are two negative consequences of teenage sex that condoms can help prevent, there are other consequences that they can't. Teenage girls commonly have sex not because they want to, but because they feel pressured into it. Researchers found that among 279 teenage girls they interviewed, many said they'd given in to unwanted sex at some point because they were afraid their boyfriend would get angry. Unwanted sex can lead to depression, anxiety, and post-traumatic stress disorder. The findings, published in the *Archives of Pediatrics & Adolescent Medicine*, indicate that rather than promoting safe sex through condom distribution, school districts should be educating girls on not giving in to sexual pressure and lecturing boys on not pressuring girls to have sex.

In addition, according to the article "Teenage Girls Feel Pressured into Sex" in *The Sydney Herald*, alcohol, marijuana, or other drugs are often involved in situations where girls are pressured into sex. For example, girls who had unwanted sex were more apt than their peers to have partners who smoked marijuana. School districts dispensing condoms are not going to alter the drug-related nature of many unwanted sexual encounters. In fact, they may be abetting the situation.

What about the moral issue? Most would agree that it is not right that ever-younger teenagers are having sex in record number and that it is another example of the moral slippage that our country is experiencing. That moral slippage is quite apparent when a school district is considering providing condoms for its students, an implicit condoning of the sexual behavior. Perhaps it is not fashionable today to take the moral high ground on any issue, but why can't a school district say, "We don't want our students having sex. We think that it is wrong and can be very destructive. We don't condone it and we want to educate students to its negative consequences." Providing condoms should not be part of that education.

Over sixty years ago, nearly half of American men and women smoked cigarettes, according to a 1944 Gallup Poll. Recently, a new Gallup Poll shows that percentage has been cut in half. People quit smoking because for years they have been bombarded by a national educational campaign sending the message that cigarette smoking is unhealthy. The message took. The government and health industry didn't accept that smoking was an inevitable behavior and provide smokers with a low-nicotine option. They strongly advised smokers to stop. Providing condoms to high school students is the low-nicotine option, and it's not going to get anyone to change their behavior.

There are plenty of parents in the community who don't want their high school daughters or sons sexually active, and they are doing what they can as parents to see that it doesn't happen. Then all of a sudden they see the school district dispensing condoms to high school students to practice safe sex. It's as if the school district is condoning a behavior among students that many parents are trying to combat. Mother says, "We don't think it's in your best interests to be sexually active at this age," and daughter says, "But the school district provides condoms so students can practice safe sex." Is it right for a school district to work at cross purposes with parents?

There is no question that practicing safe sex dramatically reduces the incidence of pregnancy and STD's among any population. And of course, that is the justification the school district is using when considering dispensing condoms. "They're going to have sex anyway, so we should help to ensure that they do it responsibly," goes the argument. Shouldn't the district also provide rides home to students who have been drinking at parties? The district knows that many students drink alcohol, so shouldn't it at least help them to drink responsibly? The point is this: a school district should never enable behavior that is not acceptable or right, whether it be teenage drinking, drugs, or sex. Teenage sex is not acceptable behavior, and it is wrong for any school district to enable such behavior by dispensing condoms. The emphasis should be on reducing the incidence of teenage sex, not increasing it.

Prewriting

As with previous "Prewriting" sections, this section provides you with a number of suggestions in preparation for writing the first draft of your essay. Use these suggestions in ways that fit your personal writing process and best prepare you to write the first draft. This may mean using the prewriting suggestions as a structured framework for generating material and providing direction for your essay or as a general guide for thinking about your topic and how you might develop it. Writers vary greatly in how they prepare to write an essay, and the prewriting suggestions enable you to prepare in whatever ways you find most beneficial.

Since the writing emphasis in this unit is on incorporating moral evidence, a primary consideration is selecting a topic which has a moral component, where judgments of right and wrong may come into play. In addition, you have a range of evidence to draw from in writing your essay that you have incorporated in previous essays: empirical, factual, logical, comparative, and causal. No doubt you will be able to use some or all of these types of evidence to help develop your essay most effectively.

Topic Selection

To select a topic for your upcoming essay, consider the following suggestions.

1. **Select a topic that people have differing opinions on.** Your topic may come from any field - education, health, politics, children's issues, fashion, technology, sports, social issues - and at any level - local, state, national, international.

2. **Select a topic that has a moral component**. When considering different topics, ask yourself, "Is there an issue(s) of right-and-wrong involved with this topic? While some topics have a clear moral component, such as euthanasia, abortion, or capital punishment, there are many topics which may raise matters-of-conscience issues, such as hiring illegal aliens, nepotism in employment, mandatory retirement age, reverse discrimination in college acceptance, affirmative action, private school vouchers, racial profiling, legalizing marijuana for medical purposes, or requiring a tax on merchandise sold online.

3. **Select a topic that interests you and that may interest or affect others.** Perhaps the biggest step towards writing an interesting essay is selecting a topic that you really want to write about. Take your time to discover that particular topic.

4. **Select a topic that is specific enough to develop effectively in an essay-length paper.** While the topic "America's War on Drugs" could fill a book, the narrower topic, "Massachusett's Educational War on Heroin" might be well rendered in an essay.

Activity 6.5

Considering the suggestions for topic selection, select a topic for your upcoming essay.

EXAMPLE

Topic selection: A play-off system for college football

Thesis

It is useful to generate a tentative thesis statement - your opinion on the topic - relatively early in your prewriting preparation in order to begin marshaling supportive evidence. Sometimes you have a good idea of your opinion before investigating your topic, and other times your thesis may evolve as you learn more about your topic through your research.

To generate a thesis for your upcoming paper, consider the follow suggestions.

1. **Generate a thesis that you believe in.** If you strongly believe in what you are writing, you will have the passion and desire to convince readers of the rightness or validity of your belief.

2. **Generate a thesis that clearly expresses your opinion on the topic**. Your thesis should be clear and definite so that readers have no question as to what position you are taking and defending in your essay.

3. **Generate a thesis that you can convincingly support.** For most readers, the strength of a thesis lies in the support that the writer provides. The stronger and more convincing your support, the more likely that readers will consider your thesis seriously.

4. **Generate a thesis that is consistent with the evidence**. If in researching your topic, you find that some or all of the evidence does not support your thesis, you may want to reconsider or revise it. It is certainly better to revise your thesis than to stick with a thesis that has questionable support.

Activity 6.6

Generate a tentative thesis statement for your essay. First, you may want to do some research and learn more about your topic before forming an opinion.

EXAMPLE

Topic: A play-off system for college football

Tentative thesis statement:
It is time for the NCAA to implement a play-off system for Division I football to determine the true champion.

Support

Your support for your thesis includes all of the reasons that you believe as you do on your topic and the evidence that validates each reason. Together, they form the nucleus of your paper and are largely responsible for how readers respond to your thesis.

As you write your paper, reasons and evidence often go hand-in-hand in a natural manner. For example, in her upcoming paper, for one of the reasons that she supports a college play-off system, a writer writes, "National play-offs are common in intercollegiate sports, and Division I football should be no different." She then follows with the comparative evidence to support her reason, indicating the various intercollegiate sports that have national play-offs, including intercollegiate football at the Division II and III levels. Her reason leads naturally to her comparative evidence in a manner that fulfills the readers' expectation and produces a nicely developed paragraph (See sample draft on page 291.)

To generate support for your thesis, consider the following suggestions.

1. **Generate a number of reasons in support of your thesis.** You may already have some reasons in mind that support your thesis, and you may find more as you research your topic. You may not use all of the reasons in your essay - some may turn out unsupportable and others relatively insignificant -, so it's useful to generate a good number.

2. **What evidence - empirical, factual, comparative, logical, causal, moral - might you use to support each reason?** For each reason, run through the different types of evidence to determine which appears most appropriate and compel-

ling. You might use more than one type of evidence to support a particular reason.

3. **What is the moral component(s) for your topic, and what evidence will you provide?** What issue(s) of right and wrong might you raise regarding your topic, and what moral evidence could you provide to further your thesis?

    For example, the writer advocating for a national play-off system for college football raised and answered the following questions of fairness: If it right for the NCAA to ignore the overwhelming support for a play-off system expressed by fans, players, and coaches? Is it fair that a computer-generated system determines who plays for the national championship rather than have it determined on the field? Is it right that a small group of NCAA administrators can dictate how a national collegiate champion will be determined? Is it fair to players for the NCAA to "pick" what two teams get to play for the national championship and leave everyone else out?

4. **What opposing arguments to your thesis should you address in your essay?**

    As you know, countering opposing arguments can be crucial in swaying readers who may hold opposing views and want to see those views acknowledged. For example, one opposing argument that the writer supporting a football playoff system knew that she must address in her essay was, "A play-off system will destroy the traditional bowl system that has been in existence for over sixty years."

Activity 6.7

Generate some reasons in support of your thesis, some potential evidence to support each reason, including moral evidence, and some opposing arguments to address in your essay. Do the necessary research to become most knowledgeable on your topic and generate the best reasons and evidence.

EXAMPLE:

Topic: college play-off system for football

Thesis: It is time for the NCAA to implement a play-off system for Division I football to determine the true champion.

Reasons:

1. A play-off is the only way to determine the true champion.
2. The current system is fatally flawed in determining the champion.
3. Fans, players, and coaches all favor a play-off system.
4. Play-offs are common in collegiate sports.
5. A viable play-off system template already exists.

Evidence (For each of the five reasons):
1. Use logical, empirical, and causal evidence
2. Use logical, comparative, and moral evidence
3. Use moral and logical evidence
4. Use comparative evidence
5. Use causal and comparative evidence

Opposing arguments to address:
1. Play-off would destroy traditional bowl system.
2. Play-off would extend the season too long.

Audience and Purpose

Two important prewriting considerations are, "Who is the reading audience for your essay?" and "For what purpose are you writing to them?" Determining your audience and writing purpose are important because they shape your paper in ways that help you accomplish your purpose: how you write the paper, what you choose to include, what tone you use, what you choose to emphasize, and how you connect with your readers.

To determine your audience and purpose for the upcoming essay, consider the following questions:

1. Whom do I want to read this essay: people that need the information? people that can have an impact on the topic? people that have opposing viewpoints?
2. What do I need to keep in mind about my readers: their age? ethnicity? gender? educational level? interest or opinion on the topic?
3. How might I connect with my readers? What might we have in common, and what might we agree upon? How can I best address any opposing argument they may have?
4. What is my purpose in writing to this audience: to educate or enlighten? to move to action? to change their minds?
5. What tone should I use to help accomplish my purpose?
6. Given my audience, how can I best accomplish my purpose? What do I need to emphasize to make the greatest impact?

Activity 6.8

Answer the six questions above to help determine your audience and purpose for the upcoming essay.

EXAMPLE

    Topic: play-off system for college football

    Thesis: It is time for the NCAA to implement a play-off system for Division I football to determine the true champion.

1. I'm going to write this essay for the NCAA committee, who will determine whether there is a college play-off system.
2. They are a tough audience because they have continuously defended the current BCS (Bowl Championship Series) system which they created. I need to put together the best possible arguments and evidence, and I also need to keep in mind that they are human and are feeling the pressure of angry public opinion.
3. I don't know how or if I can connect in any way to the audience. I can probably acknowledge what a difficult position they are in and how changing a system that has been in place for a long time isn't easy. There may be one area of agreement to include: that they too must want a system that determines the true champion.
4. My purpose is to get them to implement a national play-off system, and nothing short of that is an option.
5. My tone needs to be respectful but firm. I need to show how passionate I am about the subject - they need to see this is a big issue with a lot of people.
6. I'm not sure how I'm going to best accomplish my purpose. Hopefully as I write the first draft I'll get a better feel for how I can change these people's minds. I'll have to see what seems to be the most effective arguments as I develop the paper.

Drafting

For most writers, prewriting preparation gives them something to work with as they begin writing: a sense of direction and some ideas to develop. However writing the draft usually goes well beyond just connecting the prewriting dots.

Writing is in part a process of discovery, and writers need to be open to the ideas that come to them as they work through a draft: connections between ideas that they hadn't considered, new reasons in support of their thesis, an opposing argument they hadn't thought of, a new line of supportive evidence. For many writers, the process of writing itself generates ideas that help to develop and enrich the essay.

In addition, writers use their creative talents to compose fresh and interesting openings, to juxtapose their ideas in effective ways, to produce evocative comparisons, to express their ideas interestingly and cogently, and to create endings that make a lasting impact on readers. No matter how well thought-out a prewriting plan is, it is the writing process itself that breathes life into the plan through the writer's creative presence.

Drafting Guidelines

As you write the first draft of your essay, consider the following suggestions.

1. **In your opening paragraph(s), introduce your topic, engage your readers' interest, and either include your thesis statement or provide readers with a sense of direction.** In your opening, you might create a scenario, reveal a powerful real-life incident, introduce some interesting, relevant facts, or provide a compelling anecdote. Ask yourself, "How can I introduce my topic in the best way to grab my readers' interest?" (See the opening paragraphs of the upcoming sample draft.)

2. **To help readers best understand your topic, you might begin your middle paragraphs with some background information and explanations that will enhance their understanding of the essay.** What do readers need to know about the topic to get the most from the essay? What might you need to explain to them?

3. **In the middle paragraphs, present your reasons in support of your thesis and the evidence to validate each reason, and address some crucial opposing arguments.** Be open to new ideas that come to you as you write: a new supportive

reason, some additional evidence, a timely comparison, a more effective way to refute an argument. In addition, make sure to include some moral evidence, appealing to the readers' sense of what is right or fair regarding the topic.

4. **Conclude with an ending that follows logically from what has come before and makes an impact on readers.** You might summarize main points, save a final compelling point for the conclusion, present or reinforce your thesis, emphasize your purpose, provide a solution to a problem, or present a scenario for the future. Whatever you write, bring something new to the conclusion that helps to create your desired response from readers.

5. **Keep you audience and purpose in mind.** As you write, remember whom you are writing for and why you are writing to them. Make connections with your readers that are genuine and could further your writing purpose, and use the most effective writing tone to convey your thoughts.

Activity 6.9

Read the following sample first draft, noting the opening, the background material, the supportive reasons and evidence (including moral arguments), the response to opposing arguments, the connections with readers, and the conclusion. Then write the first draft of your essay.

Sample First Draft (Audience: NCAA committee that governs college football)

A Real Play-off System for College Football

Each year, there is a televised national spelling bee where kids spell against each other until everyone but the eventual winner is eliminated by misspelling a word. The tension mounts as one contestant after another is eliminated until there are just two contestants left standing, vying for the national championship. It is an exciting competition, even if you're not into spelling, and the winner is certainly deserving, prevailing over some marvelously talented challengers.

Imagine, though, the competition done differently. Based on previous performances in other competitions, just two contestants are chosen in advance to compete for the national championship. The rest of the contestants are paired off against each other, but the competition means nothing since only one of the two anointed candidates can win the national title. How fair would that be to the rest of the candidates, and how boring would that be for anyone watching on television? That is exactly, however, how the national Division I college football champion is decided.

For many years, there was nothing resembling a play-off system in college football. There were a number of post-season bowl games, with the more powerful teams usually competing in the most prestigious bowls - Rose, Orange, Sugar, and Cotton Bowl -, and the national champion chosen by different national press and college coaches' polls, which sometimes contradicted one another. With fans clamoring for a better system, the NCAA devised the Bowl Championship Series (BCS) a few years ago. Five bowls are designated as BCS games, and the top ten rated college teams based on the BCS formula, which includes complex computer ratings, press and coaches' polls, along with subjective decisions by the BCS committee, play in the five games. The catch, however, is that only the top two rated teams play for the national championship. The rest are basically relegated to playing for pride. There is no play-off system at all since no team plays its way into the championship game. No matter who is ultimately "crowned" the national champion, there is the sense that it is a phony tribute, one that is given more than earned.

Is there a better way to decide a national championship in college sport? Of course, and most college sports have true national play-offs, including baseball, basketball, tennis, track, swimming, volleyball, and even Division II and III football. The national champion in each of those sports earns the title by defeating a number of top teams during the post-season play-offs. Many teams are given the opportunity to compete for the title, and few can say they have been unfairly left out. With today's BCS system, every Division I football team but two are left out.

National poll after poll reveals that the large majority of fans, players, and coaches all want a national play-off, yet the NCAA doggedly and stubbornly sticks to its infamous BCS format. They come up with their reasons, which amount to so many excuses, for thumbing their noses at the fans, players, and coaches. In essence, it is the tyranny of the few and powerful ignoring the will of the vast majority. Perhaps that type of decision-making is accepted in totalitarian countries like China, but it flies in the face of American democracy and is simply not right.

The BSC committee claims that a football playoff system would dismantle the traditional bowl system. That does not have to be the case, however. Several supporters of a play-off system have provided online scenarios where the major bowls would be used for play-off games. Using the bowls for play-off games would enhance the bowls, adding greatly to the fan interest and television ratings. NCAA basketball play-off games are among the most highly rated sports' television programs annually, and it stands to reason that bowl game play-offs would generate the same kind of interest. Another argument from the NCAA is that a play-off system would extend the season too long and therefore be educationally detrimental to the student-athletes. However, a playoff system doesn't have to last any longer than the current football post-season. Today's post-season bowls are spread out over a month's time, from early December to early January. A four-to-five week play-off system would fit within the same time frame and would affect fewer student-athletes each week as the field was pared down to a few remaining teams. In addition, many coaches have expressed a willingness to reduce the regular football season by one game to provide more time for a play-off. The NCAA's educational argument simply isn't valid.

Of course, a football play-off system couldn't involve sixty-four teams playing two-three times per week like the basketball play-offs. A credible football play-off scenario, one that has been supported by many fans, pundits, and coaches, would involve sixteen top teams in the country, which would include conference champions and outstanding at-large teams, playing over three weeks until the final two teams are left standing. Then after a week's break, the championship game would occur, culminating a five-week play-off schedule ending in early January. All of the current BSC bowl sites could be used for play-off games, so who would be left dissatisfied? As to the twenty-some other bowl games that occur every year, they could be played as usual among the teams that are not among the sixteen play-off teams. These games would lose no stature from the play-offs since they are already rendered meaningless by being outside the BCS bowl system.

What would a play-off system mean for college football? First it would mean that a national champion would be chosen by play on the field rather than by a committee, which is the only fair, non-controversial way. Second, it would mean that sixteen teams rather than two would be vying for the national championship through the play-offs, giving a number of outstanding teams a chance, and guaranteeing that the final prevailing team would deserve to be called champion. Third, it would mean that the will of the vast majority of fans, coaches, and players would prevail over a handful of NCAA administrators, which is only right in a country that espouses democratic principles.

Finally, a football play-off system would bring a level of excitement to the football post-season that would rival basketball's March Madness and the NFL's Super Bowl. For most fans, the BSC post-season is a yawner, with only one game having any real meaning, and that game badly tainted by the teams not having to play their way in. Imagine the interest in the best sixteen teams in the country going head to head, the excitement building each week until the two final teams were left standing.

The state of Utah is suing the NCAA for monopolistic practices in not allowing teams to compete for the national championship, their undefeated University of Utah team of 2007 having been left out of the "championship" game. Were the Utes good enough to be national champions? What about the undefeated Boise State teams of past years? Was USC the most dominant team of 2008 despite an early loss that kept them out of the championship game? No one can answer those questions, but a college football play-off system could. Let's decide the national champion on the field, not in some NCAA back room. No matter how fair the BSC committee tries to be, the BSC system is flawed beyond repair, and everyone seems to agree but the NCAA.

Although writers may have some sense of what needs revising as they work through a draft, they have a better perspective after having completed the draft and viewing it as a whole. We have all probably done enough drawing to know what it is like to step back and see how disproportionate a picture can become, our horse's legs grotesquely short and stubby or too long and spindly for its substantial body. First drafts can display similar disproportions as we become engrossed in their individual aspects, and viewing the draft as a whole often reveals the problems to us.

For example, on rereading her draft on the college football play-offs in the preceding section, the writer realized that parts of the draft sounded pretty harsh and probably would offend the NCAA audience she was trying to win over. She didn't think about it as she was writing, venting her frustrations over the current system and pretty much ignoring her readers. During revision, she toned down some of the stridency and "talked" more directly to her audience without diminishing or changing her message.

Transitions

An important, subtle aspect of writing an effective essay is using *transitions* to connect parts of the essay and help create a coherent whole. Transitions - words and phrases that tie thoughts together and show relationships among them - provide signposts to readers to let them know what is coming and how it relates to what has preceded.

No doubt you use transitions naturally in your writing without notice. When you juxtapose contrasting ideas, you might introduce the second idea with an "however:" "We are often taught in school that our founding fathers were staunch revolutionaries who defied England and the Crown. *However*, men such as Benjamin Franklin were English loyalists who for years did everything possible to keep the colonies peacefully within the realm." You also might use transitions such as "first," "second," or "next' to denote separate steps in a process or different reasons in support of a thesis, or you might begin your conclusion with a "finally" or "as you can see."

If you are already using transitions in your writing, why devote a section to them? First, having a greater awareness of transitions and their role may help you use them even more effectively in your writing. For example, you may ask yourself, "Could beginning this paragraph with a transition help to show that I am introducing a new supportive reason?" or "Would transitions help readers delineate the steps in the electoral process better?" Second, in evaluating your use of transitions, you may find that you may overuse a few transitions at the exclusion of other useful options, which this section will provide. (Note the use of transitions in this paragraph: "First" and "Second" to introduce two reasons for devoting a section to transitions, and "For example" to introduce questions you may ask yourself.)

Using Transitions Effectively

To use transitions most effectively in your writing, consider the following suggestions.

1. **Consider using transitions when you begin new paragraphs**. A transition in the first sentence of a paragraph helps readers in two ways: it shows what, if any, relationship the new paragraph has with the previous one, and it gives them a sense of what to expect in the new paragraph. For example, if a new paragraph begins with the transition "On the other hand," readers suspect that what is coming will be in contrast to the previous paragraph.

2. **Consider the variety of transitions available to connect sentences and paragraphs and show relationships among ideas:**
    Series: *first, second, third, next, then, finally*
    Adding: *in addition, also, moreover, furthermore, another, in fact*
    Contrast: *however, nevertheless, despite, on the other hand, in contrast*
    Cause/effect: *therefore, consequently, thus, ergo, due to, because of, to that end, for that reason*
    Concluding: *finally, lastly, in conclusion, as you can see, in the end*
    An aside: *incidentally, by the way, as a matter of fact*
    Definite: *of course, naturally, certainly, after all, surely, needless to say, without question, as we know, obviously*
    Introductory: *for example, for instance, such as*
    Time frame: *meanwhile, in the meantime, for the time being, during that time, recently, previously*
    Comment: *fortunately, unfortunately, sadly, amazingly, unexpectedly, decidedly*

3. **Vary your transitions to avoid overusing a few favorites**. If you find yourself relying on "however" to contrast ideas, try some appropriate options. If your draft is full of "therefores," consider an occasional "consequently" or "thus."

4. **In using transitions, more isn't necessarily better**. Some-

times when writers become more aware of transitions, they tend to pile them on to distraction. When used most effectively, transitions help guide readers through an essay without their awareness.

Activity 6.10

For practice using transitions, fill in the spaces in the following essay with appropriate transitional words and phrases, varying your choices.

EXAMPLE

Running her first Boston Marathon, the young Finnish entrant blazed through the first few miles, distancing herself from the competition. <u>Needless to say</u>, she paid for her inexperience later, fading badly and barely completing the race.

Outsourcing American Jobs

_____, the corporate outsourcing of jobs to other countries has put many Americans out of work. Jobs as varied as telemarketing, medical transcription, auto manufacturing, and tax accounting are now being done by employees in countries such as India, Mexico, and China. The reason for the outsourcing is obvious: cheaper labor in Third World countries, meaning greater profits for companies.

_____, many American corporations are more concerned about cutting overhead and maximizing profits than keeping jobs in the country. Since American workers cannot compete with poorly paid foreign employees, the outsourcing trend will continue and expand as potential employees in other countries are trained and educated to perform more and greater skilled jobs. The result, _____, will be even greater job loss in America and the jolting displacement of employees set adrift.

Some jobs, _____, would be immune to foreign outsourcing. _____, you're not going to Venezuela to see a physician, right? Wrong. Medical insurance companies are _____ seeing the financial advantages of outsourcing, and are sending patients to physicians in other countries where surgeries can be done less expensively, saving the insurance companies money. If even medical care can be outsourced to other countries, what job can't be?

_____, the government can't force companies to keep jobs at home or keep American consumers from buying the cheaper products that foreign employees can produce. No one can expect American employees to work for the pathetically low wages that foreign employees are paid.

_____, it was America that helped spawn the economic globalization that lead in part to the outsourcing, and it has certainly helped the economies of many poorer nations, but at what expense to American workers?

_____, no one knows the answer. There is always the optimistic talk about American ingenuity and our ability to adjust to changing economic situations. _____, the vast majority of us made our living in agriculture less than a hundred years ago, and now agriculture makes up roughly two percent of the workforce. When we lose jobs in one area, we create them in another. _____, the world is a very different place than it was even twenty or thirty years ago.

_____, America has lost its quality edge. At one time no country could manufacture products that matched American quality. Today, countries all over the world can match that quality and in many cases surpass it. _____, American has lost its technological edge. We have been a very generous country in passing on our mechanical, computer, and agricultural technology to other countries, and they can now manufacture the technological devices and produce the high quality crops that we formerly had a corner on. One reason that our import-to-export ratio is so out of whack is that countries don't need the American goods that they once needed. They can make them themselves or buy them more cheaply elsewhere.

_____, America has lost its competitive edge. The driving desire to get ahead and stay ahead has long been a force in sustaining our economic development. Today that driving desire is more evident in countries like China and India, where people are more willing to work harder and longer and make more sacrifices to get ahead. In America, we have had it good for so long that it seems each generation is looking for an easier, more care-free life: shorter work weeks, more leisure time, more creature comforts, more instant gratification. _____, we have grown softer while other countries are growing stronger.

Only time will tell how America weathers the outsourcing storm and a world of competitive nations that are striving to have what we have. _____, we will keep buying cheaper goods at the Wal-Marts whose products are manufactured abroad and eating Chilean grapes that taste just as good as their California counterparts. As corporations have no loyalty to American employees, Americans have no loyalty to American-made goods. We're all looking for the best deal we can get, and we don't really think about the consequences. We have become a consumer-oriented nation, and _____, the producers are coming at us hard.

Revision Guidelines

As you evaluate and revise your current draft, consider the following suggestions.

1. **Opening.** Your goal in the opening is to introduce your topic clearly, create interest for readers, and present your thesis or give readers a sense of the direction of your essay. From your readers' perspective, how effectively would the opening get their attention? Do they sense the seriousness or gravity of the issue, or how it may affect them? How strong is your thesis statement? Make any changes to the opening that will make it more compelling for readers.

2. **Middle.** If you opened the middle section by providing background or explanatory information on your topic, make sure that you have included everything necessary to help readers understand the topic, including defining key terms. Revise this section to make your topic as clear to readers as possible.

Next, read each individual paragraph to see how it might be improved. Is the topic of each paragraph clear? Are your supportive reasons for your thesis strong, and do you provide compelling evidence to validate each reason? Do you provide a source reference for any researched material?

Third, check the overall organization of your middle paragraphs to see whether you have presented your main supportive points in the best order. Does each paragraph flow logically and smoothly from the preceding one? Make any revisions in the order of your paragraphs that will strengthen the organization.

Fourth, did you present and address one or two opposing arguments? Did you do so in a way that will influence readers who may agree with those arguments? What might you add or revise to refute the arguments even more convincingly?

3. **Moral evidence.** Read the draft to determine whether you have provided the strongest moral evidence to help make your case. Will readers clearly see that your thesis is on the side of what is right and fair? What else might you do to bring readers to that side?

4. **Ending.** Read your ending carefully and evaluate its impact on readers. Is it long enough to balance with the other sections and provide a powerful conclusion? Does it reinforce the thesis strongly? Does it leave readers will a clear understanding of the seriousness of the issue, why it should concern them, how they may be affected, or how they should respond? How might you revise the ending to make it stronger, more compelling, or more memorable?

5. **Sentence Wording.** Read each sentence to see how its wording might be improved. Eliminate unnecessary or repetitious words or phrases, reword awkward sentences, clarify vague sentences, and replace questionable word choices. Revise sentences to make them as smooth and clear as possible.

6. **Transitions.** Read your draft to evaluate your use of transitions to connect paragraphs and sentences within paragraphs. Would an added transition here or there help move readers more smoothly from one paragraph to the next or show an important connection between ideas? If you have repeated the same transition(s) numerous times, consider using some different transitions covered in this section.

7. **Paragraphing.** Check your paragraphing one last time to make sure that you are changing paragraphs as you move to different aspects of your essay - a new supporting reason, a response to an opposing argument, a different part of the essay - and that you don't have any overly long paragraphs or strings of short, related paragraphs.

> **8. Audience and purpose.** Read the draft from your readers' perspective, considering how your audience might respond to each paragraph. Revise your paper in ways that will elicit the best response from readers.
>
> Finally, evaluate how well you have accomplished your purpose. Read each part of the draft to see how it relates to your purpose, and make any changes that will strengthen your intent.

Activity 6.11

Applying the revision guidelines, evaluate the following first draft and note possible revisions you might suggest to the writer. Then revise your own draft with the guidelines in mind.

Life at the Zoo (audience: general public)

Imagine that in your inner-planetary travels you are captured by a group of superior beings called Zolots and encaged along with fellow earthlings in their planetary species zoo. You have room to move around in the cage, you are provided food and water, and your most basic needs are met. Adult Zolots and their offspring come everyday to gaze at you, an exotic and rare creature. Your fate, unknown to you at the time, is to remain in this cage until you die, as is the fate of any children you may sire or conceive in captivity.

This wretched, horrific fate is no different than that of every caged animal in a public zoo. We the superior species encage them for our amusement, much as the Zolots encage humans, and rationalize that they are just as happy and perhaps better off than in a free environment, a favorite Zolot rationalization. If we humans feel we would be happier and better off encaged for life by the Zolots, then we may have an argument for encaging wild animals. However, if we believe that life in a Zolot zoo would be one of the worst imaginable fates, then we need to do away with all zoos.

Wild animals placed in zoos are subject to life imprisonment without having done anything wrong. How just is that? What right do we have as humans to imprison animals for life, as well as their offspring, for our own amusement and entertainment? Do we somehow consider it our right just because as the superior specie, we have the power to do it? Two-hundred years ago, Americans justified slavery by rationalizing that Africans were better off as slaves than in their "savage" natural habitat, and that they fared best under the "guidance" of their captors. Do we not use similarly tragic arguments today to imprison animals in cages?

The national organization PETA, People for the Ethical Treatment of

Animals, points out some of the obvious problems of keeping animals in captivity. PETA opposes zoos because zoo cages and cramped enclosures deprive animals of their most basic needs. In general, zoos and wildlife parks preclude or severely restrict natural behaviors, such as flying, swimming, running, hunting, climbing, scavenging, foraging, exploring, and partner selection. The physical and mental frustrations of captivity often lead to abnormal, neurotic, and even self-destructive behaviors, such as pacing, swaying, head-bobbing, bar-biting, and self-mutilation, many of which any zoo visitor can observe on any day.

In addition, according to PETA, animals are regularly bought, sold, borrowed, and traded without any regard for established relationships, similarly to how slaves were treated. Animals are often bred because babies bring in money, but their fate is often bleak once they outgrow their "cuteness." And many zoos still capture and encage animals from the wild.

Dale Jamieson, Director of Environmental Studies at New York University, makes the case that it is morally wrong to take animals from their natural environment, transporting them great distances and keeping them in alien environments in which their liberty is severely restricted. Being taken from the wild and confined in zoos, animals are deprived of a great many goods. For the most part they are prevented from gathering their own food, developing their own social orders and generally behaving in ways that are natural to them. These activities all require significantly more liberty than most animals are permitted in zoos. Unless how we treat animals has absolutely no moral import, to which Jamieson strongly disagrees, then confining them in cages is morally reprehensible.

Are animals better off in zoos than in the wild? Zoo advocates argue that animals in captivity eat better, are free from predators, and often live longer. The same, however, can be said of prison inmates. Who among us would trade our freedom for imprisonment in order to eat better, live longer, or avoid many of the vagaries of a free life? If animals had the ability to express their thoughts, would they feel any differently about choosing freedom over captivity?

Other zoo proponents argue that zoos protect species from extinction. Most animals in zoos, however, are not endangered. For those that are, captivity does nothing, according to Jamieson, to protect wild populations, and returning captive-bred animals to the wild is usually impossible since they have learned no survival skills and often have no natural habitat to return to because of human encroachment. Saving endangered species is clearly not a valid justification for the existence of zoos.

The 2008 article "The Case for Freeing Captive Elephants" on Encyclopedia Britannica's Advocacy for Animals website provides a good example of why zoos are terrible for elephants. In the wild, an elephant lives in a family group that may include her mother, sisters, and aunts and their children as well as other, unrelated females and pre-adolescent males. With this group she wanders for miles every day, grazing on a variety of plant material. She drinks at waterholes and rivers and bathes when she can. Through she is in proximity to many species of animals, some of them predators, she finds security in the company of many of her kind and is rarely threatened. She learns the skills for survival from the example of her elders and participates in caring for calves in preparation for her role as a mother. If she is injured or sick her herd will comfort and support her, and she may live for sixty or more years.

Consider then the life of an elephant in a zoo. She will likely have the company of only one or two unrelated other elephants, or she may be alone. If she was born at the zoo, she may have been separated from her mother and siblings, making a long, incomprehensible journey by truck to her zoo home, or she may have been caught in the wild and made an even more terrifying trip across the continents. She lives in a building and has access to the outdoors only in mild weather. Otherwise she stands on a concrete floor and looks out through bars at the crowds of unfamiliar faces that look back at her, often chained by the leg for long periods of time and forced to stand in one place. When she has access to the outdoors she usually has only a small, confined area in which to move about and interact with the other elephants. At any time she may be sent to another zoo and have to accustom herself to new surroundings, caretakers, and companions.

When you apply this experience to the similar experiences of most animals in a zoo, you get a devastatingly depressing and bleak picture of zoo animals' lives. The only way we can allow this to continue is to ignore the reality of their tortured existence. How can anyone visit a zoo without feeling guilty for the crime against animals that we silently help to perpetuate?

Returning to your zoo captivity by the Zolots, your emotions over a period of time have run the gamut from terrified to angry to hopeful to despairing to depressed to hopeless to numb. After months of captivity, you stare vacantly out of your cage day after day, the same vacant stare that we see in zoo animals, and you vegetate. You become something else, your humanity stripped from you as your memories of family and a free life grow dimmer and dimmer. Your former life eventually becomes dead to you, and you have nothing to live for but your next meal shoved under the bars. Welcome to the zoo.

Editing

By this time in your writing experience, you are probably quite adept at editing your drafts for errors and making the necessary corrections. No doubt you successfully ferret out the types of errors you are most prone to make, leaving you with a few inadvertent slips to clean up.

The most common of these unconscious gaffes - e.g. writing "there" when you mean "their" or "of" when you mean "off" - have been catalogued by a number of writing analysts. While writers are well aware of the correct forms and usages, they will still occasionally blunder, concentrating more on a sentence's content than its wording.

Common Errors

The following errors are among the most common that writers tend to make. While you undoubtedly know the correct forms and usages, it is still wise to check your drafts for those inadvertent slips that all writers make.

1. **Comma Usage:** Omitting commas after introductory clauses or phrases, before coordinating conjunctions in compound sentences, and before and after nonrestrictive relative clauses: The Nuclear Phase I Disarmament Treaty which reduces nuclear stockpiles by twenty percent was approved by the U.S. and Russia. (Commas required after "Treaty" and after "percent" to set off nonrestrictive relative clause). In addition, adding unnecessary commas in places where they aren't required: before "and" connecting two phrases or clauses, before a subordinate conjunction in the middle of a sentence, with restrictive relative clauses.

2. **Pronoun Usage:** Lack of pronoun-antecedent agreement and vague pronoun reference.

3. **Sentence Problems:** Faulty sentence structures involving dangling and misplaced modifiers, two sentences run together without an end mark or with a comma rather than a period between them (comma splice), and incomplete sentences punctuated as sentences (fragments).

4. **Quotation Problems:** Quotations punctuated incorrectly or poorly integrated into a sentence.

5. **Unnecessary or Missing Apostrophes:** Missing apostrophes

in contractions and possessive nouns and unnecessary apostrophes in plural words that *aren't* possessive.

6. **Verb Problems:** Unnecessary shift in verb tense within a paragraph or sentence, typically present to past or past to present. Example: Privately run metropolitan museums have a hard time supporting themselves, and they have often needed the help of the city. (Needless change in tense from present to past.) Revised: Privately run metropolitan museums have a hard time supporting themselves, and they often need the help of the city.

7. **Capitalization:** Unnecessary and missing capitalization. Example: The arch-conservative Senator from Wyoming often clashed with governor Carlyle, who was a liberal democrat. ("Senator" incorrectly capitalized, and "governor" and "democrat" require capitalization.) Revised: The arch-conservative senator from Wyoming often clashed with Governor Carlyle, who was a liberal Democrat.

8. **Wrong Word**: Using "there" for "their," "no" for "know," "its" for it's," "your" for "you're," "accept" for "except," "effect" for "affect," or "hear" for "here."

Activity 6.12

Keeping in mind the most common writing errors and your own error tendencies, proofread your current draft and make the necessary corrections.

Readings

Taking a Bite out of Cheating
By Kim Clark

Teachers, long behind in the cheating arms race, may finally be catching up. They are using new technologies, including text-matching software, webcams, and biometric equipment, as well as cunning stratagems such as Web "honey pots," virtual students, and cheat-proof tests. The result: It appears to be getting harder for students to plagiarize from websites, text-message answers to friends during tests, or get others to do their homework.

The percentage of students who admit to cheating, which had risen from about 20 percent in the mid-1900s to top 50 percent in 2002, has dropped about 10 percentage points, according to one of the nation's leading cheating experts, Donald McCabe of Rutgers. Some of that recent decline may be because of students redefining "cheating" to exclude the increasingly common practice of cutting and pasting material from the Internet, McCabe believes. But the tide may also be turning, at least in part, because of anticheating technology blitzes like those at the University of Central Florida, where many business students now take their tests on cheat-resistant computers in a new, supersecure testing center. UCF students report much less cheating than students at other campuses. "We've scared the living daylights out of them," explains Taylor Ellis, associate dean for undergraduate programs and technology at UCF's college of business.

Professors at the forefront of the cheating war say they have had to scramble to catch up to youngsters who have proved brilliant at using new technology to get A's without studying. There are hundreds of websites that offer custom-written papers. YouTube has dozens of student-made videos teaching how, for example, to scan a Coke bottle label into a computer, replace the nutrition information with physics notes, and paste the label back onto a bottle to create a cheat aid unlikely to be caught by teachers. And students say it is easy to load notes into cellphones or programmable calculators and sneak peeks at the devices during tests. Some say they've used their devices' infrared, Bluetooth, or texting capabilities to share information with other test takers.

A recent Ohio State University graduate said he often walked into tests with three calculators in his backpack so that he could turn one in if the professor tried to crack down by asking students to turn in their calculators. He said other students hid powerful calculators in the bodies of old, basic ones that are permitted in exams.

"Cheating is super easy now. College classes are way too big, and you can pull out anything on your desk," he says. And it is widespread, he says, because students are busy, hungry for good grades, and often skeptical of the lifetime benefit of learning what many professors put on tests. The student, who worked nearly full-time during school, said it took him only an hour or so to program his calculator with notes. That saved him as much as 20 hours of study time. "I don't really consider what I did cheating...because in the real world I would be using that device...I see that as just being more efficient."

Of course, most schools are still trying to fight cheating by old-fashioned methods, such as appealing to students' sense of fairness. And, in fact, studies show that well-designed and enforced honor codes can make big dents in improper behavior.

Unfortunately, student pledges are not a cure-all. So, instructors and school administrators say they have little choice but to join the technological arms race. The instructors are hoping to encourage students to do their own original work by using the same technology that students use to cheat.

Teachers say they are catching a surprising number of plagiarizers by simply Googling unattributed phrases they find in students' papers. Often, they say, they find passages lifted improperly from Wikipedia, free essay sites, or other Web pages.

Several new software companies are giving instructors even more firepower to fight cheating. Turnitin.com, SafeAssign, and a few other new companies have built up databases of millions of school papers, books, articles, and Web pages that they compare against homework. Millions of students around the world now turn in their homework electronically to the companies so that the programs can highlight parts that match other sources. Teachers sign on to the companies' sites to look at the results and decide how much similarity is too much.

These software programs have been boons to professors like Rick Lotspeich, who teaches economics at Indiana State University in Terre Haute. Until ISU signed up for Turnitin.com a few years ago, Lotspeich says he often spent hours in the library trying to document suspicions of student plagiarism. Now, he just clicks on his computer. "The electronic revolution cuts both ways. It makes plagiarism a lot easier, and checking a lot easier," he says.

The software isn't perfect, of course. A group of Virginia high schoolers is suing Turnitin.com for allegedly taking their papers for its own profit without compensating them. This group (and other students) also says the software doesn't work well because it sometimes accuses students who use common phrases or repeat something they themselves happened to write or blog about previously. And some students say they can beat the program by simply replacing every third word or so from copied material. Turnitin officials say that while a good paraphrase of someone else's material might squeak through, programmers have fixed most of the commonly exploited flaws. CEO John Barrie says that the company is making fair use of the students' papers. "Institutions that have used Turnitin for five or more years have, on average, experienced an over 80 percent decrease in levels of unoriginal student work," he claims. And that, he says, "is a significant public good."

The Graduate Management Admission Council announced this summer that it will start testing palm-print readers to make sure students who sign up for the GMAT are the ones who actually take the tests. Peg Jobst, senior vice president of the GMAT program, says upgrading from fingerprints to palms will allow their computers to flag anyone whose current name and palm don't match previous records. Earlier programs that matched photos didn't always work, although several years ago they did catch a man who wore a wig and dressed as a woman, Jobst said. "We know that cheaters invest heavily in technology, so we invest more," she says.

In addition, more universities are requiring online students to install equipment and software that will make it nearly impossible to cheat on tests. Troy University in Alabama encourages online students to install on their home computers a $150 anticheating package that includes a 360-degree webcam so that proctors can remotely monitor all sights and sounds in their rooms and software that locks down computers for anything but tests during exams. Other schools, such as UCF and Penn State, are installing test centers in which students sit at video-monitored desks and complete their exams using computers that have been cheat-proofed by blocking all ports and Internet access.

Gavin Keirans, president of Penn State's student government, remembers feeling dismayed the first time he had to sit at one of the school's video-monitored testing   computers. "I wasn't too happy.... It was almost out of the world of *1984*." But he and most other students now appreciate the way the center rewards those who study. "I think it deters cheating a great deal," Keirans says.

Barbara Christe, program director of biomedical engineering technology at Indiana University-Purdue University in Indianapolis, says she usually catches three or four students a year with her Web "honey pots." She sets up phony Web pages that specifically answer questions in her homework assignments and tests with blatantly out-of-date or inaccurate information. Because they are tailored for her course material, her sites typically show up first in Google searches. It's easy then for Christe to snag those students who took the bait and simply cut and pasted information. Instead of automatically flunking the guilty students (who are typically freshmen), in most cases she tries to use the incidents as a chance to teach how to correctly vet a source.

Christe also often signs up as a student for her own online courses under an assumed name. That way, she says, her alter ego gets many of the E-mails her students send to each other. Occasionally, she's caught students posting answers. More often, she says, she'll see an E-mail from a student complaining or asking for help. Then she'll contact the student and say, "I heard from a student that Assignment 7 is really giving you a challenge," and offer to help.

The Educational Testing Service, which administers the SAT and AP tests, says it is ratcheting up security. It doesn't allow any food, bottles, or electronic devices, including cellphones, in testing rooms. Penn State's new testing center requires students to take off or turn around any hat with a brim; that's to prevent students from using notes written on the underside of their caps. Students also must take off zipped jackets or sweatshirts - clothing items that offer plenty of cheat-note storage space - before starting tests. UCF's College of Business has banned chewing gum at its secure test center after catching a student hiding a Bluetooth cellphone earpiece behind her long hair and talking to a helper by pretending to chew gum. UCF also plugged up the computers' USB ports after proctors caught a student hiding a flash drive inside a pen.

A growing number of professors are creating computerized banks of test questions so that they can randomly assign different questions to different students. That way, there's no advantage to looking at a neighbor's paper. In addition, professors are experimenting with timed short essays that can be aced only by students who really know their stuff, since it would take too long to look up the information.

Some professors, such as Indiana State's Lotspeich, require students to turn in outlines and rough drafts before the final paper deadline so that they can see each student's progress. That quickly flags students who might have downloaded completed essays from the Web.

Some professors are even reducing cheating by creating more real-world assignments that point out the stupidity of cheating. Clayton Lewis, a University of Colorado computer science professor, now allows students to collaborate on homework. It's silly to consider that "cheating," he believes. "We're gradually waking up to the fact that in real life, it is all about working together," he says.

Lewis's assignments are often little more than: ""Think of something you would like to do with a computer, and show me that you could do it.' It isn't going to eliminate cheating, but the incidence is going to be really reduced," he says. After all, Lewis notes: "What's the point of cheating on something you want to do?"

DISCUSSION

1. What is the thesis of the essay?
2. What evidence does the author provide to support her thesis, and how effective is it?
3. What examples are provided of ways in which colleges and teachers reduce student cheating? Do the measures appear rather drastic or defensible given the size of the problem?
4. What issues of right and wrong are addressed in the essay, and how do they relate to the thesis?
5. From the amount of cheating that purportedly goes on, cheating does not appear to be a moral issue for many students. Why do you think that is?
6. What student justifications for cheating are presented in the essay? Do you feel they are valid, and why?

Same-sex Marriage Not the End of Morality
by Philip Gailey

The abortion wars have been raging for three decades, with no end in sight. Now it appears we are headed toward another emotional and divisive fight over whether to legalize homosexual marriage. The debate on this issue was relatively low-key until the U.S. Supreme Court struck down a Texas anti-sodomy law a few weeks ago. None other than Justice Antonin Scalia spoke for religious and cultural conservatives who see the decision as the end of sexual morality, the family and civilization itself. In his dissent, Scalia warned the majority ruling called into question "state laws against bigamy, same-sex marriage, adult incest, prostitution, masturbation, adultery, fornication, bestiality, and obscenity." Oh my, the end really is near.

So now we have Republicans calling for a constitutional amendment to ban homosexual marriage, Democrats running for political cover and churches tearing themselves apart over what God would do about it. Most of the Democrats running for president say they support civil unions for gays but not marriage. Sen. John Kerry of Massachusetts put it this way in a recent interview with the Washington Post: "Marriage is an institution between men and women for the purpose of having children and procreation. . . . I've been willing to take my lumps on everything that I think enhances people's rights and gives people equality, but I think there is something special about the institution of marriage - the oldest institution in the world."

I wonder if Kerry really believes that the institution of marriage would crumble if gays had the legal right to tie the knot? Heterosexuals would keep on getting married and having children and getting divorced. Religious leaders would continue to denounce same-sex unions as a sin and refuse to bless them. The big difference would be that gays would be entitled to all the legal benefits and protections straight couples enjoy. Of course, they could realize most of those benefits from a civil union, which only Vermont recognizes.

Same-sex marriage and abortion have at least one thing in common: Much of the opposition to both is rooted in religion, which if anything makes the public debate even more contentious. It's hard to reason with people who claim to take their orders straight from God. The deity seems to be sending mixed signals: Most religious leaders oppose homosexual marriage, but others support it.

The worldwide Anglican Church community, which includes the Episcopal Church USA, appears on the verge of splitting apart over the issue of gay bishops and same-sex unions. Conservative Episcopal leaders in this country have aligned themselves with Anglican archbishops from Africa, Asia and Australia who oppose accepting a gay bishop or blessing a same-sex union. I assume Episcopal bishops on both sides of this issue are reading the same Bible.

As for the Roman Catholic Church, there's no point in even raising the subject of gay marriage. The church considers homosexuality itself a sin and a lifestyle choice. But the Catholic hierarchy has lost much of its moral authority to speak out against gay marriage or any other sin involving sex. The Catholic church has its own sex scandal to explain. Last week, the Massachusetts attorney general said his 16-month investigation concluded that at least 789 children and probably more than 1,000 have been sexually abused by priests and other church workers in the Roman Catholic Archdiocese of Boston since 1940. And that number included only victims who reported their abuse. What's really unforgivable, however, is that the abusive priests were protected by church leaders.

It was not that long ago that most states had anti-miscegenation laws. The arguments against interracial marriage then are similar to the arguments against homosexual marriage now - that it was "unnatural," that it was forbidden by the Scriptures, that it would harm children and offend public decency. Of course, as we know now, it really was more about prejudice than anything else.

A recent poll by the Pew Research Center for the People and the Press found that opposition to gay marriage has dropped significantly among Americans in recent years, with 53 percent opposing same-sex marriages and 38 percent supporting them. In 1996, 65 percent were opposed, with 27 percent favoring. The strongest opposition to gay marriage is among African-Americans, 65 percent today, the same percentage as in 1996.

Gay marriage is not about civil rights. It is about society's evolving social and cultural values. This is an issue that can't be settled in the courts or in the political arena. Getting used to the idea is going to take time. Hearts and minds will change slowly, and in time even people who are uncomfortable with the idea may come around, not so much to support same-sex marriage as to tolerate it. I wonder if our children and grandchildren will look back on this debate and ask what all the fuss was about.

DISCUSSION

1. What is the implied thesis of the essay?
2. What evidence does the author provide in support of her thesis, and how effective is it?
3. What moral arguments are presented in the essay, and how do they relate to the thesis?
4. The essay uses a poll to show that the percentage of Americans opposed to same-sex marriage has dropped significantly since 1996. What do you think has brought about the change?
5. What is your opinion on same-sex marriage, and what if any influence did the essay have on your viewpoint?
6.

Animal Rights
by Amanda Wright

Do animals, like humans, possess certain inalienable rights? A growing movement in America believes they do.

Concern for animals has a long history. The ancient Greek philosopher and mathematician Pythagoras argued against cruelty to animals. St. Francis of Assisi, who founded the Franciscan Order of Catholic monks in the middle ages, taught that animals are our brothers. In 1641, Massachusetts Puritans wrote a code of laws called

"The Body of Liberties." One of the laws in this code said, "No man shall exercise any tyranny or cruelty towards any brute creatures which are usually kept for man's use." This law seemed to imply that animals, at least farm livestock, had the right to a life free of unnecessary suffering.

The American Society for the Prevention of Cruelty to Animals started in New York in 1866. Through its efforts, New York drafted an animal protection law that became a model for most of the other states. This law prohibited any needless torture, overloading, beating, mutilation, or killing of "any living creature." It still permitted, however, "properly conducted scientific experiments" involving animals. The Society for the Prevention of Cruelty to Animals and similar organizations worked for many years at the state and local levels to monitor animal dealers, circuses, zoos, movie makers, and pounds.

In the second half of the 20th century, a new wave of more aggressive animal-rights activists formed. They differed from previous activists because they do not simply want people to stop treating animals cruelly. They believe that animals, like humans, have certain inalienable rights. Peter Singer, author of *Animal Liberation*, is one of these activists. He argues that all animals are equal. By this he does not mean that all animals should vote or have freedom of speech. These rights would be meaningless for animals other than humans. Nor does he mean that all animals should be treated the same. He means that all animals should have equal consideration for their well-being. The well-being of a pig and a human are far different, he says. A pig belongs with other pigs where they can eat and run freely. A child needs to learn how to read.

Singer says that it is morally irrelevant that animals cannot speak and are not as intelligent as humans. He points out that we still accord human infants and mentally retarded people equal consideration. According to Singer, the characteristic that gives a being the moral right to equal consideration is the capacity for suffering and enjoyment. "If a being suffers, there can be no moral justification for refusing to take that suffering into consideration. No matter what the nature of the being, the principle of equality requires that its suffering be counted equally with the like suffering . . . of any other being." Singer has a term for those who allow the interests of humans "to override the greater interests of members of other species." He calls them "speciesists."

Few argue with Singer that we should take an animal's suffering into account. Those disagreeing with him, however, believe that human life is worth more than animal life. R.G. Frey, a philosopher and author of *Interests and Rights: The Case Against Animals*, says that most people believe that the value of animal life varies. He notes that most people value dogs, cats, and chimps more than mice, rats, and worms. He gives the example of a dog and a human on a raft. If only one can be saved, he says, few would disagree that it should be the human.

The reason he thinks human life is more valuable is that it has more potential richness to it. He says that unlike animals, "there are whole dimensions to our lives - love, marriage, educating children, jobs, hobbies, sporting events, cultural pursuits, intellectual development and striving, etc. - that greatly expand our range of absorbing endeavors and . . . significantly deepen the texture of our lives."

The debate over animal rights, however, does not usually occur in the abstract. It has taken place over a series of issues. In the 1980s, groups like People for the Ethical Treatment of Animals (PETA) protested the use of animals in cosmetics testing. Revlon tested the safety of its eye makeup by applying substances directly on the eyes of rabbits. Protesters carried signs saying, "How many rabbits does Revlon blind for beauty's sake?" Within six months Revlon agreed to a permanent ban on animal tests. Over the next 10 years, protests forced more than 500 other cosmetic companies to give up animal tests.

Other protests targeted medical research. During the early 1960s, investigators revealed that laboratory test animals were often forced to live under filthy conditions in cages that were too small without any veterinary care to ease the pain caused by the experiments. A movement soon emerged to ban all testing on animals. But alarmed medical researchers argued that animal testing played a necessary role in ending diseases such as polio, making human organ transplants possible, and developing many kinds of life-saving drugs.

Congress passed the first federal law regulating the treatment of lab animals in 1966. The Animal Welfare Act did not become effective, however, until Congress passed strengthening amendments in 1985. The amendments require humane treatment and adequate feeding, sanitation, shelter, and vet care for lab animals. The amendments also call for "a physical environment to promote the psychological well-being of primates." Farm animals as well as birds, rats, and mice (which are used the most in laboratory experiments) are not covered by this law. The strengthened Animal Welfare Act applies not only to research facilities, but also to animal dealers and exhibitors like zoos.

The dispute boils down to two main issues: First, does animal research improve human health? Dr. Michael E. DeBakey, chairman of the Foundation for Biomedical Research, states: "Not one advancement in the care of patients - advancements that you use and take for granted every day - has been realized without the use of animal research."

PETA disputes this. It says that rats and mice are so different from humans that studies on them tell little about humans. It asserts that "sophisticated non-animal research methods are more accurate, less expensive, and less time-consuming than traditional animal-based research methods." The second issue is: Even if it helps humans, is it ethical? It is clearly not ethical to conduct medical experiments on humans. Is it all right to conduct them on animals?

Before World War II, animals meant for food usually lived outdoors, except in extreme weather. Today, these animals live on what animal-rights activists call "factory farms." Chickens, an important part of the American diet, live in small cages stacked one on top of another in temperature-controlled, windowless barns. Often their beaks and claws are trimmed so they cannot harm one another if they fight. They are fed a special diet that promotes their growth and includes antibiotics to control disease. Other food animals--pigs, turkeys, and calves--live in similarly controlled environments.

Animal-rights activists consider these environments unnatural, inhumane, and incredibly exploitative of animals. They say that the food producers are treating the animals as machines, ignoring their pain, frustration, and natural desires. The Humane Society of the United States says: "Factory farms deny animals many of their most basic . . . needs. . . . Such artificial conditions cause animals to suffer from boredom, frustration and stress, which often leads to abnormal behavior, including unnatural aggression." The society claims hundreds of thousands of chickens die every day due to these conditions, but the companies simply consider this a cost of doing business.

Farmers deny all this. They say that their most important concern is the health of their animals because their businesses depend on this. They point out that American food production is the envy of the world. They say that animal-rights activists overly idealize animal life on a traditional farm. The Animal Industry Foundation, a national organization for animal agriculture, says: "Housing protects animals from predators, disease, and bad weather or extreme climate. Housing also makes breeding and birth less stressful, protects young animals, and makes it easier for farmers to care for both healthy and sick animals. Modern housing is well ventilated, warm, well-lit, clean and scientifically designed for the specific needs of the animal, such as the regular availability of fresh water and a nutritionally balanced diet."

Animal experimentation and intensive animal production are the two issues in the forefront of the animal-rights movement. But they are not the only ones. Animal-rights activists have also questioned the value of hunting animals, horse and dog racing, using animals for entertainment (in films, circuses, and zoos), eating meat, wearing fur, and even owning pets. Although the movement may take dubious positions on some issues, such as pet ownership, there is little question that animal-rights activists shed a constant and critical light on issues of animal cruelty that would otherwise go unnoticed.

DISCUSSION

1. What is the thesis of the essay?
2. What historical background information does the essay provide, and why is it important to the essay?
3. What evidence does the author provide to support her thesis, and how effective is it?

4. What moral issues are presented in the essay, and how do they relate to the thesis?

5. Based on the essay, what is your viewpoint on the animal-rights movement? What do you believe is the best "balance" between human and animal rights?

Your next critique-writing experience involves comparing two essays or articles with different viewpoints on the same topic. Newspapers frequently run point-counterpoint editorials to provide readers with two sides to a topical issue to evaluate. Your critique will analyze two such essays and evaluate their relative merit.

In critiquing two essays, you are essentially doing separate evaluations of the two and then based on those evaluations, comparing their relative effectiveness in supporting their theses and convincing readers of the efficacy of their viewpoints. The new critiquing elements - analyzing two essays rather than one and doing a comparative evaluation of the two - add a new level of complexity that will further your critical reading, analytical, and critique-writing skills.

Writing the Critique

The following suggestions should help you write your comparative critique:

1. Read each essay carefully, noting differences and similarities in their treatment of the topic.

2. For each essay, identify the thesis, evaluate the quality of evidence and support provided, and consider the essay's strengths and weaknesses.

3. Formulate your opinion on the effectiveness of each individual essay and what specifically you base that opinion on.

4. Based on your opinion of each essay, compare their relative effectiveness, and the specific reasons for one essay being more effective than the other. (Or specific reasons that the two are similarly effective or ineffective.)

5. In writing your critique, first introduce the two essays and their topic, the importance or relevance of the topic, and present your thesis: your viewpoint on the relative effectiveness of the two essays. (Or you may save your thesis until after you have summarized and evaluated the individual essays.)

    Next, summarize and evaluate each essay's main supportive points and evidence, which will comprise your middle paragraphs. Finally, based on your evaluations, compare the efficacy of the two essays, highlighting the strengths of the more effective essay and the weaknesses of the less effective one.

Activity 6.13

Write a critique comparing two essays or articles that have different viewpoints on the same topic. Consider different topical issues that would be of interest to readers, and find essays or articles with different viewpoints on these issues. You might find essays in the text, online, or in newspapers or periodicals.

Unit Seven
Synthesis

In this last unit, you write a final essay drawing upon everything you have learned about effective writing. The main difference between this essay and previous ones is that you are writing a "full-blown" research paper complete with parenthetical references and bibliography.

Everything you accomplished in your previous essays is relevant to your final writing assignment:

- Substantial pre-writing preparation.
- Generating a thesis reflecting your viewpoint on an issue, and developing and supporting your thesis in the essay.
- Incorporating several types of evidence in your writing - empirical, factual, logical, comparative, causal, and moral - to validate your points, and providing source references for your evidence.
- Paraphrasing - putting into your own words - most of the research material incorporated in your essays, and using quotations for particularly striking or critical comments.
- Providing background and explanatory information to help readers understand a topic.
- Acknowledging and responding to opposing viewpoints to further your purpose.
- Writing effective openings and endings to make the greatest impact on readers.
- Establishing a purpose for each essay and crafting the essay for a specific audience.
- Revising your drafts to produce the most effectively worded and organized essay.

You are certainly no stranger to research papers, having employed critical elements of research writing in your previous essays. In this unit you learn what you need to know about parenthetical references and bibliography entries, two additional requirements for a properly documented research paper.

Since this is your final essay, you will be provided only the broadest guidelines for planning and writing your paper. You have done enough prewriting planning, drafting, and revising throughout the course to have developed a process that no doubt works well for you. You have also done significant research, learning how to mine the richest resources for a topic. Use the guidelines presented in this unit in ways that fit your personal writing process and will help you write the most effective paper.

This final "Prewriting" section provides some guidelines to help you prepare for your upcoming research paper. Use the prewriting suggestions to whatever purpose you find most useful.

Topic Selection

As you know, topic selection is a critical part of writing, one that can lead to an interesting or mundane writing experience. Finding a topic of interest is a major step towards writing an engaging essay.

For your upcoming research paper, select an issue or problem that interests you and that you would like to know more about. It may come from any field and be of local, state, national, or international concern. Since you are writing a research paper, select a topic for which you can find information from various sources. You might consider two or three different topics and evaluate the research sources available before making a decision.

Activity 7.1

Select a topic that you feel would make a great subject for your research paper.

EXAMPLE

Topic selection:

I am going to look into a few different topics before making a decision. One is the national health care plan that is now law. One problem is that it is so complex that it is difficult to understand all the ramifications. I am a bike racing fan, and doping in professional bike racing is a big issue. The trustees of the state college board are proposing a 20% increase in tuition for next school year to make up for a big funding deficit. There are also two propositions on the state ballot for September that are getting a lot of attention, one to legalize marijuana for recreational use, the other to legalize gambling off of Native American land, where it is currently restricted to. I'm going to look into some of these issues, but I may also look further.

Researching

Thoroughly researching your topic is a critical part of the prewriting preparation for a research paper. Through your investigation, you will learn more about the your topic: its history or background, specifics aspects of the issue, causes and effects of a problem, and who may be affected. In addition, you may discover differing viewpoints on the issue and arguments that support those viewpoints. You will also find out how much information is available on the topic and whether you can develop a paper from it. Finally, based on your research, you may form an opinion on the topic, which may become the thesis for your paper.

Research Guidelines

As you research your topic, consider the following suggestions.

1. **Read broadly to learn as much as possible**. Look for differing viewpoints on the topic and the evidence that supports them, and see whether there are also areas of agreement that run through the research. The best-written papers often have a number of different sources, showing the breadth of the writer's investigation. A paper that relies primarily on two or three sources may have readers questioning the thoroughness of the research and what the writer may have overlooked.

2. **Check the date of publication for each article or book that you read**. In general, the more current the publication, the more credible and reliable the information. For example, findings on the rate of teenage pregnancy or violent crime in the U.S. from articles written in 1998 may show very different, and inaccurate, pictures compared to similar articles written in 2010. The more dated the information, the more suspect it is for describing or reflecting the current situation.

3. **As you read from your sources, take notes on anything that may be relevant to your paper.** If you are writing about a particular problem, look for causes, effects, who is affected, and possible solutions. If you are writing about an issue, look for different viewpoints and the support for each viewpoint. As with your previous essays, look for evidence to validate each cause, effect, or supportive reason. Before beginning your research, ask the question, "What kinds of things do I need to find out about the topic to write the best paper?"

   As you take notes, it is useful to put information from different sources on separate note cards to keep the sources for all researched material clear. Later you can "organize" your note cards by topic area, which can help in writing your first draft.

4. **Document all of your source material thoroughly**. You will use this documentation for source references within the body of your paper and in your "Works Cited" bibliography at

the end. As you take notes, document each individual source of information, including the page number(s) on which the information is found.

To document your research material, include the following source information on your note cards for each piece of information. (The examples are in their "Works Cited" form.)

Book: Author (last name, first). title of book, publishing location: name of publisher, date of publication.

Fleming, Thomas. *Liberty: The American Revolution.*
New York: Viking, 1997.

Article

Newspaper: Author (last name, first). "title of article." Name of newspaper, date article appears, page number(s).

Holden, Stephen. "Frank Sinatra Dies at 82; Matchless Stylist of Pop."
New York Times 16 May 1998, A3.

Magazine: Author (last name, first). "title of article." Name of magazine, date article appears, page number(s).

Gawande, Atul. "The Man Who Couldn't Stop Eating."
New Yorker 9 July 2001: 66-75.

Journal: Author (last name, first). "Title of article." Name of journal, issue number (year of publication), page number(s).

Kralj, Mary. "Getting Out of the Box." *Consulting Psychology Journal: Practice and Research* 46.2 (1994): 27-28.

Online Article

Newspaper: Author (last name, first). "Title of article." Name of newspaper, date of article, date of website where article appeared, online address.

Wright, Steven. "Curriculum 2000 Draws Criticism." *The Chronicle: the Independent Daily at Duke University.* 25 Jan. 2001. Web. 7 Nov. 2001. http://www.dukechronicle.com/news.

Magazine: Author (last name, first). "Title of article." Title of online magazine, date of article, date article appeared online, online address.

Saletan, William. "The Ethicist's New Clothes." *Slate.com*. 16 August 2001. Web. 17 August 2001. http://slate.msn.com.

Journal: Author (last name, first). "Title of article." Name of journal, volume number (date). Page number(s), date of article, date article appeared online, online address.

Evnine, Simon J. "The Universality of Logic: On the Connection between Rationality and Logical Ability." *Mind* 110.438 (2001): 1-2. Web. 31 July 2001. http://www3.oup.co.uk/mind.

Activity 7.2

Considering the suggestions presented, research the topic for your upcoming paper and collect information that may be relevant for your essay.

Thesis and Support

As with your previous essays, the thesis for your upcoming paper reflects your viewpoint on the topic based on your knowledge and understanding of the issue. Your essay is written in *support* of your thesis, explaining why you believe as you do and presenting evidence to validate your viewpoint.

To decide on a thesis for your upcoming paper and generate some potential support for it, consider the following suggestions.

1. **Research your topic and analyze your findings before deciding on a thesis**. Sometimes a writer with a preconceived thesis will research his paper specifically to support that thesis rather than looking at all of the available material. Such selective researching can lead to *cherry picking*: using material that supports a particular viewpoint and ignoring anything that may contradict it. Cherry picking can result in a slanted and inaccurate appraisal of a topic and leave readers unimpressed.

2. **Decide on a thesis which your research findings support**. Since your paper is intended to reveal the validity of your thesis, your research evidence should point clearly towards it. The more evidence you can provide to support your thesis, the stronger your case. If your thesis is strongly vali-

dated by the research, it will certainly make your job easier.

3. **To validate your thesis, find the best reasons to support it.** These reasons are usually *alleged facts* which your research evidence will support. The more reasons you can provide and substantiate with evidence, the stronger your case.

4. **To validate your thesis for a problem-oriented paper, make sure that the thesis is supported by all aspects of the research: the causes, effects, people or things affected, and solution.** For example, if the thesis of a particular paper is that a particular problem is difficult but not impossible to solve, the causes should reveal the difficulties, the effects should show why the difficulties must be overcome, and the solution should appear powerful enough to meet the challenge.

Activity 7.3

Based on your research and understanding of the topic, generate a thesis for your upcoming paper that the research can support.

EXAMPLE

Topic: Uninsured Children in America

Possible thesis: Every child in America deserves to have medical coverage.

Evidence

As mentioned throughout the text, the strength of your essay often lies in the evidence you provide to reveal the truth or validity of your statements. In each previous unit, you focused on one particular type of evidence: empirical, factual, logical, comparative, causal, or moral. For your upcoming essay, you can marshal all types of evidence to help make your case.

As you consider various reasons in support of your thesis, be mindful of the types of evidence you might use to validate each reason. For example, if you were writing about a proposed tuition increase and its effect on students, you might state that a 20% tuition increase will cause a drop in enrollment. You may use the following types of evidence to validate your statement: *comparative*, showing the effect on enrollment that a similar tuition increase had five years earlier; *factual*, revealing studies that show a strong correlation between significant tuition increases and drops in enrollment; and *empirical*, presenting your personal knowledge that a number of students will drop out if the tuition increase is implemented.

What evidence you ultimately use to validate a particular point will depend on what is available and what you feel is most compelling. All types of evidence have their strengths, and the more evidence you can muster, the better. As you mull over how you might convince readers of the validity of a particular point, consider each type of evidence, how it might be used to help validate the point, and where you might find such evidence.

Activity 6.4

Based on your research and personal knowledge, consider the types of evidence you have available to help make your case and how you might best use this evidence.

EXAMPLE

Topic: Uninsured Children in America

Possible thesis: Every child in America deserves to have medical coverage.

Evidence:

Factual evidence shows:
1. Many children in the U.S. don't have health insurance.
2. There are reasons why so many children don't have insurance.
3. The effects on children who don't have medical coverage are devastating.

Comparative evidence shows:
1. Other countries have fewer uninsured children than the U.S.
2. There are ways to provide medical coverage for all children.
3. Insured children are healthier than uninsured children.

Causal evidence shows:
1. Clear-cut reasons for children not being insured.

Moral evidence shows:
1. We have a moral obligation to ensure that every child has access to health services.
2. America should be just as concerned about the health

of its children as other nations who provide guaranteed medical coverage.

3. A small increase in taxes would be a small price to pay to do what's right for America's children.

Differing Viewpoints

As with your previous essays, acknowledging and responding to differing viewpoints is an important part of your research paper. If readers with opposing viewpoints don't see them addressed in a paper, they may wonder if the writer is even aware of those viewpoints and find no reason to reconsider them.

In researching your topic, you will no doubt come across differing viewpoints, one which you might decide upon as your thesis. For opposing viewpoints, look closely at the evidence that supports them and the people who embrace them. How can you best respond to those viewpoints to get readers to reconsider or abandon them? As you research your topic, make note of the most crucial opposing viewpoints and their underlying arguments.

Activity 7.5

Consider opposing viewpoints to your thesis and how you might respond to them in your paper.

EXAMPLE
Topic: Uninsured Children in America

Possible thesis: Every child in America deserves to have medical coverage.

Opposing viewpoints:
1. Government should not get involved in health insurance, leading to more socialism.
   Response: Government is already involved in Medicare and Medicaid programs, which help millions of Americans with health coverage.
2. Any new program will create higher taxes.
   Response: Studies show that any tax increase would be minimal. It would be a small price to pay for guaranteeing insurance to all children.

Audience and Purpose

Your reading audience and writing purpose for your upcoming essay may be clear from the beginning or may emerge as you learn more about your topic and how best to approach it. There is little need to consider audience or purpose before you have a good understanding of the topic and your viewpoint has begun to crystallize.

For example, let's say you are writing an essay on America's military involvement in Afghanistan. At this point, you may not have an opinion on whether such involvement is necessary or what the military goal is. If you decide ultimately that an American military presence in Afghanistan is needed, your reading audience could be quite different than if you decided that the military presence is a waste of time, money, and lives. In addition, your purpose would be entirely different based on whether or not you supported America's involvement.

It is worthwhile to have a sense of audience and purpose before writing your first draft. Once you are clear on your thesis, your audience and purpose usually come into sharper focus.

Activity 7.6

Consider a potential reading audience and purpose for your upcoming paper.

EXAMPLE

Topic: Uninsured children in America

Thesis: Every child in America should have medical coverage.

Audience: general public, who must understand problem and support solution

Purpose: to educate readers to the problem and motivate them to support legislation and programs that will help solve the problem

Drafting

In this section you are introduced to two elements of research writing - parenthetical references and bibliography - required by the MLA (Modern Language Association) research writing style that you will be using. Next, you are provided some basic considerations for writing your first draft. While most of these considerations have been covered previously, applying them to a new draft on a different topic is always unique.

Citing Sources

Since you have been referencing sources in all of your essays, you should have no problem including parenthetical references and a "Works Cited" section that are required in the MLA-style research paper. The purpose of citing your sources is the same as in other essays: first, to distinguish between the research information and your own ideas and responses, and second, to help lend credibility to the information and enable readers to verify the sources if they would like.

Citing Sources within the Body

To cite sources properly within the body of your paper, follow these guidelines.

1. **Provide a parenthetical reference for each piece of researched information.** Most typically, the parenthetical reference will include the author's last name and page number where the information was found, with no comma separating them:

   The rapid melting of glaciers in the Arctic regions could never have occurred through natural causes (Foster 14).

   If the source has two authors, include them both in parenthesis along with the page number: (Sherman and White 6). If there are several authors, include the first two authors listed followed by "et al.," signifying additional authors: (Sherman and White et al. 6). Frequently with online sources, there is no page number. In those cases, provide the author's name without a page number following it: (Gibson).

2. **If you reference the author's name within the sentence, provide only the page number in parenthesis where the information was found:**

   According to climatologist Handley Foster, the rapid melting of glaciers in the Arctic regions provides powerful evidence of global warming created by humans (14).

In addition, if you reference information from the same source successively but from a different page, provide only the page number in parentheses:

Nothing explained the change in temperament of the young chimpanzee Zelda (Houghton 13). She just wasn't her usual energetic self. It wasn't until a video camera caught an older chimpanzee who had been added to the compound abusing Zelda that zoo keepers discovered the reason (16).

3. **If there is no author given for the source, include the title and page number:**
    Demographics across America's colleges show an increasing percentage of women attending college and a decreasing percentage of men ("Changing Gender Demographics in American Colleges" 2).

4. **If a secondary source is quoted within your source, include "qtd. in" (for "quoted in") within parentheses along with the author's name and page number:**
    According to sociologist Gretchen Woods, "In some American sub-cultures, the stigma that was attached to teenage girls getting pregnant no longer exists" (qtd. in Flanagan 14).

5. **Although you aren't required to provide a source reference *within* the sentence when using parenthetical citations, it is still a good idea when that reference will lend credibility or weight to the information.** For example, if the author is a noted expert on the topic, or if the information came from a significant study, it is worthwhile to let readers know it:

Noted archaeologist Marcus Freeman believes that the greatest archaeological discoveries of early man still lie ahead due to the fertile digging grounds around the world that have yet to be excavated (6).

A ten-year Harvard Biological Institute study of identical twins separated at birth reveals a remarkable similarity in their personalities, interests, vocations, and life circumstances, strong evidence for the overwhelming influence of genetics (Green 23).

Works Cited

The bibliographical "Works Cited" section at the end of your research paper includes a source reference for every source that you used in your paper. The entries are listed alphabetically and are formatted and provide information in conformance with the MLA style. To document and format your "Works Cited" section correctly, see the documentation examples on pages 323-324 and the "Works Cited" section at the end of the sample essay on page 333.

As with parenthetical citations, if no author is indicated for a source, your "Works Cited" entry begins with the title of the article; if a source has two authors, include both of them in the entry; and if a source has more than two authors, include the first two authors followed by "et al."

First Draft

While your upcoming research paper may be the longest, most complex paper you have written for the course, it is essentially an elongated version of other essays you have written. Since you have done research for most of your essays, you are already experienced at incorporating research material in your papers, providing source references, paraphrasing and quoting from sources, using researched evidence to validate your points, presenting source information for your particular writing purpose, and weighing in on the research material with your own ideas and opinions. Therefore, drafting your research paper will not be that different from what you have been doing.

Drafting Guidelines

Consider the following suggestions in writing your first draft.

1. **Opening.** Introduce your topic clearly and in a way that will capture your readers' interest, and present your thesis. Let them know why they should care about the problem or issue you are writing about. Since your research paper will probably be longer than the other essays you have written, each section, including the opening, may also be proportionately longer.

2. **Middle.** If necessary, open the middle paragraphs by providing background or explanatory information that will help readers understand your topic and its significance. Define any terms, such as "victimless crime" or "assault weapons," that are critical to your topic.

   In the middle paragraphs, make the case for your thesis. If you are writing about a problem, present the causes, effects, and who or what is affected in the most effective order. If you are writing about an issue, present the strongest supporting points for your thesis. Use the most compelling evidence from your research to help verify the causes and effects and validate your supporting points.

Most typically, you will also acknowledge and respond to opposing viewpoints in the middle paragraphs, although they can also be addressed in your conclusion. Put your responses wherever they fit most naturally in your draft and will make the greatest impact.

3. **Ending.** Conclude your draft in a manner that reinforces your thesis and helps to accomplish your purpose. If you wrote about a problem, provide the best possible solution in a way that will convince readers to support it. If you wrote about an issue, leave your readers with a clear understanding of your position, why they should consider it, and what their stake is in the issue. You might also include different scenarios in your ending: what will happen if the problem is solved or your thesis is supported, or what will happen if it isn't. Like your opening, your ending may be longer than in previous essays, in proportion to the longer paper you are writing.

4. **Writer's voice.** As you write, make sure that readers feel your presence by providing your own thoughts and responses, paraphrasing source information, using that information to further your purpose, and showing an awareness of your readers. The paper should not read merely like an accumulation of researched information.

5. **Source references.** Include parenthetical source references for each piece of research information presented, and also introduce sources within your sentences when they will lend credibility and weight to the research.

6. **Providing evidence.** Provide the best possible evidence - empirical, factual, logical, comparative, causal, and moral - to validate your points and convince readers that you are presenting credible information.

7. **Opposing viewpoints.** Make sure to acknowledge and respond to significant opposing viewpoints to help persuade readers and further your purpose.

8. **Audience and purpose.** Keep your audience in mind as you write - their knowledge of the topic and attitude(s) towards it - and write in ways that will help accomplish your purpose.

Activity 7.6

When you are ready, write the first draft of your paper, double-spaced in accordance with the MLA style. You may first want to read the following sample first draft and note how the writer introduces her topic and thesis, emphasizes the seriousness of the problem, presents its causes and effects, incorporates and references her research material, responds to opposing viewpoints, shows an awareness of her audience, presents her solution, makes her purpose clear to readers, and concludes the paper.

Sample first draft

The Children's Health Care Crisis in America (Reading audience: general public)

Two boys died within one week in 2007 because their mothers didn't have health insurance. Deamonte Driver, age twelve, died because his mother couldn't afford to pay $80 to have his tooth extracted. The tooth abscessed and bacteria spread to his brain. After two surgeries and six weeks in the hospital, Deamonte was dead. Devante Johnson, age fourteen, died the same week of kidney cancer after he spent four months uninsured while his mother tried to renew her Medicaid coverage. She filed one application after another and appealed to a state legislator. Soon after the coverage was restored, Devante lost his battle with cancer (Fields).

These are just two examples of the tragic results that can happen when children in America don't have health insurance, an all-to-common occurrence. Over eight million children under age eighteen in the U.S. are uninsured ("Going Without: America's Uninsured Children" 6). However, that number doubles to sixteen million when you include children who have gaps in coverage - weeks or months when they are uninsured - during the year (Wilbert). In a comparison of children's health care in thirty industrialized countries, the U.S. ranked third lowest among the thirty nations in the percentage of children covered by health insurance ("Providing Health Insurance for U.S. Children"). That abysmal showing is inexcusable considering that the U.S. is among the wealthiest nations. There is no reason why children in the U.S. should not be cared for as well as any children in the world, which means providing medical coverage for all children.

How important is it for children to be covered by health insurance? Research shows that there is nothing more important for a child's well-being. According to the Kaiser Commission Report on Medicaid and the Uninsured, uninsured children are much more likely to lack a usual source of care, to delay care, or to have unmet medical needs than children with insurance. Uninsured children with common childhood illnesses and injuries do not receive the same level of care and are at a higher risk for preventable hospitalizations and for missed diagnosis of serious health conditions ("The Uninsured: A Primer" 7). Uninsured children have poorer health, receive poorer quality care, are significantly less likely to have a personal doctor, and shockingly, are ten times as likely to go without needed medical care as children who are insured (King 2). And not surprisingly, uninsured children have a greater risk of death during childhood than insured children.

⑭ According to an exhaustive Institute of Medicine report, children with health insurance, on the other hand, are more likely to have a regular source of care, immunizations and check-ups, needed medications, asthma treatment, and basic dental services. In addition, serious childhood health problems are more likely to be identified early, and insured children have fewer hospitalizations, improved asthma outcomes, and fewer missed days of school ("Health Insurance Essential for Health and Well-being"). The difference between the health care situation for insured and uninsured children is dramatic and the results profound. Every child in America should have the same opportunity for a healthy life, and that can only occur when every child is insured.

⑤ Who are these eight million children without insurance, and why aren't they insured? Surprisingly, more the eighty percent of the uninsured come from working families. Uninsured workers are more likely to work for small firms and in industries where few employers offer coverage. Despite belonging to the work force, about two-thirds of the uninsured are from families with incomes below twice the poverty level ($21,203 a year for a family of four in 2007), and private insurance is generally unaffordable for these families ("Going Without: America's Uninsured Children" 10).

⑥ According to William O'Hare, a senior fellow at the Annie E. Casey Foundation, a charitable organization devoted to helping disadvantaged children, "Economic status is the driving force regarding whether a child has health insurance. Marginally employed parents are more likely to be racial and ethnic minorities, and they are concentrated in urban and distressed rural areas." In addition, says O'Hare, "More and more jobs, particularly low-paying jobs, do not offer health insurance at all" (qtd. in Zuehlke).

⑦ Of the over eight million children who are uninsured, children of ethnic and racial minorities make up more than sixty percent of the uninsured: 3.3 million Hispanics, 1.6 million African-American children, and 670,000 children of other non-white ethnicities ("Going Without: America's Uninsured Children" 6). Clearly, there is a strong correlation between poverty and children being uninsured, and it is clear that there is a great disparity in the health care situation for Hispanic and African-American children compared to white and Asian children. It is clear where the strongest focus must be in getting children into the ranks of the insured ~unnecessary

Of course, the escalating cost of health insurance over the past twenty years has contributed to the problem of families not being able to afford health insurance. A study by the Economic Research Initiative on the Uninsured estimated that nearly two-thirds of the decline in health insurance coverage from 1990 to 2000 was attributable to rising health care costs ("Health Insurance Coverage: Overview and Strategy"). Those costs have continued to rise over the past nine years, and making health insurance more affordable needs to be a part of any solution to the health care crisis for America's children and families.

Every child in America deserves the best available health care. No child can pick his or her parents or economic situation, and that some children have no health insurance as a result is unconscionable in a country like America. There may be adults that some would say deserve what they get, but children have no control over their life circumstances, and their medical fate should never hinge on their parents' ability to pay. Whatever the ultimate solution to the crisis of uninsured children in America may be, the goal must be clear: to insure every child in America.

move to and 17a

Too often the discussion of reforming health care in America is politicized. Rather than talking about how to insure our children, the discussion turns to socialized medicine, government intervention in people's lives, the hardships of compelling employers to provide health insurance, the role of the free market in driving down health costs, and the self-interest of many in the medical profits' business - insurance companies, pharmaceuticals, physicians, and hospitals - who make arguments to maintain the profitable status quo. That most industrialized nations have found ways to insure the vast majority of their children and also keep insurance costs far below those of the U.S. should be very encouraging ("Providing Health Insurance for U.S. Children"). However, such success stories have had little impact on the medical situation in the U.S.

It is clear that providing health care for America's children cannot be left solely in the hands of employers. That the majority of the forty-eight million uninsured Americans are in the work force is ample evidence that employment alone does not guarantee health coverage.

That is why strong public support for the ongoing governmental programs to help ensure children is so critical.

11   Children from poorer families receive health insurance through two government programs: Medicaid, which provides health care for families, and SCHIP, the State Children's Health Insurance Program, which focuses exclusively on uninsured children. The SCHIP program, created and funded primarily by the Federal government, was recently expanded under President Obama to reach an additional four million children by raising the income threshold to allow more children to qualify (Zuehlke). *Nonetheless* Both Medicaid and SCHIP come under scrutiny whenever Federal and state governments experience revenue shortfalls, and it is incumbent on all Americans to support those programs adamantly with their elected officials to make sure that their funding isn't reduced through budget cuts and that they are expanded to include more children whenever possible.

12   However, such social safety-net programs are not enough to provide coverage to all of America's children, and even with Medicaid and the extended aid that SCHIP's expanded coverage provides, nearly five million children remain without health insurance. According to O'Hare, "The expanded coverage will help, but there are still millions of children without health insurance, and millions more without adequate health insurance (qtd. in Zuehlke).

13   What is needed to cover all of America's children is some form of universal health care: guaranteed health care coverage for all Americans. Universal health care can take different forms, but its goal is to ensure access to health insurance to all residents of a country. Universal health care is provided in many industrialized nations including Canada, Great Britain, France, and Germany, and there is no reason that it can't be provided for all Americans.

14   The best option available at this time to ensure health care coverage for all children is the health care legislation currently being considered. The legislation provides for a public plan option that any American can buy into, and rather than being a centralized, government-controlled plan, it is a network of choices that can be offered at a lower cost due to the number of individuals enrolled (Fritscher 1). Clearly, it is a compromise with the strong forces in America which oppose any centralized government plan such as that provided in Canada or Great Britain, but at least it provides a health insurance option for all Americans at a more affordable cost. That the current legislative plan will cover more working families, and hence more children, is encouraging, and it needs every American's support.

15   Opposition to the legislation relies on the same scare tactics that are always used against universal health care: government intrusion into our

lives, government's ineptness at running anything, the slippery slope that leads to a socialized America. However, the longstanding success of government-sponsored health care programs such as Medicare, Medicaid, SCHIP, and FEHB (Federal Employees' Health Benefits) flies in the face of such criticism. Successful government-sponsored health care programs have long been a reality in America.

(16) Despite the encouraging health care reform legislation and its intent to insure very child in America, there is still no guarantee. As the legislation stands, families would still have to buy into a plan, albeit it at a more affordable cost, rather than have it provided by the government. Therefore, there is no guarantee that every child will be covered, which is a clear weakness in the current legislation. As the legislation works its way through the House and Senate, senators and representatives need to know from their constituents that guaranteed health coverage for every child needs to be written into the bill. To pass monumental, sweeping health care reform without such a guarantee is simply unacceptable and wrong.

(17b) There is no question that providing health insurance to children improves their lives dramatically. They have serious health problems identified earlier, have fewer avoidable hospital stays, have better asthma outcomes, have fewer missed days of school, and receive more preventive services such as immunizations. Shouldn't every child in America experience the positive results of such basic health care?

Contrarily, being uninsured is hazardous to a child's health and well-being. Over eight million American children are at risk every day, and they don't need to be. Every American can play a part in ensuring that no child in America goes without health care, and the stronger and more frequently that politicians hear that message, the nearer the day when it becomes a reality. We owe nothing less to our children.

Works Cited

Fields, Monique. "Deamonte's Toothache." *The Root*. 5 Feb. 2009. 30 Aug. 2009. http://www.theroot.com/views/deamonte-s-toothache.

Fritscher, Lisa. "Understanding the Obama Health Care Plan." *About.com*. 25 July 2009. 1 Sept. 2009. http://phobias.about.com/od/treatment/a/obamaplan.htm.

"Going Without: America's Uninsured Children." *Covering Kids and Families*. Aug. 2005. 27 August 2009. http://www.coveringkidsandfamilies.org/press/docs/2005BTSResearchReport.

"Health Insurance Coverage: Overview and Strategy." *Robert Wood Johnson Foundation*. 2009. 30 Aug. 2009. http://www.rwjf.org/pr/topic.jsp?topicid=1049&p=os.

"Health Insurance Essential for Health and Well-being." *Office of News and Publications for the National Academies*. 24 Feb. 2009. 29 Aug. 2009 http://www8.nationalacademies.org/onpinews/newsitem.aspx?RecordID.

King, Meredith. "The SCHIP Shortfall Crisis: Ramifications for Minority Children." *Center for American Progress*. 21 March 2007. 26 August 2009. http://www.americanprogress.org/issues/2007/03/pdf/schip_report.pdf.

"Providing Health Insurance for America's Children Would Be Cheaper Than Expected." *Science Daily*. 16 June 2009. 29 Aug. 2009. http://www.sciencedaily.com/releases/2009/06/090616122108.htm.

"The Uninsured: A Primer." *The Henry J. Kaiser Family Foundation*. Jan. 2006 http://www.kff.org/uninsured/upload/7451.pdf.

Wilbert, Carolyn. "Many Children Lack Health Insurance." *WebMD*. 21 Oct. 2009. 29 Aug. 2009. http://children.webmd.com/news/20081021.

Zuehlke, Eric. "Economic Recession Presents Further Challenges to Uninsured Children in the U.S." *Population Reference Bureau*. April 2009. 28 August 2009. http://www.prb.org/Articles/2009/usuninsuredchildren.aspx?p=1.

Revising the first draft of a research paper is a sizable task given the length of the paper and the numerous considerations involved with research writing. However, the process itself is little different from how you revised your previous essays; it just may take a little longer. After setting aside your draft for a while, block out some time to work on your revisions so that you won't feel rushed and can give your draft the attention it deserves.

Revision Guidelines

To revise your paper effectively, consider the following suggestions.

1. **Opening.** Your goal in the opening is to introduce your topic clearly, create interest for readers, and present your thesis. Read your opening from a readers' perspective. How effectively does it get their attention? Do they sense the seriousness or gravity of the issue? How strong is your thesis statement? Make any changes to the opening that will make it more compelling for readers.

    In addition, with a research paper that runs several pages, there should be some balance in length among the different sections. For example, an extremely short opening may seem out-of-proportion in a paper that runs six or seven pages. While the middle paragraphs comprise the majority of the paper, make sure your opening is substantial enough to introduce the topic in a manner befitting a research paper.

2. **Middle.** If you opened the middle section by providing background or explanatory information on your topic, make sure that you have included everything necessary to help readers understand the topic, including defining key terms. Revise this section to make your topic as clear to readers as possible.

    Next, check the overall organization of your middle paragraphs to see whether you have presented your main supportive points, the causes and effects of your problem, and responses to opposing viewpoints in the best possible order. Does each paragraph flow logically and smoothly from the preceding one? Make any revisions in the order of your paragraphs that will strengthen the organization.

    Third, read each individual paragraph to see how it might be improved. Is the topic of each paragraph clear? Is the research evidence incorporated effectively? Do you provide your own responses and comments in appropriate places? Do any sentences seem out of place in the current location? Make changes that will improve and strengthen individual paragraphs.

3. **Evidence.** Read the draft to determine whether you have provided the strongest supportive evidence for each point in a convincing manner. Make revisions to strengthen the existing evidence and to make sure you have provided evidence for each supporting point, cause, or effect.

4. **Source references.** Read the draft to check on your source references. Have you provided a parenthetical source reference for each piece of research information in your paper? Have you included the author's last name and page number in parenthesis if they were available? Have you included the title of the article in parentheses if the author wasn't named? Do readers always know when you are presenting research material and when you are providing your own thoughts and responses? Make any revisions to ensure you have followed the MLA parenthetical reference guidelines and distinguished research material from your own ideas.

In addition, make sure that you have introduced some of your sources within your sentences: e.g. According to meteorologist Dr. Ivan Slidell, In a five-year study by the University of San Francisco Medical Center, With agreement among eighty leading international biological scientists, etc. Use source introductions (rather than just providing a parenthetical reference) when they will add credibility and weight to your findings. Make revisions, if necessary, to include some source introductions in your paper.

5. **Opposing viewpoints.** Readers are not inclined to forsake their own viewpoints just because they are presented a different one. Check to see whether you have acknowledged some significant opposing arguments and responded to them in ways that will influence readers. Revise your paper to let readers know you are aware of differing viewpoints and have considered and rejected them for good reasons.

6. **Ending.** Read your ending carefully and evaluate its impact on readers. Is it long enough to balance with the other sections and provide a powerful conclusion? Does it reinforce the thesis strongly? If the paper is problem-oriented, does it present the solution clearly and convincingly? Does it leave readers with a clear understanding of the seriousness of the issue, why it should concern them, how they may be affected, and how they should respond? How might you revise the ending to make it stronger, more compelling, or more memorable?

7. **Writer's voice.** Read your draft to see whether your writer's voice is clear throughout the paper. You accomplish this by opening and concluding the paper primarily with your own thoughts, by paraphrasing the majority of the research findings, by using the research material for your own purposes, by including your own comments and responses throughout the paper, and by showing an awareness of your readers. Revise your paper to strengthen your voice so that it doesn't read like a compilation of research information.

8. **Sentence Wording.** Read each sentence to see how its wording might be improved. Eliminate unnecessary or repetitious words or phrases, reword awkward sentences, clarify vague sentences, and replace questionable word choices. Revise sentences to make them as smooth and clear as possible.

9. **Paragraphing.** Make sure that you change paragraphs as you move to something new in your paper: a different section, a new point, a different example, a new piece of research information, a different cause or effect. Divide overly long paragraphs into two, and combine or develop pairs or strings of short paragraphs.

10. **Audience and purpose.** Read the draft from your readers' perspective, evaluating how well you have presented and explained your topic and supported your thesis. Make any changes that will help to elicit the best response from readers.

    Finally, evaluate how well you have accomplished your purpose. Read each part of the draft to see how it relates to your purpose, and make any changes that will strengthen your intent.

11. **Works Cited.** Check your "Works Cited" section to make sure that you have an entry for each source used in your paper, that you have alphabetized all sources, and that you have provided the required information following the MLA format.

Activity 7.7
Revise your draft keeping in mind the suggestions provided.

Editing

Along with your regular editing considerations for any essay, with the research paper, you also need to do a "format check" to make sure that you have formatted your paper according to MLA style requirements. The last entry in the "Editing Checklist" provides some suggestions for detecting and correcting any formatting errors.

Editing Checklist

The following checklist will ensure that you cover every aspect of grammar usage, punctuation, and spelling as you proofread your paper for errors.

1. **Spelling.** Use the spell check on your word processor and also proofread your paper for spelling errors. Most spell checks do not flush out words that are spelled correctly but used incorrectly (e.g. *Their* motives aren't as altruistic as one might imagine.), so pay particular attention to *homophones*, words that sound the same but are spelled differently, and similar sounding words.

2. **Punctuation.** Check to make sure you used the following correctly:

    End marks (periods, question marks, exclamation marks) to designate the end of each sentence. As you read your sentences, look for any *run-on sentences, comma splices, or sentence fragments,* and punctuate them correctly to eliminate the problems.

    Commas to separate words or phrases in a series; after introductory dependent clauses and prepositional, participial, and gerund phrases; after conjunctions in compound sentence; after "interrupters" such as "by the way," "incidentally," or "of course" at the beginning or within a sentences; before and after appositives or unrestricted relative clauses; to set off ending participial phrases, or at a point in a
    sentence where a pause is essential for the sentence to be read and understood correctly.

    Semi-colons to connect two closely related sentences or to separate phrases within a series that also contain commas within the phrases.
    Colons to set off a summary, series, or example following a main clause.

Dashes to set off a summary, series, or example *within* a sentence: The most difficult part of helping a child with school work - letting her learn from her own mistakes - is also one of the most important.

Apostrophes to identify possessive words and contractions.

Quotation marks to set off direct quotations.

3. **Grammar.** Check to make sure that your verbs agree with their subjects, pronouns agree with their antecedents, the correct pronoun subject and object forms are used, the correct comparative and superlative adjective forms are used, the correct adverb forms are used, and the correct irregular past tense verb forms are used.

4. **Parallelism**. Make sure that in sentences that contain a series of two or more words, phrases, or clauses, frequently joined by "and" or "or," all parts of the series are *parallel* in construction.

5. **Active/Passive Voice**. Make sure that most of your sentences are in the active voice, and use the passive voice only for special emphasis.

6. **Dangling/Misplaced Modifiers**. Check your sentences for any dangling or misplaced modifiers and make the necessary revisions.

7. **Correct Formatting**. Check to make sure you have formatted your paper correctly:

    Source references in parenthesis at the end of a sentence with *no comma* between author's last name and page number.

    For quote from secondary source, parenthetical reference includes "qtd. in" primary source: (qtd. in Hanover 14).

    "Works Cited" entries correctly alphabetized.

    Second and subsequent lines of a "Works Cited" entry indented five spaces.

    Title of book, newspaper, periodical, or online site *italicized*.

A period (.) at the end of each "Works Cited" entry.

An online address for each "Works Cited" entry for an Internet source.

Activity 7.8

Proofread your research paper for errors and make the necessary corrections.

Ending Oil Dependence
by David Sandalow

Seldom in American politics has consensus produced such little action. The United States is a divided nation, and deep disagreements often dominate our political dialogue. Consensus eludes us on countless topics.

Yet on oil dependence, an astonishing array of voices agree. National security hawks raise alarms about the vast sums of money sent each year to the Persian Gulf. Environmentalists warn about global warming. Farmers see new fortunes in the transition to ethanol. Consumers cry out when oil prices rise. Politicians as different as Senator Richard Lugar (R-IN), Senator Tom Harkin (D-IA) and Democratic National Committee Chair Howard Dean all call for an end to the United States' oil "addiction." In doing so, they echo the words of former presidents of both parties, who have been decrying our dependence on foreign oil for more than three decades

Yet today oil provides more than 97% of the fuel for our transportation fleets, barely different than a generation ago. Few experts expect that figure to change by more than a few percentage points during the next several years. Oil use continues to grow steadily in the United States and around the world.

Still, a confluence of factors – including a broad political consensus, game-changing technological advances and strong interest from private investors – creates the conditions for transformational change. These conditions offer the prospect of a lasting legacy to the leaders who make oil dependence a priority. But it will take just that – making the issue a priority. Easy rhetoric and small initiatives will not be enough. With sustained commitment, we can end the United States' debilitating dependence on oil.

The Oil Paradox

First, a question: how did a product so widely used become so widely resented? After all, oil is a high-energy content, easily transportable fuel. Trillions of dollars of infrastructure is already in place to convert it into services people want around the world. Oddly perhaps, this extraordinary success lies at the heart of the problem. Oil's dominance as a transportation fuel is so total, it shapes relations among nation-states. Oil's reward is so rich, it shapes entire economies. Oil's emissions are growing so rapidly, they are warming the planet.

Call it the Oil Paradox. Oil is a spectacularly successful product, used by billions of people daily. Yet oil's enormous success creates epic problems. Because we depend so completely on oil, we devote extraordinary political and military resources to securing it, at staggering cost. We empower oil-exporting nations that wish us ill. We pour vast quantities of heat-trapping gases into the atmosphere each year.

In one sense, the solution to these problems is straightforward : develop substitutes for oil and use less of it. Give drivers a choice between oil and other fuels. Invest in promising technologies - such as plug-in hybrid engines and cellulosic ethanol - which would do just that. Yet the challenge is immense. Oil's near-total dominance as a transportation fuel is the result not only of its inherent properties, but a century of favorable government policies and deeply ingrained cultural patterns. Furthermore, much of the oil infrastructure (pipelines, service stations, conventional vehicle manufacturing facilities) has already been built and paid for, while much of the infrastructure for alternative fuels must be built and financed.

Three facts underscore the challenge. First, modern vehicles depend almost completely on oil. This fact is so basic – so utterly taken for granted – it's worth pausing for a moment to consider. If you're thirsty and don't feel like a soda, you can drink water or orange juice. If you'd like to relax and don't feel like a movie, you can watch television or read a book. But if you want to travel more than a few miles and don't want to use oil, you're almost certainly out of luck. Perhaps you can buy 85% ethanol fuel (sold at less than 1% of U.S. gas stations) or biodiesel (even less available). Perhaps you can bike or ride an electric train. In most situations, though, you'll almost certainly need oil.

Second, oil's dominance is deeply entrenched, in part because capital stock turns over slowly. In the United States, new car sales account for roughly 6.5% of the total auto fleet every year ("Automobile and Truck Statistics"). That means it takes roughly 15 years for the fleet as a whole to turn over. Designing and testing new oil-saving technologies, and then re-tooling production facilities, can take several years at least.

Third, oil's dominance reflects a century of favorable government policies. For more than a century, eminent domain authority has been used to help build a network of pipelines for moving oil at low cost. Favorable tax treatment has promoted domestic oil drilling. Federal highway funds have vastly exceeded federal support for mass transit. Perhaps most significant, the U.S. military protects the flow of oil at key locations around the world, providing incalculable benefits to oil markets ("As Threats to Oil Supply Grow").

Previous efforts to address oil dependence have failed for lack of ambition. Solving the problems created by oil dependence will require substantial change in our stock of vehicles, approximately 260 million cars and trucks, and fuel delivery infrastructure ("Automobile and Truck Statistics"). It will require not just minor improvements in fuel efficiency, which are desirable, but a more far-reaching transformation so that drivers can choose between oil, electricity and biofuels to move their vehicles. It may require steps by other oil-consuming nations as well ("Transforming Oil Diplomacy").

We cannot meaningfully address the problems created by oil dependence by tinkering at the margins. These changes will not happen overnight. They will not happen at all without substantial and sustained bipartisan cooperation. Yet we ignore these problems at our peril.

Problems with Oil Dependence

The United States is in a long war. Islamic fundamentalists struck our shores and are determined to do so again. Like the Cold War, this struggle has many causes and will last for generations. Unlike the Cold War, oil dependence plays a central role in the struggle. Oil dependence lies behind the jihadist threat – not as the only cause, but as an important one. For example, according to Brent Scowcroft, National Security Adviser at the time of the first Gulf War, "... what gave enormous urgency to [Saddam's invasion of Kuwait] was the issue of oil" (Jaffe). After removing Saddam from Kuwait in 1991, U.S. troops remained in Saudi Arabia where their presence bred great resentment. Osama bin Laden's first fatwa, in 1996, was titled "Declaration of War against the Americans Occupying the Land of the Two Holy Places."

Today, deep resentment of the U.S. role in the Persian Gulf remains a powerful recruitment tool for jihadists. That resentment grows not just from the war in Iraq, but from the U.S. relationship with the House of Saud, the presence of U.S. forces throughout the region and more. Yet the United States faces severe constraints in responding to this resentment. With half the world's proven oil reserves, the world's cheapest oil and the world's only spare production capacity, the Persian Gulf will remain the indispensable region for the global economy so long as modern vehicles run only on oil. To protect oil flows, the U.S. policymakers will feel compelled to maintain relationships and exert power in the region in ways likely to fuel the jihadist movement.

Oil-exporting nations from other regions pose problems as well.

President Hugo Chavez of Venezuela – the world's fifth largest exporter -- fans anti-American sentiments throughout Latin America. Oil revenues not only help maintain his grip on power, they allow him to finance policies that put U.S. assets at risk in countries such as Bolivia and Argentina (Deutch and Schlesinger).

Global Warming

Oil is one of Earth's principal reservoirs of carbon. When oil is burned, this carbon is transformed into carbon dioxide, which stays in the atmosphere - trapping heat - for more than a century. Today, oil accounts for 42% of the world's energy-related carbon dioxide emissions ("What are the Sources of Greenhouse Gases?"). The average car in the U.S. puts more than 1.5 tons of carbon into the air every year. Total emissions from oil use are climbing sharply, both in the United States and around the world.

In June 2005, the U.S. National Academy of Science joined with ten other national academies from around the world in declaring that "The scientific understanding of climate change is now sufficiently clear to justify nations taking prompt action. It is vital that all nations identify cost-effective steps that they can take now, to contribute to substantial and long-term reductions in net global greenhouse gas emissions" ("Global Response to Climate Change").

Oil is also a major cause of urban smog and, as a result, of asthma and heart disease. Oil spills have damaged marine ecosystems around the world. Oil dependence also exposes the United States' economy to the volatility of world oil markets.

Because oil price increases can occur suddenly, consumers and businesses may be unable to adjust behavior and forced to incur higher expenses when prices rise. The impacts on low-income families and oil-intensive businesses may be especially severe (Cooper 7). The oil price spikes of the 1970s have often been blamed for the recessions that followed (Hamilton).Nevertheless, the climb in oil prices during the past few years imposed considerable costs. In 2006, U.S. payments abroad for oil were more than $250 billion ("Exhibit 9: Exports, Imports, and Balance of Goods").

Solutions

Recall the Oil Paradox. Oil's enormous success creates epic problems. To solve these problems, we must end the near-total dependence of our vehicles on oil. This means creating a transportation infrastructure in which drivers have a choice between oil and other fuels. Since the

1970's, "ending dependence on foreign oil" has been a regular applause line in U.S. politics. However, the challenge is more fundamental. Several problems often associated with dependence on *foreign* oil are in fact caused by dependence on oil more broadly.

Unfortunately, many national security vulnerabilities created by oil would remain even if U.S. oil imports fell. The United States hasn't purchased a drop of oil from Iran in 25 years, but that fact doesn't prevent Iran from playing its oil card to advance its nuclear ambitions. In an interdependent global economy, in which our prosperity depends on the economic well-being of allies and trading partners, the U.S. will retain a vital interest in the Persian Gulf so long as global transportation fleets run almost entirely on oil.

Cutting oil imports can help with some problems, such as the trade deficit. But many of the most important national security, environmental and economic problems created by oil cannot be solved by cutting imports alone. To solve these problems, we must end oil's near-total dominance of the transportation fuels market. We must give drivers a choice between oil and other fuels. Today several technologies offer the promise of doing just that.

Plug-in Hybrids

To reduce oil dependence, nothing would do more good more quickly than making cars that could connect to the electric grid. The United States has a vast infrastructure for generating electric power. However, that infrastructure is essentially useless in trying to cut oil dependence, because modern cars can't connect to it. If we could build cars that ran on electricity and plugged into the grid, the potential for displacing oil would be enormous.

Fortunately, we can. Several small companies are already doing this, with a first generation of "plug-in hybrid" engines designed to run both on gasoline and electricity from the grid (Boschert). General Motors recently announced plans to produce light duty plug-ins.

Historically, electric cars have been limited by several factors, including a short driving range (think golf carts), battery weight and cost. The driving range problem is solved by hybrid engines, which draw energy first from the battery packs and then from the gas tank when batteries are depleted. The weight problem is being addressed with new kinds of batteries made with nickel or lithium. Upfront costs are still high – roughly $5,000-$6,000 more than a standard internal combustion engine – but well within range of commercial acceptability. (Conventional hybrids cost $2,000-$3,000 more than a standard internal combustion engine and have demonstrated strong consumer appeal.) Purchase costs are expected to drop sharply once plug-in hybrid electric vehicles (PHEVs) are in mass production ("Plug-in Partners").

The potential benefits are enormous. Electric utilities typically have substantial unused capacity each night, when electricity demand is low. Furthermore, utilities maintain reserve generating capacity – known as "peaking power" – for days of unusually high demand. This unused and excess capacity could provide an important cushion for vehicles in case of a sudden disruption in oil supplies or steep rise in oil prices. Furthermore, driving on electricity is cheap. Even a first-generation plug-in hybrid car would travel about 3-4 miles per KwH -- equivalent to about 75 cents per gallon ("All About Plug-in Hybrids).

Plug-in hybrids would dramatically cut local air pollutants and would even be better from a global warming standpoint than a standard internal combustion engine. True, the energy to recharge a plug-in vehicle needs to come from somewhere, and in much of the United States that somewhere would be a coal-fired power plant. However, the thermal efficiency of even an old-fashioned pulverized coal plant is roughly 33-34%, while the thermal efficiency of an internal combustion engine is roughly 20% ("Effectiveness and Impact of Fuel Economy").

How much oil could plug-in hybrids displace how quickly? A lot – although the data available on U.S. driving habits only allows a rough estimate. According to the Department of Transportation, 40% of Americans travel 20 miles or less per day and 60% of Americans travel 30 miles or less each day (Raskin and Shah). In one realistic scenario, plug-ins hybrids could replace one-third of the oil in U.S. light duty vehicles by 2025. This assumes strong policies supporting early deployment of plug-ins and steady penetration in the vehicle fleet thereafter. Finally, tens of millions of PHEVs could be added to the fleet without the need for new electric generating capacity, since PHEVs could recharge at night when electric loads are low. According to one estimate, even with PHEVs making up 50% of the vehicle fleet, electricity demand would increase by only 4-7% ("Electric Drive Vehicles").

Biofuels

Over the next several decades, biofuels have the potential to replace a significant fraction of the United States' oil use. Estimates range from 25 to 100 billion gallons per year by 2025, roughly 20%-70% of 2005 consumption. Ethanol imported from the Caribbean, Latin America or Brazil could add to these totals. In 2006, the U.S. industry produced roughly 5 billion gallons of ethanol – more than 3% of U.S.

liquid fuels ("Renewal Fuels Association News Release"). Almost all ethanol in the U.S. is blended into gasoline. A small but growing number of U.S. gas stations are selling E85, a fuel made up of 85% ethanol and 15% gasoline.

The U.S. ethanol industry is growing rapidly, with double digit growth rates and at least 73 plants under construction. (At a recent conference, former CIA Director Jim Woolsey quipped that "You can't stand on a street corner in the Silicon Valley today without some venture capitalist throwing money at you for an ethanol plant" ("A High Growth Strategy for Ethanol"). When plants currently under construction are complete – projected for 2008-2009 - total capacity of the U.S. industry will exceed 11 billion gallons per year (Collins). Many experts think 15 billion gallons per year is the capacity for corn-based ethanol production in the U.S.

Conventional Efficiency Technologies

Many existing technologies can improve fuel efficiency. Most important is the "conventional" hybrid engine. The fact that hybrid engines can now be considered "conventional" reflects the technology's remarkable success in the past few years. The first hybrid engines were introduced into the U.S. market several years ago amidst some skepticism they would find a market. Since then consumers have regularly sought more hybrids than are available on the market, and the technology is rapidly moving into new models.

Analysts at Alliance Bernstein state that "The world is on the cusp of a major transition to hybrid-power vehicles…This is a game-changing technology that promises to increase energy efficiency substantially, make a broad range of fuels available for powering vehicles, and meaningfully reduce demand for oil from the transportation sector"(Raskin and Shah). These analysts see a long-term decline in global oil demand as a result of the rapid penetration of conventional hybrid engines (noting that the advent of plug-in hybrids would accelerate this trend).

Beyond hybrid engines, there are many existing or emerging technologies that can substantially reduce fuel consumption without sacrificing performance, safety or comfort. The National Academy of Sciences released a comprehensive assessment of these technologies in 2002, concluding that "Technologies exist that, if applied to passenger cars and light-duty trucks, would significantly reduce fuel consumption within 15 years. Auto manufacturers are already offering or introducing many of these technologies in other markets (Europe and Japan, for example)…" (NAS CAFÉ report). Based on this data, the Union of Concerned Scientists found that raising the average fuel economy of new passenger cars and light trucks from today's level of 24 miles per gallon to 37 miles per gallon within 10 to 15 years would be technically feasible and cost effective for the consumer with gasoline at $2.50 a gallon ("Clean Vehicles).

Hydrogen-powered Cars

Hydrogen is the most abundant element in the universe. It burns cleanly, without local air pollutants or heat-trapping gases. Yet there are few if any experts who believe hydrogen fuel could have a significant impact on U.S. oil dependence for at least several decades. First, although hydrogen is abundant, it does not exist in nature in usable form. To be used in a vehicle, hydrogen would need to be separated from the compounds in which it occurs naturally (such as water), which requires vast amounts of energy. Second, hydrogen cannot be distributed through the liquid fuel tanks found in service stations. The temperature required to convert hydrogen to a liquid is minus 423 degrees Fahrenheit, only 36 degrees above absolute zero (Wiser 6).

Massive change in the nation's fuel distribution infrastructure - including pressurized gas tanks at service stations - would also be required to accommodate hydrogen-powered vehicles. Continuing with advanced research in hydrogen may have benefits, but there is little basis to believe that hydrogen can help in any material way to reduce oil dependence during the next 25 years (Romm).

Conclusion
Can federal leadership make a difference in ending oil dependence? Yes - indeed it is essential. The following six categories of policy options could end oil dependence in a generation: transforming the auto fleet, transforming the fuel supply, protecting the climate, investing in research, transforming oil diplomacy, and establishing an Oil Addiction Index, determining annually oil's share of the transportation fuels' market. The government can play a leading role by providing funding, research, and legal mandates that tie alternative transportation options, cleaner air, and a significant reduction in oil dependency together.

Ending oil dependence doesn't mean ending oil use. It means ending our near-total reliance on oil as a transportation fuel. It means giving drivers a choice between oil and other fuels. The solutions are available for the United States to end its debilitating dependence on oil in a generation given the political will and the willingness of Americans to change to electric, hybrid, and alternative fuel vehicles.

Under reasonable assumptions, plug-in hybrids could replace more than 45 billion gallons of gasoline per year by 2025 and biofuels could replace roughly 40 billion gallons of gasoline in the same time frame. This would require production of roughly 60 billion gallons of ethanol, due to ethanol's lower energy content. Efficiency technologies could cut fuel use by a third. The result would be a transformed market for transportation fuels.

Oil dependence lies behind several of the most important problems facing the United States. The strong consensus about the gravity of the problem and new technologies provide an opportunity for transformational change.

Works Cited

"A High Growth Strategy for Ethanol," Report of an Aspen Institute Policy Dialogue, (2006) http://www.aspeninstitute.org/atf/cf/ DEB6F227-659B-4EC8-8F84 8DF23CA704F5}/EEEethanol1.pdf.

"All About Plug-in Hybrids," *CalCars*, http://www.calcars.org/vehicles.html.

"As Threats to Oil Supply Grow, A General Says U.S. Isn't Ready," *The Wall Street Journal*, December 19, 2006.

"Automobile and Truck Statistics," Plunkett Research http://www.plunkettresearch.com/Industries/AutomobilesTrucks/Automobileand TrucksStatistics/tabid/90/Default.

Boschert, Sherry, "Plug-in Hybrids: The Cars that Will Recharge America" (New Society Publishers, 2006).

Collins, Keith J., "Testimony at Senate Agriculture Committee," Jan. 10, 2007 (http://www.usda.gov/oce/newsroom/congressional-testimony/Collins_011007.pdf).

Cooper John C.B., "Price Elasticity of Demand for Crude Oil: Estimates for 23 Countries," *OPEC Review*, Vol. 27, pp. 1-8, March 2003 http://ssrn.com/abstract=416815.

"Effectiveness and Impact of Corporate Average Fuel Economy (CAFE) Standards," *National Academy of Sciences*, (2002) p. 31. http://www.nap.edu/catalog/10172.html.

"Exhibit 9: Exports, Imports, and Balance of Goods, Petroleum and Non-Petroleum End-Use Category Totals,"http://www.census.gov/foreign-trade/PressRelease/currentpressrelease/exh9.pdf.

"Global Response to Climate Change," Joint Science Academies Statement: (June 7, 2005) http://nationacademies.org/onpi/06072005.pdf.

Hamilton, James, "This Is What Happened to the Oil Price-Macroeconomy Relationship," *Journal of Monetary Economics* 38 (1996), pp. 215-220.

Jaffe, Amy Myers, "US and the Middle East," report prepared for the National Commission on Energy. http://www.energycommission.org/files/contentFiles/I.1.b.

"National Security Consequences of U.S. Oil Dependency," Independent Task Force Report No. 58, p. 26.

John Deutch and James R. Schlesinger, co-chairs (Council on Foreign Relations Press 2006) 4 88.

"Plug-in Hybrids," *Plug-In Partners,* http://www.pluginpartners.org/plugInHybrids/frequentlyAskedQuestions.cfm.

Raskin, Amy and Shah, Saurin, "The Emergence of Hybrid Vehicles: Ending Oil's Stranglehold on Transportation and the Economy," *Alliance Bernstein,* http://www.calcars.org/alliance-bernstein-hybrids-june06.pdf.

Renewable Fuels Association news release (December 20, 2006) http://www.ethanolrfa.org/objects/documents/919/yearend2006.pdf.

Romm, Joseph, *The Hype About Hydrogen: Fact And Fiction In The Race To Save The Climate* (Island Press, 2004)

"What are the Sources of Greenhouse Gases?" *Energy Information Administration,*www/eoa/dpe/gpvpoaf1605/ggccebro/chapter1.html.

Wiser, Wendell H., *Energy Resources - Occurrence, Production, Conversion, Us,* (Springer-Verlag New York, Incorporated, 1999), p. 6.

1. What is the thesis of the essay?
2. The essay follows the traditional problem/solution format. What specifically is the problem, what are its causes, and what are its effects?
3. What evidence is provided to show both the seriousness of the problem and its profound effects? How effective is the evidence in convincing readers?
4. Why is the oil problem referred to as a "paradox," and how has its paradoxical nature contributed to the lack of progress in solving the problem?
5. What solutions to the problem are provided in the essay, and what evidence is provided to support the solutions? How realistic do you think the solutions presented are in solving the problem, and why? What other possible solutions should be considered?

Index

E

F

G

H

L

M

O

P

Notes

Notes